HEALTHY COOKING

ROSEMARY STANTON

HEALTHY COOKING

R OSEMARY S TANTON

The best of Rosemary Stanton's recipes
for health and energy

M U R D O C H B O O K S®
Sydney • London • Vancouver • New York

Contents

CONTENTS

Why a healthy diet is important

We are what we eat. The human body is an amazing piece of machinery. If we feed it properly, exercise it, rest it and allow it time for relaxation and fun, it is likely to go well. If we ignore it, forget to refuel it or fail to acknowledge its needs, the chances are it will let us down. That is the theory. In reality, no one can guarantee you perfect health even if you try to put every good health habit into practice. Mostly, however, you get your just desserts. As many medical researchers have shown, taking care of yourself reduces the risk of ill-health.

HEALTH TIP

The following foods have the same calorie value: 6 medium apples (1 lb 12 oz); 6 bread slices (6½ oz); 2⅔ oz chocolate; 2¾ level tablespoons margarine (2 oz).

Opposite: Frittata (page 30) served with salad and fresh fruit makes an ideal brunch. On its own it is a tasty breakfast dish.

Everything in your body was once food. Feed yourself junk and you cannot expect your body to stay in top running order. Feed your body well and it is likely to last longer and work better.

Of course there are exceptions. Some people abuse their bodies and seem to suffer few ill-effects from the neglect. There are also some people who drive their cars in a dangerous way without ever having an accident but it is not behavior any sane person would recommend. Yet some people use this same argument with health, perhaps quoting a friend who had drunk heavily, smoked and eaten a diet of junk food but lived to be 85! Just as some idiotic drivers can be lucky, so can some people take risks with their health without suffering from any unfortunate consequences. Most can't. Generally, people who look after themselves live longer – and are healthier during their longer lives than those who do not.

Food is an integral part of health. It is the fuel for energy. It provides the nutrients we need for growth and repair of body tissues. And ultimately it controls every reaction of our complex body machinery. It is also a social lubricant and a daily source of pleasure. Depending on our choice of foods, we can satisfy some or all of these aspects of our health.

The best part of eating a healthy diet is that it makes you feel so good. If you have known the feeling of energetic exuberance which comes with eating well and being fit, you will know what I am talking about. If you constantly feel worn out and drag yourself through the day, you may need to make some changes so you can experience the vitality which comes from an ideal supply of nutrients.

Many women, especially, have put up with substandard nutrition so long that they regard a certain sinking feeling of fatigue as almost normal. It isn't. You should, and you can, feel full of energy – and upgrading your diet is a great way to go about it.

Many people think healthy eating is a complicated matter of charts and figures. In this book, we do provide some of those so you can make food choices intelligently. Other people believe healthy eating is a series of prohibitions, and that healthy eaters have to cultivate a puritanical attitude to life. In fact, healthy eating is a pleasure – for the senses as well as the body.

Most healthy foods also taste delicious. There are hundreds of examples of the mouth-watering taste sensations of healthy foods. In contrast, many of the foods which cause diet-related health problems are not always taste turn-ons. How many half-cold French fries, soggy pie crusts, ordinary cookies and uninspiring sauces have you eaten – just because they were there? Many fat-laden foods and most of the bland processed and take-out foods are quite ordinary and do not live up to our preconceptions of their flavor. Most people eat these foods for convenience, not taste. Once your taste buds experience the delights of fresh natural foods simply prepared and beautifully served, it is hard to go back to eating many of the mundane offerings dished up by sections of the food industry.

Some foods are inherently delicious by virtue of their fat or salt or sugar and it is not always possible to make healthier versions of many of these. There is no real substitute, for example, for good chocolate, rich creamy ice-creams and some wonderful, but fatty, cheeses. Some traditional recipes also cannot be changed without losing their essential character. But a healthy diet does not mean you should never have any of these indulgences. A well-balanced diet simply means eating more of some foods and less of others. And many recipes can be adapted to fit a healthier lifestyle without sacrificing their nature or taste.

It's true that some healthy foods do take a little more time and trouble to find and prepare. Does that matter? Is it worth

HEALTH TIP

Both margarine and butter have the same high calorie count – 150 cal per tablespoon.

living life in such a rush that we do not have the time to devote to preparing for one of life's greatest pleasures – eating?

Setting appropriate limits

We all stop eating at some stage. Some people are good at setting appropriate times; others are not.

Just as we set some limit on how much we eat, so we should recognize that some foods need lower limits. Quality rather than quantity! To eat well and live longer, you may need to reset your limits on some foods. However, the many foods which are still delicious when prepared in a healthier way can become the mainstay of the diet. The occasional indulgence then does no harm. Just make sure the indulgences do not come too thick and fast, or your waistline will do the same!

The balanced diet pyramid

A well-balanced diet is simple. Nothing is forbidden, but some foods need a higher profile than others. No foods are 'good' or 'bad'. It is the total intake that counts. Eat healthfully most of the time and there is no valid reason why you cannot indulge occasionally in some less nutritious foods. However, you should avoid a steady diet of junk foods. It is a little like sleeping. If you get enough sleep most of the time, you can take an occasional lack of sleep. But if you habitually deny yourself enough rest, your body is likely to react badly.

Fruits, vegetables, all foods made from grains, legumes and seafoods are all low in fat and provide a wide range of vitamins and minerals. All except fruits and vegetables are important sources of protein and all except seafoods are valuable for their dietary fiber. Grains, breads, cereals, vegetables, fruits and legumes are important sources of energy-giving carbohydrate.

Chicken or turkey, lean meat, nuts, seeds, eggs, milks and cheese and yogurt are valuable for their protein, minerals and vitamins. All except dairy products are good sources of iron

and zinc, while dairy products earn top marks for their high calcium content. Although these foods all supply fats (in varying amounts), their fats accompany important dietary nutrients. Nevertheless, they should be eaten in moderation and should not dominate the diet.

Apart from some fats such as olive oil, most fats, sugars, salt and alcohol have little nutritional worth. Many processed and prepared foods have large amounts of fats and sugar. These are cheap 'filler' ingredients. In small quantities, these do most people no harm. But in the large quantities present in the average person's weekly shopping, they can cause health problems, including:

❑ excess weight
❑ coronary heart disease
❑ high blood pressure
❑ adult-onset diabetes
❑ liver diseases
❑ constipation (millions of laxatives are sold each year)
❑ and certain types of cancer (especially breast and bowel)

Health authorities have calculated that 60 per cent of all deaths in Western countries are related to the food we eat. We all have to die at some time, but the concern is that many of these deaths are occurring in relatively young people.

Changing the diet

Some people want to follow diets which others find extreme. Some of these are discussed in this book. For most people, the risk of diet-related health problems can be reduced significantly by making a few small, simple changes to food choices.

Some people complain that the modern food supply lacks vitamins. That is not true. There are plenty of wonderfully nutritious foods with more than enough vitamins. Contrary to the cries of the scaremongers, there is no need to rush out and buy pills and expensive dietary supplements. Everything most people need can be found in food. It's a matter of balance.

Cooking

Most people lead busy lives and there is often little time left for cooking. This is why so many take-out and highly processed foods are popular. It's not their taste that is the attraction, it's the simplicity of buying a ready-made meal instead of having to plan what to make, do the shopping, cook the food and clean up afterwards. Many of these tasks traditionally have been left to women. Although men are increasingly doing more of these chores, surveys show that most food preparation is still done by women.

If we are to live longer, we have to go back to the kitchen. But not for hours and hours. There are plenty of healthy meals and snacks which can easily be prepared in a minimum of time. If a microwave oven is used, the cooking and clean-up time will be reduced even more. And if all the family members share the tasks, preparing food can be a relaxing and enjoyable part of life rather than a chore assigned to one person.

Benefits of a healthy diet

❑ Feeling on top of the world

❑ Plenty of energy for exercise or play

❑ Ideal body weight – not too high and not too low

❑ Blood fats (cholesterol and triglycerides) normal

❑ Blood sugar normal

❑ Strong bones

❑ Improved ability to cope with stress

❑ Reduced risk of many common health problems

❑ A healthy immune system

❑ Looking younger

HEALTH TIP

Cruciferous vegetables may give protection against certain types of cancer. Included in the cruciferous category are bok choy, broccoli, Brussels sprouts, cabbage, cauliflower, kale, kohlrabi and turnips.

The Balanced Diet Pyramid

Eat Least
of sugar, fats,
alcohol and salt.

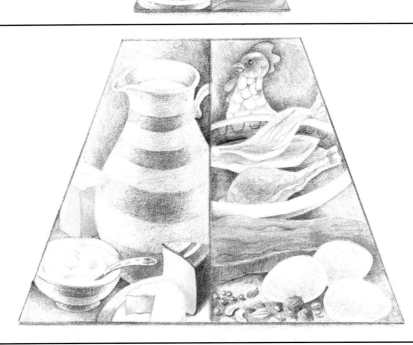

Eat Moderately
of chicken, turkey,
lean meat, nuts, eggs
and dairy products

Eat Most
of fruits,
vegetables,
breads, cereals,
grains, legumes
and seafoods.

Energy: what is it?

Energy means different things to different people and the various interpretations can be confusing. In nutrition, the energy content of a food refers to the number of calories released during the digestion process. More energy is not necessarily better, for, if a food supplies too much energy, the body is unable to use it all and converts some to stored energy – or fat. And some energy-rich foods can, in fact, make us feel sluggish.

The term 'energy' is one of the most difficult to use because of the fact that it has different meanings for different people and in particular contexts. Some people use 'energy' in a psychological sense to mean 'vitality'. Others use it to signify a spiritual force, while scientists think of energy as a capacity for work. In the scientific sense, energy comes from solar, chemical, mechanical and electrical sources.

The different interpretations given to the word energy can be confusing. In nutrition, the energy content of a food refers to the number of calories released when the food is 'burned' in the body. More energy is not necessarily better, for, if a food supplies too much energy, the body is unable to use it all and converts some to stored energy. The popular meaning of energy as vitality gives many people the idea that energy is a good thing while they think calories are to be avoided. One is a measure of the other.

We need to consider what happens to various foods within the body. During digestion, proteins are broken down to amino acids; fats to fatty acids and carbohydrates to glucose. The smaller particles formed during digestion then combine with oxygen in a series of combustion reactions to release energy. Alcohol can also be 'burned' directly to release energy.

About 40 per cent of the energy from the combustion of food is stored as chemical energy and about 60 per cent is dissipated as heat. This makes the human body more efficient than, say, a steam engine, in which only about 30 per cent of the energy produced is captured and used for work.

The energy produced from different foods is measured in calories. This energy can be used to provide fuel for millions of reactions to work the cells of the brain, muscles (including the heart muscle), the lungs, kidneys and other vital organs, and to produce essential secretions and hormones. Even when we are sitting doing nothing, many of these tissues need energy to keep them 'firing'.

The various chemical reactions involved in the release of energy from protein, fat and carbohydrate need enzymes. These enzymes are protein molecules which contain vitamins and minerals as part of their structure. The vitamins and minerals do not provide energy themselves but work as catalysts, so the reactions which release energy in the body can proceed.

The energy from some foods is preferentially used by muscles to move the body. If you are physically active, your muscles will use large amounts of energy from carbohydrates to perform at their peak. In fact, carbohydrates are the only fuel your body can use for energy for some types of physical activity (see page 152).

Some energy is also needed to repair body tissues which are constantly being broken down and reformed. Children need lots of energy for growth of new body tissues and so do pregnant women. Once all the body's needs for calories of energy have been met, any leftovers are

converted to body fat, a form of stored energy.

The rate at which we take in foods to provide energy is important. So is the type of food we eat. In theory, fats supply the most energy – 9 calories per gram. However, that does not mean we should eat lots of fat to get lots of energy. The body finds it easy to convert fat calories to body fat. Carbohydrates, on the other hand, are mainly used to replenish blood sugar levels and to give fuel to muscles. Carbohydrates give you a feeling of power to go, and probably best fit the popular meaning of the term 'energy'. Foods rich in carbohydrate are the best energy foods for physical activity.

There are complications, however. Not all foods containing carbohydrate are equal. Some, such as sugar, are pure carbohydrate and have none of the vitamins and minerals (often called micronutrients) needed in the production of energy. If you eat a lot of sugar, the body must then 'rob' these micronutrients from some other food. That may not be a problem because many of the foods we eat contribute more of these micronutrients to the body than necessary. Bread – even white bread – for example, has larger amounts of the B vitamins than the body needs to digest and absorb the carbohydrate in the bread itself. As long as you eat bread (or some other nutrient-rich food), you can cope with some sugar. But it makes much more sense to eat carbohydrates which come with their own micronutrients than to eat a nutritionally inferior food such as sugar.

The ins and outs of energy

There are two sides to the energy equation: getting it and disposing of it. We get it from foods and drinks. We dispose of it in metabolism, for growth (during childhood and pregnancy), to keep the body temperature normal, in repairing body tissues and for physical activity. Any leftover energy is tucked away in fat stores, a reserve of energy in case of lean times later.

3 g protein at 4 Cals/g	= 12
0.7 g fat at 9 Cals/g	= 6
12 g carbohydrate at 4 Cals/g	= 48
total calories	= 66
If you prefer to work in Kilojoules	
3 g protein at 16 kJ/g	= 48
0.7 g fat at 37 kJ/g	= 24
12 g carbohydrate at 16 kJ/g	= 192
total kilojoules	= 264

The ins

Proteins, fats, carbohydrates and alcohol all supply calories of energy. When burned in the body, these macronutrients give different amounts of energy as shown in the chart, below right.

It is easy to see why a diet high in fat and alcohol so easily leads to excess weight. Carbohydrates, on the other hand, have the least calories. Of course, some carbohydrates, such as sugar, are easy to consume in large quantities without you noticing, most of it hidden in the processed foods we buy.

Calories

In America energy is measured in kilocalories (usually abbreviated to calories, sometimes with a capital C to indicate the 'kilo'). The metric equivalent is the kilojoule (abbreviated as kJ, with a capital J to represent Joule, the physicist after whom the unit was named). If you want to convert one to the other, remember that there are 4.2 kJ to every calorie.

Most foods contain mixtures of proteins, fats and carbohydrates. Once you know how much of each of these ingredients a food contains, you can calculate its calorie value. For example, a thick slice of whole wheat bread has around 3 grams of protein, 0.7 grams of fat and 12 grams of carbohydrate. You can calculate the calories in a slice of bread as shown in the chart above.

More accurate tables of calorie levels come from burning each food in an instrument called a Bomb Calorimeter and measuring the heat produced.

The outs

Metabolism

Much of our energy is used to keep the body's processes ticking away, 24 hours a day. The sum total of essential, continuous processes is known as metabolism. For the average person, metabolism uses up over 1500 calories of energy a day. This is much the same as the amount of energy used by leaving a 75-watt light bulb on all day. (A 75-watt bulb uses 75 calories a second or 1550 calories a day.)

Throughout the day and night, the heart keeps pumping away to send blood throughout the body, the lungs expand and contract, taking in oxygen and getting rid of carbon dioxide; the brain keeps functioning with dreams and memories (including one to wake us up); the liver keeps breaking down and building up various substances; and the kidneys keep on filtering hundreds of pints of fluid.

The body can vary how much energy it uses for these processes of metabolism depending on how much food is available. If you eat very little, the body cuts back its metabolic rate to make the energy supply go further. This often happens with strict diets – they do not work because they simply slow down the body's metabolic rate. Any diet with less than about 1000 to 1200 calories per day will slow down the energy used for metabolism. When this happens you lack energy and feel tired. And, because you are not burning up many calories, you are unlikely to begin breaking down fat stores to any extent. This is why diets which are too strict are useless for weight reduction.

1 gram of fat gives 9 calories
1 gram of protein gives 4 calories
1 gram of carbohydrate gives 4 calories
1 gram of alcohol gives 7 calories

Temperature control

Some energy is needed to keep the body temperature normal. If the weather is cold, you shiver. The physical activity of shivering burns energy and produces heat. Anyone living in a cold climate, therefore, burns much more energy each day just to keep the body temperature normal. Those in hotter areas use far fewer calories each day. This is probably why bracing outdoor air sends the appetite soaring.

1 calorie = 4.2 kJ
An apple has around 50 cals or 210 kJ (50 x 4.2)

HEALTH TIP

Make up casseroles and soups ahead and chill them in the refrigerator. It is then a very simple matter to remove all the fat that rises and solidifies on the top.

HEALTH TIP

The average person loses ⅔ gallon of water a day without any obvious sweating. Some of this will be replaced from food but 6–8 glasses of water are also needed.

Pasta is a good source of carbohydrate – and comes in a wonderful variety of flavors and shapes.

Meals

Every time we eat, the process of digesting, absorbing and metabolizing the meal uses energy. This used to be called the Specific Dynamic Action of food but now is usually referred to as food-induced thermogenesis. It is one reason eating makes you warm. It may also be one way in which people differ in their disposal of energy. One study found that some people produced far more calories of heat after eating than others did. Those who habitually eat a lot and do not put on weight may be lucky in wasting much more of the energy from their food. In a crisis of starvation, such people would not be good survivors. In a society where it is easy to overeat, they are the lucky ones.

Muscles and physical activity

Muscles also need energy, even when they are not actively working. The more muscle you have, the greater the energy you will use. Comparing a man and woman of the same height and weight, the man burns up more energy because he has more muscle. Fat uses almost no energy – it is inactive tissue. Muscle is active tissue and burns up many more calories. Of course to get the muscle first, you must be physically active and that too burns up many calories. Extra fat deposits in women are useful to provide energy during pregnancy if needed and also make them better suited to any lifestyle where food supplies are likely to be limited. Women who are short or do little exercise, and therefore have little muscle, burn up far fewer calories.

The more you exercise, the more energy you burn up. Exercise has multiple benefits in controlling weight. During the exercise you burn up energy and after you stop, the muscle you have developed keeps on burning it up. As a bonus, exercise speeds up the body's basic metabolic rate for some time after you finish the exercise itself. Thus, if two people of the same height and weight are sitting at their office desks but one has been out walking or swimming before arriving, that person will burn up more calories even while they are both sedentary. Exercise is one of the key features of controlling energy output.

Up to half the men and women in affluent Western countries are overweight. Various studies have also shown that 20 to 30 per cent of children and teenagers are also carrying too much body fat. Men and women become overweight at different ages, in different places and from slightly different causes. There is also a great difference in their perceptions of excess weight.

Men tend to become overweight in their 20s and 30s, whereas most women stay slim at these ages and put on weight rapidly during their 40s and 50s.

Other factors affecting metabolism

There are other factors which affect how much energy we use.

❏ *Size* The larger your body frame size (i.e. the taller and broader you are), the more muscle tissue you have. This does not apply to fat. Some overweight people claim they are 'large-boned' when their bones are of average size but are well padded. Most men have larger frames than women, and this means they have more muscle and use more calories, even without considering the effect of male hormones on the body's muscle. A tall woman burns up more calories of energy than a short woman.

❏ *Dieting* If you cut your calorie intake too low, the body uses less energy. Metabolic rate falls whenever calorie intake falls below 1000 to 1200 calories.

❏ *Pregnancy* During the last six months of pregnancy, the metabolic rate increases, so pregnant women use up more calories. This is usually offset in most pregnant women because they reduce their physical activity as they become bulkier.

❏ *Fever* If your body temperature is above the normal 98.4°F, you burn up more calories. This is why anyone with a prolonged fever has severe wasting. It may seem 'natural' not to eat when the body's temperature is high, but nature does not always protect sick creatures.

Weight – not too high, not too low

Men tend to accumulate excess weight around their abdomen and upper body – a very fat man may still have skinny legs.

Women normally have more fat than men on the lower body and this is where excess fat tends to accumulate. As they grow older, women may adopt the male pattern of putting on weight around the middle.

Weight around the waist and on the upper body presents the greatest risk to health. Weight around the hips and thighs, with little or no excess fat on the upper body, is not a health risk for any of the conditions listed. The only problems from fat on the lower half of the body are the extra strain on joints caused by any excess weight and our society's perception of lower body fat as undesirable.

Both men and women have difficulties with their perceptions of body size, but in opposite directions. Many men who are too fat will pat their tummies proudly and declare 'it's all muscle'. Some see what they refer to as a 'beer gut' as nothing more

Health risks associated with upper body fat:

❏ heart disease
❏ high blood pressure
❏ diabetes
❏ gallstones
❏ colon cancer
❏ hormone-dependent cancers such as prostate or breast cancer

than that. In fact, the typical beer gut is simply a heap of fat around the abdomen. If a man (or woman) drinks a lot of beer and is not physically active enough to burn up all the calories from the beer, the excess are stored as fat. Men tend to store fat around the waist and the beer gut is not from a distended stomach but is a large deposition of fat. It is certainly not 'muscle'. And it is a health risk.

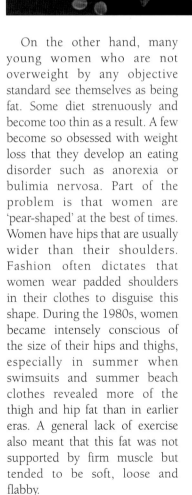

On the other hand, many young women who are not overweight by any objective standard see themselves as being fat. Some diet strenuously and become too thin as a result. A few become so obsessed with weight loss that they develop an eating disorder such as anorexia or bulimia nervosa. Part of the problem is that women are 'pear-shaped' at the best of times. Women have hips that are usually wider than their shoulders. Fashion often dictates that women wear padded shoulders in their clothes to disguise this shape. During the 1980s, women became intensely conscious of the size of their hips and thighs, especially in summer when swimsuits and summer beach clothes revealed more of the thigh and hip fat than in earlier eras. A general lack of exercise also meant that this fat was not supported by firm muscle but tended to be soft, loose and flabby.

The less muscle present, the more the fat hangs in 'lumps', commonly called cellulite. Contrary to the claims of those who aim to pummel it away, rub it off, siphon it out or flush it away, cellulite is not 'toxic waste trapped beneath women's skin'. It

is simply fat that has little supportive muscle and therefore has succumbed to gravity and fallen into little pockets or dimples. It is the presence of this fat, even more than the reading on the scales, which leads many women of normal or even below normal weight to try to lose weight. Their efforts usually result in a loss of energy and even greater loss of muscle rather than any magic disappearance of their cellulite. Men do not get cellulite because they have less fat on their thighs and much more muscle.

So we have many men who are overweight who think their weight is just right and many women who are not overweight who think they are too fat. Studies have confirmed that men tend to be happier with their weight than women – even when the situation should be reversed.

Studies have also shown that many young women have a distorted body image and see themselves as much fatter than they really are. Many women also suffer from problems when looking in a mirror. Rather than seeing themselves as a whole person, they automatically look straight at the part of their body they do not like, usually the thighs or hips or bottom.

Pork Cutlets with Mango Sauce (page 82) is a satisfying main dish that is surprisingly low in calories.

About two-thirds of the weight of a lean person is water. Overweight people have less water but more fat.

Society's conditioning

Our society has conditioned us to think that 'thin is beautiful' and some have extrapolated this to mean that 'thinner is more beautiful'. Many of the models of the 1980s suffered from anorexia and other eating disorders and were hardly fitting role models for everyday women to copy. Many models are also very young, yet we find women in their 20s, 30s and even 40s wanting to have bodies similar to 15 and 16 year-old fashion models. It is not healthy to be fat, but neither is it physically healthy to be too thin.

The rise in the prevalence of eating disorders in women is testimony to the fact that striving for everlasting thinness is psychologically damaging.

There is no exact correct weight for good health. Instead there is a healthy weight range and you should aim for a weight somewhere within this. If you have a small frame or you have little muscle, aim for a weight in the lower half of the healthy weight range. If you are large-framed or spend a lot of time exercising to increase muscle mass, look to the higher levels of the healthy weight range.

BODY MASS INDEX

The Body Mass Index (BMI) is the most valid indication of weight status. It is calculated as follows:
[weight (pounds) ÷ height (inches)^2] x 704.5
The following classifications are used:
12 to 18 – underweight;
18 to 25 – healthy;
25 to 30 – overweight;
above 30 – obese.
Many studies have shown that men and women from 18 years onwards with BMI between 18 and 25 have the least risk of disease and death (J. Garrow – Classification of Obesity).
The National Institute of Health has taken this as the Acceptable Weight Range.

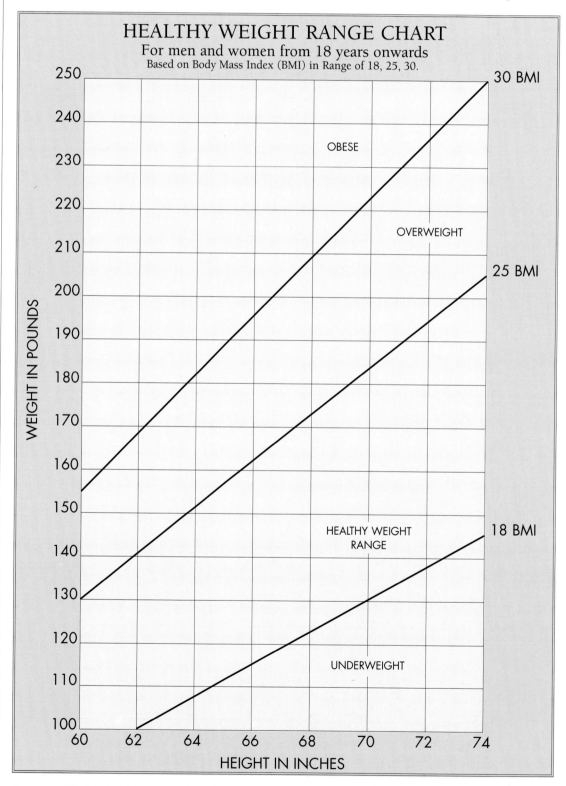

HEALTHY WEIGHT RANGE CHART
For men and women from 18 years onwards
Based on Body Mass Index (BMI) in Range of 18, 25, 30.

Resource: The National Institute of Health

The risks of being underweight

Being underweight, as shown on the Healthy Weight Range chart, is undesirable. A body starved too lean lacks strength and resistance to illness. Most people who are thin either do not eat very much, fail to exercise or are smokers. Eating more, increasing exercise and avoiding cigarettes are the most important and effective ways to gain weight.

A close inspection of the long-term eating habits of most very thin people shows that they eat much less than they think they do. For example, a thin person may see his or her meal as large when it is small by most people's standards. Some thin people eat a lot when they go out, but their food intake over the ensuing 24 hours may be lower than usual. They may either skip the next meal or eat much less at each meal for the next day or so. Some very thin people also dislike fatty foods and, as a result, their total calorie intake is correspondingly low.

Smoking suppresses the appetite and cigarettes are also used as meal substitutes. Foods lose some of their taste in a tobacco-flavored mouth so smokers tend to eat less. To make matters worse, smoking speeds up metabolism in some people so that they burn up and waste more calories from their food.

Exercise is important for normal appetite. Some people who do not exercise eat more and grow fat; others are not hungry enough to eat properly. Increasing exercise usually normalizes appetite.

There are a few people who genuinely do eat a lot, exercise regularly and do not smoke yet find they cannot gain weight. These people are rare and the reasons for their inability to gain weight are unknown. The most likely explanation seems to be an inefficient metabolism which wastes any spare calories as heat instead of storing them as fat. If you fit this group, you may have to accept your slender status for it can be more difficult for such people to gain weight than it is for the overweight to lose it.

Most very thin people, however, can gain weight if they eat more.

To gain weight:

- ❑ if you are a smoker, quit
- ❑ exercise
- ❑ try to eat more, especially concentrated foods such as nuts, meat, malted milk shakes, ice-cream and grains
- ❑ if you cannot eat larger meals, make sure you eat between meals
- ❑ get up earlier so that breakfast and lunch do not become combined into one meal
- ❑ relax while eating
- ❑ drink the high-calorie, high-protein Energy Drink regularly between meals.

Energy Drink

2½ cups milk

6½ oz yogurt

2 scoops ice cream

2 tablespoons malted milk powder

3 eggs

1 tablespoon honey

few drops vanilla extract

SERVES 3

Combine all ingredients in blender. Store in refrigerator.

Nutritional information (entire mixture): Protein 60 g; fat 62 g; carbohydrate 104 g; 1190 cals

Preparation time: 5 minutes

Cooking time: nil

Is your diet ideal for energy?

Many people do not achieve peak performance because they eat too much fat in proportion to carbohydrate. Keep a record of everything you eat and drink and, using these charts, add up protein, fat and carbohydrate. The table on page 19 shows you how to work out what percentage of your diet the nutrients form.

The typical Western diet compared with the ideal diet for energy		
	Typical diet	Ideal diet
% energy from protein	17	10-15
% energy from fat	37	20-30
% energy from carbohydrate	46*	55-70

* Much of this carbohydrate is in the form of sugar, the least nutritious food source of carbohydrate.

Opposite: Seafood Pizza (page 73) and Tuna and Pasta (page 84).

Protein, fat and carbohydrate content of some common foods (average servings used and figures taken to the nearest gram)

Food	Protein	Fat	Carbohydrate	Food	Protein	Fat	Carbohydrate
BREADS AND CEREALS				milk, whole, 8 fl oz	8	8	11
bread, 1 slice, 1 oz	3	1	12	milk, 2 per cent fat, 8 fl oz	8	5	12
bread roll, 1¾ oz	5	1	25	milk, skim, 1 per cent, 8 fl oz	8	3	12
garlic bread, 2 slices, 2 oz	6	10	32	milk, skim fortified, 8 fl oz	10	1	14
English muffin, ½, 1 oz	3	1	13	milk, goat's, 8 fl oz	9	10	11
pita bread, 1¾ oz	5	1	29	soy milk, fortified, 8 fl oz	7	5	4
croissant, 2 oz	6	15	22	yogurt, plain, 8 oz	8	7	11
bran, toasted, 1 oz	5	1	18	yogurt, plain, skim, 6½ oz	12	0	17
bran, unprocessed, 2 tbsp, ¼ oz	1	0	4	yogurt, fruit, 6 oz	7	4	32
corn flakes, 1 bowl, 1½ oz	3	0	38	yogurt, fruit, no sugar, 6½ oz	10	0	14
Granola, ¼ cup, 1 oz	2	4	21	FRUIT			
bagel, one, 2 oz	6	1	31	apple, 1 medium, 5 oz	0	0	18
rolled oats, 1 cup cooked, 7½ oz	3	2	18	apricot, 2 medium, 3½ oz	1	0	8
whole grain wheat cereal, 1 oz	3	0	19	avocado, ½, 3½ oz	2	23	0
wheat germ, 1 tbsp, ¼ oz	3	1	4	banana, 1 medium, 4½ oz	2	0	26
rice, 1 cup cooked, 6 oz	4	0	53	cherries, 5 oz	1	0	18
spaghetti, 1 cup cooked, 5½ oz	7	1	37	cantaloupe, raw, 1 cup pieces, 5½ oz	1	0	14
DAIRY PRODUCTS, EGGS				grapes, flame or Thompson, 3½ oz	1	0	16
cheese, Cheddar, 1 oz	8	10	0	grapefruit, ½, medium, 4 oz	1	0	7
cheese, cottage, 2½ oz	13	1	1	kiwi fruit, 1 medium, 3 oz	1	0	8
egg, 2 oz	6	6	0	mango, 1 medium, 5 oz	2	0	19
ice-cream, 1 scoop, 2½ fl oz	3	5	17	orange, 1 medium, 5 oz	2	0	12

Food	Protein	Fat	Carbohydrate	Food	Protein	Fat	Carbohydrate
passion fruit, 2 medium, 1¼ oz	1	0	2	spinach, English, 1 cup, 4½ oz	4	0	1
peach, 1 medium, 4½ oz	1	0	8	sweet potato, 1 piece, 4 oz	2	0	20
pear, 1 medium, 5 oz	0	0	19	sweet corn, 1 cob, 5½ oz	7	2	25
pineapple, 1 slice, 4 oz	1	0	10	tomato, 1 medium, 5 oz	1	0	3
strawberries, 1 cup, 5 oz	1	0	11	zucchini, 1 medium, 4 oz	1	0	2
watermelon, 1 slice, 6½ oz	1	0	10	CHICKEN, FISH, MEAT			
NUTS				beef, lean, casserole, 6½ oz	72	16	0
Brazil nuts, 8, 1 oz	4	18	1	beef, round, top, broiled lean, 3½ oz	32	17	0
cashews, 1 oz	5	14	10	beef, ground, lean, 3½ oz	25	18	0
peanuts, 1¾ oz	13	23	6	chicken, roast, with skin, 3½ oz	26	4	0
peanut butter, 1 tbsp, ¾ oz	6	13	3	chicken breast, lean only, 4 oz	34	2	0
walnuts, 15 halves, 1 oz	3	15	1	fish, broiled, 5 oz	30	2	0
VEGETABLES				ham, leg, lean, 3½ oz	19	4	0
asparagus, 6 spears, 3 oz	2	0	1	lamb shoulder chops, broiled, lean, 3 oz	23	9	0
beans, baked, 1 cup, 7½ oz	12	1	24	lamb leg, baked, lean, 4 oz	37	9	0
beans, green, 1 cup, 4½ oz	2	0	3	pork chop, cooked, 4½ oz	32	40	0
beans, kidney, cooked, 1 cup, 5½ oz	14	1	29	pork, lean, cooked, 5 oz	32	11	0
beets, canned, ½ cup, 3 oz	1	0	6	pork loin, lean, broiled, 4 oz	33	15	0
bell pepper, chopped, 1¾ oz	1	0	3				
broccoli, 1 piece, 3½ oz	3	0	2	tuna, canned, in water, 3½ oz	28	1	0
Brussels sprouts, 6, 4 oz	4	0	2	tuna, canned, in oil, 3½ oz	25	7	0
cabbage, raw, 1 cup, 2¾ oz	1	0	2	veal chops, broiled, lean, 2, 3½ oz	30	3	0
cabbage, cooked, 1 cup, 4½ oz	2	0	3	TAKE-OUT FOODS			
carrot, 1 cup, 4½ oz	1	0	8				
cauliflower, 1 cup, 3½ oz	2	0	2	burrito, bean, 1 item, 7 oz	15	14	63
celery, raw, 1 stalk, 3½ oz	1	0	2	chicken, 6 nuggets, 3½ oz	17	17	13
cucumber, 4 slices, 1¼ oz	0	0	1	fish, battered, 1 piece, 3 oz	12	12	13
eggplant, 1 small, 6 oz	2	0	5	hamburger, plain, 3½ oz	15	11	28
lettuce, 3½ oz	1	0	1	hamburger, big, 7 oz	25	26	42
mushrooms, 1 cup sliced, 2½ oz	3	0	1	large spring roll, 5½ oz	13	17	43
onion, 1 medium, 3½ oz	2	0	5	pizza, cheese, 2 slices, 7 oz	30	18	57
peas, 1 cup cooked, 5 oz	7	0	10	sandwich, subway club, 6 inch	25	11	45
potato, 1 medium, 4½ oz	3	0	18	ice-cream sundae, 4½ oz	7	7	35
pumpkin, 1 piece, 3½ oz	2	0	7	milk shake, chocolate, 13 oz	13	15	71
Swiss chard, chopped, 3 oz	2	0	4				

Food	Protein	Fat	Carbohydrate	Food	Protein	Fat	Carbohydrate
FAT				brownie, 4 oz	1	4	13
butter or margarine, 1 tbsp	0	16	0	Danish pastry, 3½ oz	8	16	36
cream, 1 tbsp, 20 mL	0	7	1	doughnut, plain, 2¼ oz	4	15	33
oil, 1 tbsp	0	20	0	granola bar, one, ¾ oz	2	4	16
COOKIES				muffin, cake-type, 2 oz	6	4	30
chocolate-coated, 2, 1 oz	2	10	20	scone, plain, 1¼ oz	4	3	14
cream-filled, 2, 1¼ oz	2	9	24	angel food cake, 1 piece, 2 oz	5	0	36
crackers, small, 6, ¾ oz	2	6	14	jello, ½ cup	2	0	19
plain sweet, 2, ½ oz	1	3	11	MISCELLANEOUS			
light crisp bread, 4, ¾ oz	4	1	16	chocolate, 1¾ oz	4	15	30
rye crisp bread, 2, 1 oz	2	0	13	potato chips, small packet, 1 oz	2	10	15
wheat crisp bread, 4, ¾ oz	4	2	18	fruit and nut bar, 1¾ oz	5	13	12
CAKES, PIES				gravy, ¼ cup	2	6	6
apple pie, average slice, 3½ oz	3	13	36	honey, 2 tsp, ¼ oz	0	0	10
cake, plain, average slice, 2 oz	3	1	35	jam, 1 tbsp	0	0	14
cheesecake, average slice, 5 oz	10	33	45	corn chips, 1 oz	2	9	17
chocolate cake, iced, 2½ oz	4	22	38	sugar, 1 tsp, ¼ oz	0	0	7

How to calculate dietary percentages

Using the figures in the charts on pages 17 to 19, you can add up the total amount of protein, fat and carbohydrate you eat each day and calculate both your calorie intake and the percentage of calories from each of these macronutrients. For example, if you consumed 2¾ oz (80 g) of protein, 2¼ oz (70 g) of fat and 6½ oz (200 g) of carbohydrate you would calculate the percentage as shown below. Comparing this with the ideal diet we mentioned on page 17, you can see this diet is too high in fat and protein and too low in carbohydrate.

2¾ oz (80 g) protein at 4 calories per gram	= 320 cals
2¼ oz (70 g) fat at 9 calories per gram	= 630 cals
6½ oz (200 g) carbohydrate at 4 calories per gram	= 800 cals
total calories	= 1750 cals
percentage of calories from protein	$\frac{320 \times 100}{1750}$ = 18 per cent
percentage of calories from fat	$\frac{630 \times 100}{1750}$ = 36 per cent
percentage of calories from carbohydrate	$\frac{800 \times 100}{1750}$ = 46 per cent

Diet-related health problems

More people are living longer than ever before. Much of the increase in life expectancy comes from conquering childhood diseases and infections. Women's life expectancy has increased dramatically with the advent of smaller families and safer childbirth. And the downturn in deaths from heart disease and strokes in middle-aged men is related to fewer men smoking, more men increasing their exercise and, probably, to basic changes in diet.

In many households, plate-sized fatty steaks and some other sources of saturated fats have disappeared from the dinner table and there is a conscious effort to eat less salt. Hard-liquor consumption is also dropping, with more people consuming beer, wine and even soft drinks and bottled water. However there are many small dietary changes which we could easily make to decrease further the risk of diet-related health problems.

Claims that pesticides and food additives are killing us are not supported by the facts. This does not mean we should relax our vigilance concerning these products but it does mean we do not need to avoid eating fresh fruits and vegetables.

firm muscles and brain cells which function well are much more important. And it is these factors which can be affected by diet and exercise. For those more interested in the cosmetics of ageing, it is worth noting that a stooped spine and poor muscle tone may make us appear older than do a few grey hairs.

Naturally, all bodies age. None of us is immortal. But bodies that are uncared for, or abused with smoking, poor diet, little exercise and a lack of mental stimulation age much more rapidly.

Some people maintain that the effort of keeping the body fit and youthful is not worth the trouble. "Eat, drink and be merry", they cry, assuming that one day they will simply drop dead. The reality is that the care you give your body is reflected in your health for many years before death. Some people do die of a sudden heart attack but many more suffer disabilities and restriction of their activities for 20 or 30 years prior to their death. On balance, those who care for their health when young have the last laugh when they age.

Extensive studies are being made into the effects of nutrition on delaying the ageing process. It has been known for some years that the way to extend the lifespan of rats is to restrict their food intake throughout life. Some scientists have recommended, therefore, that humans wanting to live longer should try semi-starvation rations of food. But humans do not have the same biochemistry as rats and recent long-term population studies in the Netherlands, Britain and Sweden have each found that

people who eat more do live longer. There is a catch. The long-livers don't just eat more of anything; they specifically eat more of plant-based foods (grains, breads, cereals, legumes, fruits and vegetables) and more fish. They are not necessarily vegetarian, but they do not over-indulge in animal products, with the possible exception of fish. With plant-based foods, you can eat more but not grow fat. You will also have a higher level of carbohydrates with which to fuel your muscles for exercise.

The ageing process in our internal tissues occurs because minute, highly reactive molecules – called free radicals – attack the body's cells. The free radicals are very unstable compounds and try to increase their own life by taking an electron from another molecule. In particular, they disrupt the polyunsaturated fats in the membranes around every body cell. These fats are easily oxidized and thus destroyed.

Heart disease. The major killer each year in Western society.

Heart disease

Cancer

Road Accident

Diet and ageing

When most people think of the signs of ageing, they think of grey hair and facial wrinkles. In terms of health, these are relatively unimportant.

Factors such as unclogged arteries through which blood can flow unimpeded, a straight spine,

Factors such as radiation, cigarette smoke, urban pollution, light, iron and copper as well as the presence of oxygen in tissues can all start free-radical reactions. Certain enzymes and antioxidant substances, however, can prevent free-radical destruction of tissues. There is little point in buying 'enzymes' from your health-food shop – there are hundreds of thousands of different enzymes which allow various chemical reactions to take place in the body. All enzymes are proteins and enzyme supplements will be broken down by hydrochloric acid in the stomach, so they will not reach individual cells.

However, the enzymes within the tissues which counter free radical attack depend on a balanced supply of the minerals selenium, manganese, copper and zinc. Too much of various minerals is as bad as or worse for you than too little, so high-dose supplements are not the answer to the problem. Some are useless; others are worse. Taking too much zinc, for example, can interfere with the body's absorption of iron and copper.

Vitamins A, C, E and possibly vitamin K are also important antioxidants, but whether taking supplements of these will help prevent free-radical reactions without doing any damage is still not known. All these vitamins can be harmful in excess.

The best way to combat the effects of free radicals is to avoid cigarette smoke, to breathe air which is as clean as possible and to have a diet rich in antioxidant vitamins and minerals. These are found in fruit and vegetables as well as whole grain products.

Diet for anti-ageing
Eat more fruits and vegetables, whole grain foods and fish. Eat some fruits and vegetables raw. Follow a balanced diet. Avoid too many fats, fried foods and salt. Be sure to include calcium-rich foods in your diet.

Coronary heart disease
Still the most common cause of death in Western countries,

coronary heart disease is now more common in parts of Asia where people are forsaking their traditional diet of rice, vegetables, fish and fruit for the fatty 'pleasures' of the Western diet.

Studies show that the major dietary problem for coronary heart disease is saturated fat. Other risk factors are smoking, excess upper body weight, high blood pressure and no exercise.

Women are initially protected from coronary heart disease by one of their hormones, estrogen. After menopause, production of

estrogen slows down and women gradually acquire the same high risk of coronary heart disease as men.

Coronary heart disease occurs over the years as fatty deposits accumulate in the arteries. The coronary arteries that supply the heart muscle with its vital blood supply are only the size of a drinking straw. Deposits of fat and fibrous material will narrow the area for blood flow, forcing the heart to work much harder.

It is best not to have fatty deposits develop in the first place, but there is evidence the situation can be improved by adopting a low-fat diet.

A blood test can determine your cholesterol level which, ideally, should be below 200 mg/dL. There is no point in being obsessed with reducing your level much below this. Remember that most blood cholesterol tests are only accurate to within about 10 per cent.

High blood pressure (also known as hypertension)
The heart pumps blood through the arteries to every tissue in the human body. Blood pressure refers to the strength with which blood pushes against the walls of the arteries.

If the arteries lose some of their

Above: Vegetarian Fettuccine (page 59), served with olives and Cheese and Sage Damper (page 140).

Opposite: Fresh fruits, dried fruits and nuts are important components of a healthy diet.

> ## Recommendations to reduce high blood cholesterol
> ❏ Reduce weight to the healthy weight range with a balanced diet and moderate exercise such as brisk walking, swimming or cycling.
>
> ❏ Eat less fat, especially saturated fats
>
> ❏ Eat plenty of fiber-rich foods, especially those containing soluble fiber (oats, barley, beans, apples, vegetables)
>
> ❏ Eat fish one to three times a week
>
> ❏ For cooking, use only a very small amount of oil, preferably olive oil
>
> ❏ Make the time to learn some simple relaxation techniques

Diet to reduce high triglycerides

❏ Reduce weight to normal with a low-fat diet and exercise

❏ Reduce all fats, especially saturated fats

❏ Keep sugar and alcohol intake to a minimum

❏ Eat more fish (fish-oil capsules may be required)

HEALTH TIP

When dining out or entertaining, remember that most people use their first one or two drinks to quench their thirst. It is better to do this by drinking one or two glasses of water before you move on to alcoholic or sugary drinks.

In restaurants, ask the waiter not to refill your wine glass until it is empty. This helps you keep track of how much you drink – important for avoiding exceeding the legal limit for drinking and driving, as well as for looking after your waistline and triglyceride levels.

elasticity – usually because hard, fatty deposits have built up on their walls – the heart must pump harder. And, if your body fat increases, the heart also has to pump harder to supply the additional tissue. When the diet is high in salt, extra fluid is retained in the body, forcing the heart to pump against a greater pressure. In addition, if the kidneys are not functioning properly – often because they have had to get rid of excess salt for many years – this places an increased strain on the heart and can send blood pressure soaring.

Normal blood-pressure readings should not be greater than 120/80 mm of mercury. The upper reading is the systolic pressure, or the pressure when the heart is contracting to force blood out through the arteries. The lower reading, the diastolic pressure, records the pressure when the heart is relaxing between beats. A higher level for the diastolic pressure is particularly dangerous as it means the heart is not getting its proper rest between beats.

Some people believe that high blood pressure is an inevitable part of ageing – but Bushmen in parts of Africa and isolated people in New Guinea register no increase in their blood pressure as they age. Both these groups consume a diet very low in salt, with no processed foods. Volunteers in many countries are currently following a low-salt diet to see if this can prevent the usual rise in pressure allied to age and, so far, results are very promising.

Smoking, stress and a lack of exercise are also significant. When the body is tense, small blood vessels constrict and blood pressure rises. Exercise keeps the arteries suitably elastic so that

they do not harden.

Like salt, fats can contribute to high blood pressure. The saturated ones tend to stiffen or harden the arteries, whereas the monounsaturated or poly-unsaturated fats do not. Fish fats can reduce pressure levels, possibly because they stop hard deposits forming on the walls of the arteries.

Potassium and calcium may also give protection. Potassium helps to balance sodium (from salt) and is found in vegetables (especially potatoes, sweetcorn, spinach and pumpkin), fruits (prunes, rhubarb, melons, avocado and bananas), legumes, fish and milk. Calcium comes in dairy products and fish with edible bones (such as canned sardines or salmon).

Changing to a vegetarian diet can assist in the reduction of blood pressure, but the reason for this is not yet known. Since many people who do eat a balanced diet which includes moderate quantities of animal products do not have high readings, a vegetarian diet obviously is not essential. It is however, an option that works for many.

High blood pressure tends to run in families. That does not mean it is inevitable and changes to diet, smoking, stress and exercise patterns can go a long

way to prevent it ever developing.

All adults should have their blood pressure checked regularly as high levels can lead to strokes and heart failure.

Low blood pressure

This is not a disease; it is only a problem when blood pressure suddenly falls to a low level, as may occur after surgery or blood loss. Otherwise, low blood pressure is an inconvenience, not a condition which requires any treatment. If your blood pressure is low, you may feel dizzy if you stand up quickly. The remedy is simply to stand up slowly. Eating less salt does not lower blood pressure in those with normal or low readings.

Diabetes

There are two different types of diabetes: juvenile-onset diabetes (Type 1) and adult-onset diabetes (Type 2). Type 1 diabetes occurs when the pancreas stops producing insulin, the hormone which normally takes glucose from the blood (blood sugar) into the cells where it can be used as a source of energy. If non-diabetics eat more sugar, they produce more insulin.

Type 1 diabetes does not seem to be caused by diet but adult-onset (responsible for about 95 per cent of all diabetes)

To reduce high blood pressure

❏ If overweight, lose weight with a balanced diet and exercise (this is often the only treatment required)

❏ Stop smoking

❏ Walk, swim or regularly do some other moderate exercise

❏ Eat foods rich in potassium to help balance the unavoidable sodium from salt

❏ Don't use salt in cooking or at the table and choose unsalted food products where possible

❏ Decrease alcohol consumption

❏ Eat less saturated fat

❏ Have plenty of calcium

---

is related to the quantity and quality of what we eat and drink. With this more common type, the pancreas may continue to produce insulin but the quantity may be insufficient or the action of the insulin may be blocked.

All carbohydrate foods are eventually digested to glucose. Some carbohydrates are broken down to glucose more quickly than others and may demand a large, sudden supply of insulin, while others take longer to be digested and absorbed. Soluble fiber in oats, barley, legumes and some fruits and vegetables slows down the rate at which glucose enters the blood and helps in the control of diabetes and fluctuating blood-sugar levels.

If you gain weight, your insulin supply does not increase. Although a genetic factor must also be present, adult-onset diabetes often occurs because the body is producing only enough insulin for someone of normal weight. Once excess body fat is lost, the diabetes abates.

Fats in the diet can cause cells to become resistant to the action of insulin. The body then fails to burn fats and glucose effectively as fuel and they are easily converted to body fat.

Whatever the underlying cause of diabetes, the effect is that glucose cannot get into the cells to provide energy. An untreated diabetic then feels excessively tired and lethargic. The glucose builds up in the blood and finally 'spills over' into the urine. A large volume of urine is passed and the untreated diabetic constantly feels thirsty. In some people, especially women, the frequent excretion of sweet urine can allow some bacteria to grow and cause an itch in the vulval area.

Children with Type 1 diabetes need insulin injections and will continue to need insulin throughout their life. Their dietary treatment requires the individual supervision of a dietitian. The diet will focus on foods which are high in carbohydrate and soluble fiber and which provide enough calories for growth and activity. It

Diet to avoid osteoporosis

❏ Plenty of calcium

❏ Avoid too much salt

❏ Stay within a healthy weight range and avoid excessive slimness

will avoid quickly absorbed carbohydrates, such as sugar, unless they are present in fiber-containing foods.

Osteoporosis
This condition – when bones become porous and easily broken – occurs mainly in women, especially older women. Risk factors include the drop in female hormones after menopause or with extreme slimness, a lack of calcium in the diet, smoking and a lack of exercise.

Cancer
Most research on the connections between diet and cancer has concentrated on cancers of the breast and colon – two of the most common types in Western countries. The exact mechanisms relating a high fat diet to these cancers are not fully understood but eating large amounts of fat does seem to create the right environment for cancer-causing substances (carcinogens) to gain a footing and cause cells to

multiply at an abnormal rate.

Fat on the upper body is a factor in colon cancer for both men and women, and is also related to a higher incidence of breast cancer in women over the

age of 50. Post-menopausal women who eat a high-fat diet have higher levels of hormone-related substances which are known to be cancer-forming. Dietary fat also causes a greater production of

Ricotta Cheesecake (page 124) is low in fat and a good source of calcium.

Diet for adult-onset diabetes (Type 2 diabetes)

❏ Your doctor will advise if you need insulin or if diet is the main treatment

❏ Reduce weight to the limits of the healthy weight range, preferably keeping to the low side of the range

❏ Eat carbohydrate foods which are high in dietary fiber – whole wheat bread, whole grain cereals (especially oats and barley), legumes, fruits and vegetables

❏ Divide food evenly throughout the day (a dietitian can help you plan this)

❏ Avoid fats, especially saturated fats

❏ Drink alcohol only in moderation, and never drink on an empty stomach

❏ Avoid sugar, except when present with high-fiber foods (a small serving of dessert occasionally is not usually a problem once weight is normal)

bile acids which can be converted to substances known to cause colon cancer.

Dietary fiber may offer some protection against both breast and colon cancers. Different types of fiber may be important in each of these conditions.

Soluble fiber seems to offer some protection against colon cancer and starches in some foods such as rice may have a similar action. When bacteria in the large colon digest soluble fibers, acids are formed. One of these, butyric acid, will inactivate an enzyme which colon cancer cells need in order to multiply. Some types of starch also stimulate the production of these acids in the large colon and this may help explain the low incidence of colon cancer in most Asian people who eat their traditional diet. Bananas, cold potatoes and oats cooked and allowed to cool (as in the typical Scottish porridge oats) also contain this 'resistant starch'.

With breast cancer, insoluble fibers found in whole wheat or wheat-bran products change the bacterial population in the intestine and cause some carcinogens to be excreted.

There is also evidence that many types of cancer occur less in those who eat plenty of fruits and vegetables. This may be due to carotenes and/or vitamin C in these foods. Beta-carotene takes its name from 'carrots' which are one of the richest sources, but all red, orange and green fruits and vegetables supply beta-carotene.

Vitamin C is found in all raw and lightly cooked vegetables (preferably those that have been microwaved, steamed or stir-fried) and fruits. The richest sources include guavas, bell pepper, broccoli, Brussels sprouts, pawpaw, citrus fruits, kiwi fruit, strawberries, cabbage,

Vegetables and fruits rich in beta-carotene	
Food	beta-carotene micrograms
carrots, 3½ oz	12,000
sweet potato, orange variety, 3½ oz	6780
spinach, 3½ oz	6000
mango, 1 medium	3800
pumpkin, 3½ oz	3000
cantaloupe, dark-colored, 5 oz	3000
broccoli, 3½ oz	2500
apricots, dried, 1¾ oz	1800
bell pepper, red, ½ medium	1500
apricots, 3 medium	1500
pawpaw, 5 oz	1350
dried peaches, 1¾ oz	1000
tomato, 1 medium	900

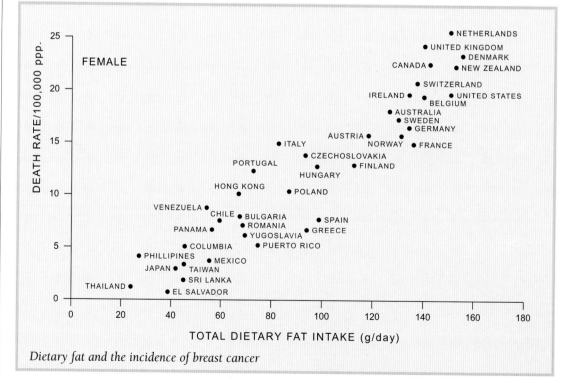

Dietary fat and the incidence of breast cancer

Diet for protection against cancer

❏ Eat less fat of all types

❏ Eat plenty of fruits and vegetables

❏ Eat plenty of whole grain products, with as wide a variety as possible

❏ Eat more fish

Note: If you have any suspicion of cancer, always seek qualified medical treatment before any self-medication with diet.

cauliflower, cantaloupe, mango, peas, potatoes and tomatoes.

Constipation and irritable bowel syndrome

Constipation is common, especially in women, and may become worse with age. It is usually caused by a lack of dietary fiber. Constipation also occurs in children, but is less common in men. Irritable bowel syndrome, with alternating constipation and diarrhoea, may occur in men or women. Stress is an important factor and many people find their bowel reacts when they contend with any nervousness or stress.

The major factors involved in constipation include a lack of dietary fiber, a lack of water and, sometimes, insufficient exercise. Laxatives may work in the short term but are inadvisable. The main treatment for constipation and irritable bowel syndrome is a high-fiber diet. However, see your doctor to make sure there are no major problems.

Gallstones

The gall bladder is involved in the digestion of fat. Every time fat is present in the small intestine, the gall bladder squirts out some bile to break it up. When the body is forced to process high levels of fat and make a lot of cholesterol, the gall bladder becomes overworked and gallstones may form. The stones themselves consist to a large extent of cholesterol.

Liver disease

All types of liver problems are potentially serious as the liver is a complex organ that processes all

Diet for protection against gallstones

❏ Reduce weight to normal with a low-fat diet and exercise

❏ Eat less of fats of all kinds

❏ Eat small amounts often rather than three large meals

Note: Always see your doctor if you suspect gallstones, as dietary treatment will not cure them.

the fats, proteins, carbohydrates and alcohol that we consume. Fortunately it has enormous powers of regeneration. As soon as it ceases to function in the proper manner, you will usually feel nauseated and should seek medical attention.

Infections of the liver cause inflammations known as hepatitis. The organ may also develop fibrous areas caused by alcohol, even in those who would be classed as 'social' drinkers.

The nausea accompanying most types of liver problems ensures that little fat is eaten. The fats in milk are usually well tolerated and a simple diet with milk drinks (skim, if needed) as well as fruits, vegetables, breads and cereals and fish, chicken or very lean meat is advisable. Avoid alcohol. Even after recovery from conditions such as hepatitis, it will take many months before the liver can cope with alcohol of any type.

Small, frequent meals are usually more appealing to anyone with liver disease than a large plate of food.

Weight
Excess weight is one of the major problems in America. Being underweight can also be a problem (see Weight – *not too high, not too low*, page 13).

Hypoglycemia (low blood sugar)
Hypoglycemia is defined in different ways. Some consider levels normal while others feel the same levels require treatment.

A drop in blood sugar level occurs in most people several times a day, usually four to five hours after a meal. This naturally stimulates the appetite. We eat and the blood sugar levels are restored to normal.

Hypoglycemia can also be reversed by breaking down lean muscle tissue and converting the protein to blood glucose.

Some people react to the normal 'lows' by feeling a sudden loss of energy, irritability, headaches, poor concentration, shakiness, depression and nausea. The temptation is to eat a sugary snack but a sounder solution to a late-afternoon energy slump is to eat smaller meals with between-meal snacks of high-fiber carbohydrate foods.

Diet to avoid or treat constipation

❏ Eat more fiber from a variety of sources (whole grain cereals and cereal products, whole wheat bread, fruits, vegetables, seeds, nuts)

❏ Drink more water

❏ Avoid excessive amounts of finely milled, unprocessed bran

Breakfast
Dishes

BREAKFAST IS AN IMPORTANT MEAL. IT RAISES THE metabolic rate and gives you energy for the day ahead. Fresh fruit, cereal and whole grain toast make an excellent, well-balanced breakfast, while more substantial dishes made with vegetables or eggs are ideal for a leisurely brunch – try Frittata, Baked Lima Beans or tasty Vegetable and Oat Patties. Check out your local health food store for a range of good quality breakfast cereals, made from oats, whole wheat or other whole grains. Avoid those with sugar and vegetable oils high in their list of ingredients – some of these products have a similar fat and sugar content to a bowl of broken-up sweet cookies. Avoid croissants and pastries, too – they are high in fat. Just one croissant has as many calories as five slices of toast.

Toasted Muesli

1½ lb rolled oats

1 cup shredded coconut

⅓ cup sesame seeds

½ cup sliced almonds

8 oz barley flakes

½ cup roasted buckwheat (Kasha)

1 cup wheat germ

8 oz mixed dried fruit

8 oz golden raisins

½ cup pumpkin seeds

½ cup sunflower seeds

SERVES 30

1 Place oats on an ungreased baking sheet. Bake in a moderate (350°F) oven for about 15 minutes, stirring several times, until oats are golden brown (take care as they burn easily). Cool.
2 Toast coconut, sesame seeds and almonds in a dry frying pan, tossing to prevent burning. Cool.
3 Combine all ingredients and store in an airtight container. It will keep fresh for at least two weeks.

Nutritional information per 1¾ oz serving: Protein 6 g; fat 7 g; carbohydrate 27 g; dietary fiber 5 g; 195 cals
Other features: A good source of thiamin (B1) and iron

Preparation time: 20 minutes
Cooking time: 15 minutes

Swiss Muesli

1 cup rolled oats

½ cup barley flakes

¾ cup low-fat milk

1 large apple, cored and chopped finely

8 oz blueberries (or use an extra apple)

1 tablespoon honey

½ cup non-fat yogurt

¼ cup toasted sliced almonds

¼ teaspoon cinnamon

SERVES 4

1 Mix oats and barley flakes with milk; refrigerate overnight.
2 Next morning, add remaining ingredients.

Nutritional information per serving: Protein 10 g; fat 8 g; carbohydrate 47 g; dietary fiber 6 g; 295 cals
Other features: A good source of vitamin C and thiamin (B1); also provides calcium, riboflavin (B2) and iron

Preparation time: 20 minutes
+ overnight standing
Cooking time: Nil

Swiss Muesli.

Baked Lima Beans

2 cups (12 oz) lima beans

5 cups water

2 bay leaves

2 tablespoons dark brown sugar

1 apple, peeled and chopped roughly

1 tablespoon dry mustard

¼ cup malt vinegar

1 large onion, chopped finely

2 medium tomatoes, diced

SERVES 4

1 Place beans, water and bay leaves in a saucepan and bring to the boil. Cover, turn off heat and leave to stand for an hour (if leaving longer, place in refrigerator).
2 Bring beans to the boil and simmer, covered, for 1 hour.
3 Drain beans, reserving ½ cup liquid. Add remaining ingredients to beans, pour into a casserole and bake, covered, in a slow (300°F) oven for 1 hour.

Nutritional information per serving: Protein 12 g; no fat; carbohydrate 37 g; dietary fiber 10 g; 200 cals
Other features: A good source of vitamin C; provides B-complex vitamins, potassium and iron

Preparation time: 20 minutes
+ 1 hour standing time
Cooking time: 2 hours

Previous page: Swiss Muesli (page 28) and Yeasty Oat Cakes (page 29).

Yeasty Oat Cakes

A delightful recipe to make for breakfast – or have with coffee.

1 cup low-fat milk

2 teaspoons honey

1 package dry yeast

¼ cup unprocessed oat bran

½ cup quick-cooking oats

½ cup oat flour
(or all-purpose flour)

1 Warm milk (30 seconds on High in microwave is ideal). Add honey and yeast and stir thoroughly until yeast is dissolved.
2 Add oat bran, oats and flour and leave mixture to stand in a warm place for 30 minutes.
3 Cook spoonfuls of mixture on a hot non-stick pan until golden brown on both sides.

Nutritional information per serving: Protein 2 g; fat 1 g; carbohydrate 7 g; dietary fiber 1 g; 40 cals

Preparation time: 15 minutes
+ 30 minutes standing time
Cooking time: 6 minutes

MAKES 16

Yeasty Oat Cakes.

Oaty Pancakes

You can make up the mixture the night before, put it in the refrigerator and have a quick and healthy breakfast next morning.

2 cups low-fat milk

1 tablespoon lemon juice

1 cup unprocessed oat bran

½ cup all-purpose flour

1 tablespoon sugar

2 eggs

1 Combine milk and lemon juice and stand for 10 minutes.
2 Place all ingredients in blender or food processor and process until well combined. Leave to stand for 30 minutes (or, preferably, overnight). If mixture is too thick, add a little more low-fat milk.
3 Grease a non-stick pan, heat and pour in some of the pancake batter, swirl to coat pan and cook until brown on each side.
4 Serve with lemon juice or poached or canned fruit (without added sugar).

Nutritional information per serving: Protein 5 g; fat 2 g; carbohydrate 15 g; dietary fiber 1 g; 100 cals

Preparation time: 5 minutes
+ 40 minutes standing time
Cooking time: 3 minutes each

MAKES 10 pancakes

Buckwheat Pancakes

Buckwheat pancakes are dark in color and have a slightly nutty flavor. They are quite heavy, so do not attempt to eat too many.

2 cups low-fat milk

2 eggs, separated

2 tablespoons honey

1½ cups buckwheat flour

½ cup all-purpose white flour

1½ teaspoons baking powder

1 In blender or food processor, combine all ingredients except egg whites.
2 Beat egg whites until stiff and gently fold into buckwheat mixture. (Add a little more milk, if necessary, to make a smooth consistency.)
3 Cook spoonfuls on a hot, greased non-stick pan until bubbly. Turn and cook other side. Serve immediately as they tend to become heavy when cold.

Nutritional information per serving: Protein 4 g; fat 1 g; carbohydrate 15 g; dietary fiber 2 g; 85 cals

Preparation time: 10 minutes
Cooking time: 3 minutes each pancake

MAKES 18 pancakes

HEALTH TIP

Lecithin is needed in the transport of fats in the body, but we are quite capable of making it as required. Commercial lecithin is about 80 per cent fat.

Vegetable and Oat Patties

Do not mash potato with milk or butter.

½ cup cooked, diced turkey
or lean ham

2 cups mashed potato

1 cup cooked peas

2 eggs, beaten

1 cup rolled oats

2 tablespoons
chopped parsley

MAKES 12 patties

1 Combine all ingredients, mix well and form into patties.
2 Cook in a non-stick pan until brown on both sides.

Nutritional information per serving: Protein 5 g; fat 2 g; carbohydrate 10 g; dietary fiber 2 g; 76 cals

Preparation time: 30 minutes
Cooking time: 12 minutes

Frittata

2 teaspoons olive oil

1 medium tomato, sliced

2 medium zucchini, sliced

6–8 button mushrooms, sliced

2 eggs

1 tablespoon fresh chopped
herbs (parsley, thyme,
oregano or chives)

2 tablespoons low-fat milk

2 tablespoons rolled oats

SERVES 2

1 Heat oil in a non-stick frying pan and cook vegetables for 4–5 minutes.
2 Beat eggs with herbs and milk. Add oats. Pour egg mixture into pan and cook over a gentle heat until egg sets and mixture is brown underneath.

Nutritional information per serving: Protein 13 g; fat 12 g; carbohydrate 16 g; dietary fiber 5 g; 220 cals
Other features: An excellent source of vitamin C; a good source of riboflavin (B2); and provides niacin (B3), iron, thiamin (B1) and carotene (vitamin A)

Preparation time: 20 minutes
Cooking time: 10 minutes

Eggs in Baskets

Lean ham may also be used in this recipe.

4 round whole wheat
bread rolls

4 slices lean turkey

4 eggs

4 slices tomato

1 tablespoon chopped parsley

SERVES 4

1 Cut a lid from the top of each roll. Carefully scoop out middle of roll to make room for an egg. Use a blender or food processor to make the bread you have removed into crumbs. Reserve one tablespoon of these crumbs (keep the rest in an airtight container in the refrigerator for some other dish).
2 Place a slice of turkey inside each roll. Break an egg into each roll and top with a slice of tomato.
3 Combine 1 tablespoon of reserved crumbs with parsley and sprinkle over top of rolls. Bake at 400°F for 15 minutes, when rolls should be crisp and eggs set.

Nutritional information per serving: Protein 17 g; fat 9 g; carbohydrate 24 g; dietary fiber 3 g; 248 cals
Other features: A good source of niacin (B3) and provides thiamin (B1) and riboflavin (B2) as well as iron.

Preparation time: 30 minutes
Cooking time: 15 minutes

Cornmeal Muffins

- 1 cup cornmeal
- ½ cup all-purpose flour
- 2 teaspoons baking powder
- ½ teaspoon baking soda
- 2 eggs, separated
- 1 cup buttermilk
- 2 tablespoons oil
- 1 tablespoon lemon juice

1 Combine dry ingredients. Set aside.
2 Beat egg yolks, buttermilk, oil and lemon juice together. Add to dry ingredients, stirring just enough to combine.
3 Beat egg whites stiffly. Fold into cornmeal mixture and spoon into greased non-stick muffin pans. Bake at 400°F for 15–20 minutes. Serve while still warm.

Nutritional information per serving: Protein 4 g; fat 5 g; carbohydrate 15 g; dietary fiber 1 g; 120 cals

MAKES 12 large muffins

Preparation time: 30 minutes
Cooking time: 20 minutes

HEALTH TIP

When milk is heated, it retains all its calcium.

Vegetable and Oat Patties, left, and Cornmeal Muffins.

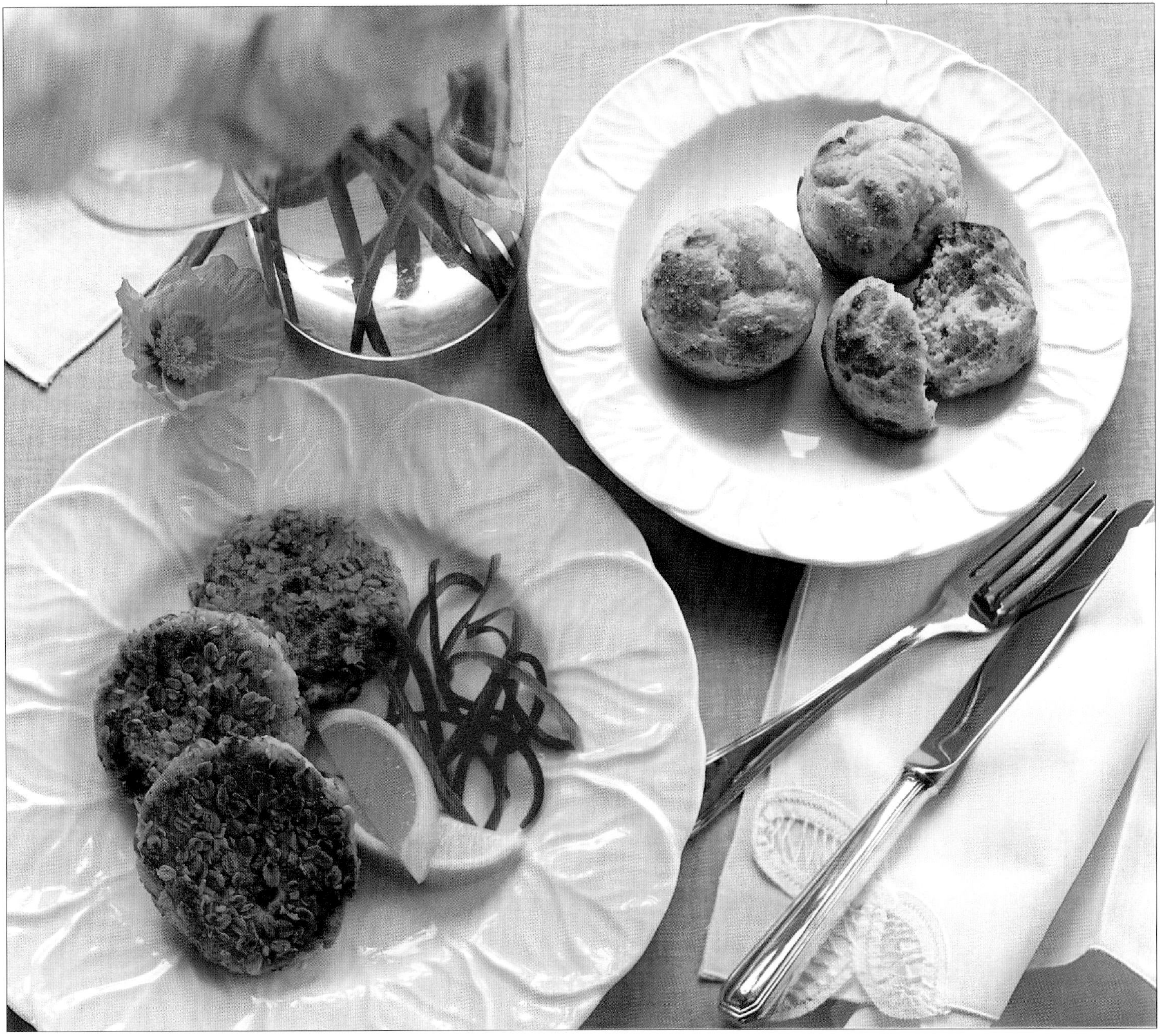

Banana Bran Pancakes

For a delicious weekend breakfast, make up the mixture for these pancakes the night before. Make sure you use a very hot pan for best results. Leftover mixture can be stored in the refrigerator for the following day, if you like.

2 cups skim milk
1 tablespoon lemon juice
1 large or 2 small ripe bananas
1 cup whole wheat flour
½ cup unprocessed bran
1 egg, separated
cinnamon

1 In blender, combine all the ingredients except egg white and cinnamon. Leave to stand in refrigerator overnight.
2 In the morning, beat egg white until stiff. Fold into pancake mixture, using a metal spoon.
3 Heat a non-stick pan, grease lightly and pour in about one sixth of mixture. Swirl to spread mixture. Cook about 1 minute then turn and cook other side. Sprinkle with cinnamon and serve immediately.

Nutritional information per pancake: Protein 8 g; fat 2 g; carbohydrate 23 g; very good dietary fiber 5 g; 140 cals
Other features: A good source of riboflavin (B2) and thiamin (B1), provides useful amounts of calcium, potassium and niacin (B3) and some iron. Low sodium (55 mg)

SERVES 6

Preparation time: 15 minutes + overnight standing
Cooking time: 10–15 minutes

Ricotta Fruit Whip

This is a good substitute for whipped cream with only a fraction of the fat. You can make it up to an hour before serving.

1 cup low-fat ricotta cheese
2 tablespoons concentrated orange juice
1 cup canned pears in pear juice, drained
½ teaspoon vanilla extract

Place all ingredients in a blender and process until very smooth.

Nutritional information per serving: Protein 6 g: fat 4 g; carbohydrate 6 g; dietary fiber 1 g; 80 cals
Other features: Useful source of vitamin C and calcium. Low sodium (95 mg)

SERVES 6

Preparation time: 5 minutes
Cooking time: Nil

Apricot and Ginger Sauce

Use fresh root ginger in this recipe.

1 lb fresh apricots, pitted and chopped
1 tablespoon orange juice
1 teaspoon chopped ginger
1 cup orange juice
1 tablespoon cornstarch
sugar substitute to taste

1 Heat apricots with 1 tablespoon orange juice and the ginger.
2 Blend 1 cup orange juice and cornstarch and stir into apricot mixture. Cook for 1–2 minutes, stirring constantly. Add sugar substitute.
3 Purée sauce until smooth. Serve warm or chilled.

Nutritional information per serving: No protein; no fat; carbohydrate 8 g; dietary fiber 1 g; 45 cals
Other features: Good source of vitamin C and a useful source of vitamin A. Negligible sodium (5 mg)

Opposite: Banana Bran Pancakes served with Ricotta Fruit Whip, and Apricot and Ginger Sauce.

SERVES 6

Preparation time: 10 minutes
Cooking time: 15 minutes

SOUPS &
STARTERS

WE TEND TO THINK OF SOUPS AS COLD-WEATHER FOOD,
but here's a selection of recipes that will take you
right through the seasons. Try hearty Veal and
Vegetable Soup on chilly days, and cooling Watercress
Vichyssoise when the temperature starts to climb.
The basis of a good, full-flavored soup is a good stock.
It's well worth making the effort to prepare your own,
and it is much easier than you might think. Many of
these soups and appetizers can become light meals
simply by adding a crisp salad and some crusty bread.
For those planning a dinner party, select a special
classic such as Sesame Shrimp or Carpaccio of Salmon.
Or, if you're looking for something striking and a little
unusual, choose Pickled Vegetables with delicious
crunchy Seeded Crisp Bread.

Fresh Tomato Soup.

Fresh Tomato Soup

The secret of making a good tomato soup is to use very ripe tomatoes and well-flavored stock. Sieve the soup and you won't need to peel the tomatoes.

2 teaspoons olive oil

1 medium onion, diced

1 clove garlic, crushed

1 teaspoon sugar

½ teaspoon chopped chili (optional)

2 lb ripe tomatoes, chopped roughly

1 tablespoon tomato paste (no added salt)

3 cups veal or chicken stock

bunch fresh herbs (try parsley, basil or thyme, mint and rosemary)

freshly ground pepper

1 Heat oil, add onion and garlic, cover and cook over a gentle heat for 3–4 minutes.
2 Add sugar, chili, tomatoes and tomato paste and stir well. Cook for a further 2–3 minutes. Add stock and herbs. Bring to the boil; cover and simmer for 10 minutes (do not overcook).
3 Remove herbs. Purée soup, then rub through a sieve to remove any pieces of tomato skin. Add pepper to taste.

Nutritional information per serving: Protein 3 g; fat 2 g; carbohydrate 10 g; good dietary fiber 3 g; 70 cals
Other features: An excellent source of vitamin C, a good source of niacin (B3) and potassium and has useful amounts of iron and vitamin A. Low sodium (40 mg)

SERVES 6

Preparation time: 30 minutes
Cooking time: 20 minutes

Black Bean Soup.

Previous page:
Fresh Tomato Soup, top, and Carpaccio of Salmon (page 44).

Black Bean Soup

Any leftovers of this wonderful dark soup can be frozen. For a thicker soup, purée a cup or two separately and stir to combine before serving.

6 cups water

10 oz black beans

6 cups chicken stock

2 chicken stock cubes

2 cloves garlic

1 teaspoon dried marjoram

2 bay leaves

1 medium onion, diced

1 medium carrot, diced

2 small celery stalks, sliced

2 tablespoons tomato paste

1 teaspoon hot chili sauce

1 tablespoon wine vinegar

2 tablespoons low-fat yogurt

chili powder

1 Soak beans in water overnight. Drain and discard water.
2 Cover beans with chicken stock. Add stock cubes, garlic, marjoram, bay leaves and vegetables. Bring to the boil and simmer 1 hour, or until beans are tender. Remove bay leaves.
3 Stir in tomato paste, chili and vinegar. Serve with a swirl of low-fat yogurt and a sprinkling of chili powder.

Nutritional information per serving: Protein 13 g; fat 1 g; carbohydrate 38 g; excellent dietary fiber 14 g; 175 cals
Other features: A very good source of iron and potassium, a good source of zinc and B-complex vitamins. Also provides some calcium. Low sodium (100 mg)

SERVES 6

Preparation time: 30 minutes
+ overnight soaking
Cooking time: 1 hour

Pumpkin and Rosemary Soup

2 lb pumpkin flesh

4 cups chicken stock

3 sprigs rosemary (or use
1 teaspoon dried rosemary)

3 bay leaves

1 cup non-fat dry milk

½ cup low-fat yogurt

freshly ground black pepper

1 In a large saucepan, combine pumpkin, stock and herbs. Bring to the boil, then cover and simmer for about 15 minutes or until the pumpkin is cooked. Remove rosemary sprigs and bay leaves.
2 Purée soup, adding dry milk. Serve in bowls, topping each with a spoonful of yogurt and a sprinkle of black pepper. Garnish with a sprig of fresh rosemary.

Nutritional information per serving: Protein 11 g; fat 2 g; carbohydrate 23 g; good dietary fiber 3 g; sodium 140 mg; 125 cals
Other features: A very good source of calcium and potassium, a good source of vitamins A and C and also provides some iron and zinc

Preparation time: 15 minutes
Cooking time: 20 minutes

SERVES 6

In the US, if a food label reads 'starch' it is safe for people on gluten-free diets as it signifies cornstarch.

Mushroom Soup

2 teaspoons butter or margarine

1 medium onion, diced

1 teaspoon French mustard

1 teaspoon dried thyme

1 lb mushrooms, preferably wild or flat, chopped roughly

3 cups chicken or veal stock

½ cup red wine

1 tablespoon light sour cream

few thyme sprigs

1 Heat butter in a saucepan and gently cook onion for 3–4 minutes, allowing it to brown slightly.
2 Add mustard, thyme and mushrooms and cook a further 2–3 minutes, stirring gently.
3 Add stock and wine, bring to the boil, cover and simmer for 10 minutes. Purée soup. Serve with a drizzle of sour cream on top of each bowl. Garnish with a fresh thyme sprig.

Nutritional information per serving: Protein 6 g; fat 4 g; carbohydrate 5 g; very good dietary fiber 4 g; 70 cals
Other features: A very good source of riboflavin (B2) and niacin (B3) and a good source of potassium. Low sodium (80 mg)

Preparation time: 20 minutes
Cooking time: 20 minutes

SERVES 4

Arrowroot and cornstarch can be interchanged in most recipes. Arrowroot gives a clearer thickening and is often used in lemon sauces for this reason.

Creamy Cauliflower Soup

2 lb cauliflower, chopped roughly

4 cups chicken stock

1 medium onion, chopped roughly

3 bay leaves

fresh mint sprig

1 cup non-fat dry milk

1 tablespoon snipped chives

1 Place all ingredients except dry milk and chives in a large saucepan. Bring to the boil and simmer 12–15 minutes, or until cauliflower is tender.
2 Remove bay leaves and mint. Purée soup in food processor or blender, adding dry milk. Reheat. Serve in deep soup bowls and sprinkle with chives.

Nutritional information per serving: Protein 11 g; no fat; carbohydrate 15 g; good dietary fiber 4 g; sodium 152 mg; 110 cals
Other features: An excellent source of vitamin C and niacin (B3), a very good source of potassium and a good source of calcium. Also supplies some iron and B-complex vitamins

Preparation time: 10 minutes
Cooking time: 20 minutes

SERVES 6

Veal and Vegetable Soup

This hearty soup is a meal in itself – serve it with fresh whole wheat rolls.

1 tablespoon butter or margarine

1 large onion, sliced

1 clove garlic

1 veal knuckle (ask butcher to cut it through)

6 cups water

1 teaspoon mixed dried herbs

½ cup split peas

½ cup pearl barley

1 large potato, peeled and diced

1 kohlrabi bulb, peeled and diced

1 leek, washed and sliced

1 large carrot, diced

1 large parsnip, peeled and diced

1 celery stalk, sliced

1 cup sliced green beans (or broccoli pieces)

1 cup sliced mushrooms

1 tablespoon chopped parsley

1 Melt butter or margarine and gently cook onion and garlic for 3–4 minutes. Add veal and cook 3–4 minutes longer, stirring occasionally.
2 Add water, herbs, peas and barley, bring to the boil, cover and simmer for 1½ hours.
3 Add potato, kohlrabi, leek, carrot and parsnip and cook for a further 20 minutes. Remove veal.
4 Add celery, beans and mushrooms to soup and simmer a further 10 minutes.
5 While vegetables are cooking, remove meat from veal bone and return meat to soup. Serve topped with parsley.

Nutritional information per serving: Protein 25 g; fat 4 g; carbohydrate 29 g; excellent dietary fiber 8 g; sodium 140 mg; 250 cals
Other features: A very good source of niacin (B3), riboflavin (B2), potassium and vitamin A and a good source of thiamin (B1), zinc, iron and vitamin C

Preparation time: 30 minutes

Cooking time: 2 hours

SERVES 6

Chilled Tomato Soup

This richly flavored soup makes a delightful summer first course.

2 lb very ripe, red tomatoes, cored

2 medium cucumbers

1 small onion

1 medium red bell pepper

2 cloves garlic, crushed

1 cup beef stock

few thyme sprigs

2 tablespoons chopped parsley

1 tablespoon lemon juice

freshly ground pepper

1 Skin tomatoes by covering with boiling water for 1 minute then plunging them into iced water. Dice finely.
2 Cut cucumbers lengthwise and remove seeds. Dice flesh finely. Dice onion and bell pepper finely (some food processors do this well). Combine with tomatoes, garlic, beef stock and thyme. Leave to stand for at least 2 hours to allow the flavors to blend. Remove thyme.
3 Add parsley and lemon juice just before serving. Add freshly ground pepper to taste. Float an ice cube on top of the soup in each bowl.

Nutritional information per serving: Protein 5 g; no fat; carbohydrate 12 g; very good dietary fiber 5 g; 65 cals
Other features: An excellent source of vitamin C, a very good source of potassium and a good source of vitamin A and niacin (B3). Also provides riboflavin (B2) and iron. Low sodium (45 mg)

Preparation time: 20 minutes + 2 hours chilling time

Cooking time: Nil

SERVES 4

Opposite: Veal and Vegetable Soup, top, and Mushroom Soup (page 37).

Scandinavian Fruit Soup

2 cups apple juice

2 cups orange juice

1 cup dried apricots

½ cup dried apples

½ cup raisins

1 piece cinnamon stick, about 2½ inches long

3 or 4 cardamom pods

½ cup white rice

½ cup low-fat yogurt

½ teaspoon finely grated orange rind

SERVES 6

1 Place juices, fruit, spices and rice in a large saucepan and leave to soak for at least 1 hour.

2 Bring mixture to the boil and simmer gently for 15 minutes. Remove cinnamon stick and cardamom pods. If serving cold, cool, then refrigerate for at least 2 hours. Serve topped with a swirl of yogurt and a sprinkle of orange rind.

Nutritional information per serving: Protein 3 g; no fat; carbohydrate 52 g; excellent dietary fiber 9 g; 220 cals
Other features: A very good source of potassium. Provides some calcium. Low sodium (70 mg)

Preparation time: 15 minutes + at least 1 hour soaking
Cooking time: 20 minutes
+ 2 hours refrigeration if served cold

Carrot and Orange Soup.

Opposite: Watercress Vichyssoise, top, and Scandinavian Fruit Soup.

Carrot and Orange Soup

1 lb carrots, sliced

1 large potato, peeled and sliced

2 cups chicken stock

1 cup orange juice

1 teaspoon chopped fresh ginger

1 teaspoon curry powder

SERVES 4

Combine all ingredients, bring to the boil, cover and simmer for 20 minutes, or until vegetables are tender. Purée until smooth. Serve the soup garnished with yogurt and dill, if you like.

Nutritional information per serving: Protein 3 g; no fat; carbohydrate 19 g; very good dietary fiber 5 g; 90 cals
Other features: An excellent source of vitamins A and C, a good source of niacin (B3) and potassium. Also provides useful amounts of iron. Low sodium (90 mg)

Preparation time: 15 minutes
Cooking time: 30 minutes

Watercress Vichyssoise

2 teaspoons butter or margarine

1 medium onion, chopped roughly

2 medium leeks, washed and sliced

2 large potatoes, peeled and sliced

4 cups chicken stock

3 bay leaves

1 teaspoon finely grated lemon rind

1 bunch watercress, washed

6½ oz low-fat yogurt

few thyme sprigs

SERVES 6

1 Heat butter in a large saucepan. Add onion, cover and cook gently for 3–4 minutes.
2 Add leeks, potato, stock, bay leaves and rind, and simmer for 15 minutes.
3 Remove coarse stems from watercress and add the leaves to saucepan. Cook 2 minutes. Remove bay leaves. Cool.
4 Purée soup, swirl in yogurt and chill until ready to serve. Garnish each serving with a thyme sprig.

Nutritional information per serving: Protein 8 g; fat 3 g; carbohydrate 20 g; very good dietary fiber 5 g; 140 cals
Other features: An excellent source of vitamin C, a very good source of potassium and a good source of iron, vitamin A, riboflavin (B2) and niacin (B3). Also a useful source of calcium. Low sodium (120 mg)

Preparation time: 10 minutes
Cooking time: 20 minutes + 2 hours refrigeration

Barley Soup

1 veal shank, cut into slices	
1 large onion, sliced	
1 cup pearl barley	
6 cups water	
3 bay leaves	
few parsley stalks	
1 teaspoon mixed dried herbs	
2 medium carrots, sliced	
2 celery stalks, sliced	
2 cups sliced mushrooms	
1 cup green beans, sliced	
1 tablespoon fresh snipped dill (or parsley)	

SERVES 6

1 In a large saucepan, brown veal and onion.
2 Add barley, water and herbs. Bring to the boil, cover and simmer for 2 hours.
3 Remove veal. Cut meat off bones and return meat to soup.
4 Bring back to the boil, add vegetables and simmer for 10–15 minutes. Sprinkle each bowl with dill before serving.

Nutritional information per serving: Protein 14 g; fat 1 g; carbohydrate 25 g; dietary fiber 5 g; 165 cals
Other features: An excellent source of carotene (vitamin A); good source of niacin (B3) and vitamin C; provides iron

Preparation time: 30 minutes
Cooking time: 2 hours 15 minutes

Potato and Leek Soup

1 tablespoon olive oil	
1 medium onion, sliced	
2 medium leeks, sliced	
1 lb potatoes, peeled and cut into quarters	
4 cups chicken stock	
2 bay leaves	
¾ cup instant non-fat dry milk	
pinch nutmeg	

SERVES 4

1 Heat oil and add onion and leeks. Place lid on saucepan and allow vegetables to 'sweat' for 4–5 minutes, stirring occasionally.
2 Add potatoes, stock and bay leaves. Bring to the boil and simmer for 15–20 minutes or until potatoes are tender. Remove bay leaves.
3 Purée soup in blender or food processor, adding dry milk and nutmeg.
4 Serve hot or chilled, garnished with fresh herbs.

Nutritional information per serving: Protein 14 g; fat 5 g; carbohydrate 36 g; dietary fiber 5 g; 236 cals
Other features: Excellent source of vitamin C, good source of potassium and calcium

Preparation time: 20 minutes
Cooking time: 25 minutes

Chicken Stock

2 lb chicken bones or 1 whole chicken	
8 cups water	
1 medium onion, chopped roughly	
2 bay leaves	
8–10 peppercorns	
1 small celery stalk, chopped roughly	
1 small carrot, chopped roughly	
few fresh parsley or thyme sprigs	

MAKES 4 CUPS

1 Place all ingredients in a large saucepan, bring to the boil, cover, simmer for 1–1½ hours. Strain, then cool and refrigerate.
2 Remove and discard any fat from top. Freeze if you like.
3 Chicken stock can be reduced by boiling rapidly without a lid until two-thirds of volume remains. (Reduced chicken stock is ideal for stir-frying vegetables.) Freeze if you like.

Nutritional information per serving: 1 cup chicken stock has 18 cals

Preparation time: 15 minutes
Cooking time: 1 hour 30 minutes

Salmon Mousse

¾ cup low-fat ricotta cheese

⅓ cup evaporated skim milk

1 teaspoon paprika

½ cup fresh cilantro

¼ cup sliced green onions

7 oz can red salmon, drained and flaked

1 tablespoon gelatin

2 tablespoons lemon juice

¼ cup boiling water

2 egg whites

1 Place ricotta, evaporated milk, paprika and cilantro in blender and process until smooth and creamy. Fold in green onions and salmon.

2 Soften gelatin in lemon juice, then dissolve in ¼ cup boiling water. Stir into salmon mixture.

3 Beat egg whites until stiff and fold into salmon. Place in four ½-cup capacity wet molds and refrigerate until set. Mousse may be flaked with a fork to serve. Serve with Seeded Crisp Bread (page 44) and a salad.

Nutritional information per serving: Protein 21 g; fat 7 g; carbohydrate 4 g; no dietary fiber; sodium 445 mg; 170 cals
Other features: A very good source of niacin (B3) and riboflavin (B2), a good source of calcium and provides some iron, zinc, potassium and vitamin A

Preparation time: 15 minutes + 2 hours setting time
Cooking time: Nil

SERVES 4

In a blender, process ricotta, evaporated milk, paprika and cilantro until smooth.

Fold drained and flaked salmon and green onions into ricotta mixture.

Dissolve gelatin in boiling water and stir into the salmon mixture.

Broiled Eggplant

2 small eggplants (about 10 oz each)

1 teaspoon sesame oil

1 teaspoon olive oil

freshly ground black pepper

2 tablespoons sesame seeds

4 small tomatoes

1 tablespoon chopped fresh basil

1 Slice eggplant. Combine oils and pepper and warm slightly (30 seconds in a microwave is ideal). Brush the eggplant slices with oil. Cover and leave for at least 30 minutes.

2 Put eggplant on foil-lined broiler pan and broil until brown.

3 Turn eggplant slices. Sprinkle with sesame seeds and broil again until brown (take care that sesame seeds do not burn).

4 Slice tomatoes and place on flat dish with eggplant. Sprinkle with basil and serve warm with focaccia or other bread.

Nutritional information per serving (without bread): Protein 4 g; fat 6 g; carbohydrate 6 g; very good dietary fiber 5 g; 85 cals
Other features: An excellent source of vitamin C, a good source of potassium and provides some niacin (B3), vitamin A and iron. Low sodium (10 mg)

Preparation time: 10 minutes + 30 minutes standing time
Cooking time: 10 minutes

SERVES 4

Cucumber Salad

2 medium cucumbers, about 8 oz each

1 teaspoon salt

1 tablespoon finely chopped mint

½ cup low-fat yogurt

freshly ground pepper

1 Peel cucumbers, cut them in half lengthwise and remove the seeds (use a teaspoon). Slice cucumber flesh thinly and place on a plate. Sprinkle with salt and leave for 20–30 minutes.

2 Rinse cucumber, drain well, squeeze out any moisture.

3 Toss together cucumber, mint, yogurt and a good grinding of pepper. Serve within 30 minutes.

Nutritional information per serving: Protein 2 g; no fat; carbohydrate 5 g; dietary fiber 1 g; 30 cals
Other features: High in vitamin C. Low sodium (50 mg)

Preparation time: 10 minutes + 30 minutes standing time
Cooking time: Nil

SERVES 4

Salmon Mousse, served with Seeded Crisp Bread (page 44).

Pickled Vegetables

1 large carrot, peeled, cut into 4 inch strips

6½ oz small onions

1 cup cauliflower pieces

2 medium zucchini, cut into 4 inch strips

1 red bell pepper, seeded, cut into 4 inch strips

1 green bell pepper, seeded, cut into 4 inch strips

2½ cups wine vinegar

2 teaspoons mustard seeds

10 peppercorns

4 cloves

MAKES 6 CUPS

1 Steam carrot, onions and cauliflower for 3 minutes. Drain.
2 Pour boiling water into a 6 cup jar. Drain.
3 Arrange all vegetables in sterilized jar.
4 Combine vinegar with mustard, peppercorns and cloves. Pour over vegetables, making sure vegetables are completely covered in vinegar. Seal and leave in refrigerator at least a week before use.

Nutritional information per serving: Protein 2 g; no fat; carbohydrate 4 g; some dietary fiber 2 g; 25 cals
Other features: Provides some potassium. Low sodium (15 mg)

Preparation time: 30 minutes + 1 week standing time
Cooking time: Nil

The Mediterranean diet (fish, vegetables, fruits, olive oil and almonds plus small amounts of yogurt and cheese) leads to a long, healthy life.

Seeded Crisp Bread

4 whole wheat pita breads

1 egg white

2 tablespoons water

2 tablespoons sesame seeds

2 tablespoons poppy seeds

1 tablespoon fennel seeds

SERVES 4–8

1 Carefully separate pita bread and lay each piece out flat.
2 Using a fork, beat egg white and water.
3 Using a pastry brush, brush surface of pita bread with egg white mixture and sprinkle with seeds. Bake on oven shelf at 350°F until crisp (7–8 minutes), taking care not to burn. Break into pieces to serve with Salmon Mousse or any dip.

Nutritional information per serving: Protein 6 g; fat 5 g; carbohydrate 13 g; some dietary fiber 3 g; sodium 165 mg; 115 cals
Other features: Provides some B-complex vitamins, vitamin E, iron and zinc

Preparation time: 10 minutes
Cooking time: 8 minutes

Carpaccio of Salmon.

Opposite, clockwise from top:
Pickled Vegetables,
Broiled Eggplant (page 43)
and Seeded Crisp Bread.

Carpaccio of Salmon

6½ oz piece of fresh salmon

lettuce, preferably butterhead, or cabbage

1 head Belgian endive

freshly ground black pepper

1½ tablespoons extra virgin olive oil

1 tablespoon lime juice (or use lemon)

1 tablespoon fresh basil leaves, shredded (optional)

SERVES 4

1 Place salmon in freezer for 30 minutes. Remove and slice it very thinly.
2 Arrange lettuce and Belgian endive leaves to one side of each plate. Spread salmon slices over remainder of plate and sprinkle with plenty of freshly ground pepper.
3 Combine olive oil and lime juice. Sprinkle over salmon and strew with basil, if you like.

Nutritional information per serving: Protein 11 g; fat 7 g; no carbohydrate; dietary fiber 1 g; 110 cals
Other features: A useful source of potassium. Low sodium (80 mg)

Preparation time: 10 minutes
+ 30 minutes for freezing the salmon
Cooking time: Nil

Sesame Shrimp

Researchers have confirmed that eating shrimp does not raise the blood cholesterol level – so you can enjoy this flavorsome dish with a clear conscience.

1 tablespoon salt-reduced soy sauce

1 tablespoon sherry

1 teaspoon sesame oil

2 teaspoons chopped fresh ginger

1 clove garlic, crushed

12 large raw shrimp, peeled, but with the tail left on

2 tablespoons sesame seeds

1 Combine soy sauce, sherry, oil, ginger and garlic. Add shrimp, cover and refrigerate for 30 minutes.
2 Remove shrimp from marinade and thread on to small bamboo skewers (soaked in water to prevent burning). Roll shrimp in sesame seeds and broil or barbecue for about 3 minutes.

Nutritional information per serving: Protein 19 g; fat 6 g; carbohydrate 1 g; dietary fiber 1 g; sodium 445 mg; 130 cals
Other features: A good source of iodine, and provides some iron, zinc, calcium and B-complex vitamins.

Preparation time: 20 minutes
(or 10 minutes if using peeled shrimp)
+ 30 minutes for marinating
Cooking time: 3 minutes

SERVES 4

Grapeseed oil is a polyunsaturated oil, like safflower, sunflower or corn oil. Olive oil is the best oil to use. Try using extra virgin olive oil on salads. Its strong flavor means you use less. If salad greens are dry, less dressing is needed.

Roasted Eggplant and Red Pepper Dip

It really is worth the effort of removing the pepper skins before making this dip – the flavor will be much sweeter.

1 eggplant, about 14 oz

2 red bell peppers

1 teaspoon coriander seeds

2 cloves garlic, crushed

2 tablespoons lemon juice

1 tablespoon extra virgin olive oil

½ teaspoon paprika

1 Place the whole eggplant on the oven shelf and bake at 350°F for 30 minutes.
2 While eggplant is roasting, skin red peppers; halve them and place, skin-side up, under a broiler and cook until blackened. Wrap blackened peppers in a clean damp cloth or kitchen towel and leave for about 10 minutes. Skin will then rub off.
3 Place coriander seeds in a saucepan, cover and heat until they begin to pop (do not burn).
4 Scoop out the eggplant flesh (discard the skin) and mix in a blender with the pepper, coriander, garlic and lemon juice. Process until smooth. Pour into a serving dish. Combine olive oil and paprika and drizzle it over the top.

Nutritional information per serving: Protein 2 g; fat 4 g; carbohydrate 5 g; good dietary fiber 3 g; 65 cals
Other features: An excellent source of vitamin C. Negligible sodium (8 mg).

Preparation time: 20 minutes
Cooking time: 45 minutes

SERVES 4–8

Opposite: Roasted Eggplant and Red Pepper Dip and, front, Sesame Shrimp.

LIGHT MEALS & SNACKS

FOR LUNCHES, WEEKEND MEALS AND INFORMAL entertaining, here is a selection of recipes you'll turn to time and again. They're quick and easy to prepare, they're delicious and very nutritious – in fact, flavorful sandwiches and crusty bread rolls are some of the healthiest foods around. Try Vegetables with Peanut Sauce or homemade Picnic Bread. You'll find these light meals appeal to every palate – making it simple to cater for vegetarians, weight-watchers and anyone on a special diet – and for all ages, including children, teenagers, adults and older family members.

Previous page: Picnic Bread (page 55) and, bottom, Vegetables with Peanut Sauce (page 54).

Italian Special

Sun-dried tomatoes in canola or olive oil are readily available in supermarkets and health food stores.

1 clove garlic

few parsley sprigs

¾ cup pitted black olives (or stuffed olives)

1 teaspoon lemon juice

2 tablespoons olive oil

freshly ground black pepper

4 crusty white rolls

4 slices mozzarella cheese

8 small sun-dried tomatoes

4 lettuce leaves

1 Place garlic, parsley, olives, lemon juice, oil and pepper in blender and process to a smooth paste.
2 Split rolls and spread with olive paste. Add cheese, sun-dried tomatoes and lettuce to each roll.

Nutritional information per sandwich: Protein 13 g; fat 20 g; carbohydrate 31 g; dietary fiber 5 g; 360 cals
Other features: Provides calcium and some iron

SERVES 4

Preparation time: 30 minutes
Cooking time: Nil

Avocado Delight

If the sandwich is not to be eaten within half an hour, brush the avocado slices with lemon juice to prevent browning.

2 slices grainy bread

1 tablespoon cottage cheese

¼ avocado

2 teaspoons toasted pine nuts

¼ cup alfalfa sprouts

Spread one slice of bread with cottage cheese. Top with sliced avocado, pine nuts and sprouts. Add remaining slice of bread.

Nutritional information per sandwich: Protein 11 g; fat 18 g; carbohydrate 23 g; dietary fiber 4 g; 200 cals

MAKES 1 sandwich

Preparation time: 10 minutes
Cooking time: Nil

Spicy Apple

Fresh seasonal pears may also be used in this sandwich.

1 large apple, peeled, cored and chopped

1 tablespoon lemon juice

¼ teaspoon cinnamon

pinch powdered cardamom

½ cup raisins

4 slices whole grain rye bread

2 tablespoons low-fat cream cheese

1 Combine apple and lemon juice. Add spices and raisins and mix well.
2 Spread bread slices with cream cheese. Divide the apple filling between two slices of bread and top with remaining two slices.

Nutritional information per sandwich: Protein 4 g; fat 2 g; carbohydrate 28 g; dietary fiber 3 g; 145 cals

SERVES 2

Preparation time: 20 minutes
Cooking time: Nil

Gourmet's Chicken Sandwich

Add some sprouts for extra crunch.

1 teaspoon chopped chili

2 teaspoons honey

1 tablespoon salt-reduced soy sauce

1 tablespoon mango chutney

¼ cup orange juice

4 boneless chicken thighs

1 French bread stick

1 cup watercress sprigs

4 lettuce leaves

8 cherry tomatoes

1 Combine chili, honey, soy sauce, chutney and orange juice. Add chicken and marinate for 30 minutes (or longer in refrigerator).
2 Remove chicken from marinade and cook in a non-stick pan for 5–6 minutes, turning once. Cool a little. If not serving straight away, cover and store in refrigerator.
3 To serve, cut French bread into four portions. Cut each piece through lengthwise and arrange a piece of the chicken, watercress, lettuce and tomatoes in each.

Nutritional information per sandwich: Protein 27 g; fat 9 g; carbohydrate 38 g; dietary fiber 3 g; 340 cals
Other features: A good source of niacin (B3); provides iron and thiamin (B1)

Preparation time: 20 minutes
+ 30 minutes standing time
Cooking time: 6 minutes

SERVES 4

TASTE TIP

If you like to take egg or tuna salad sandwiches to work or school for lunch, but don't want everyone to know about it, make up your sandwich the night before, wrap in plastic wrap and freeze. Take it out next morning and it will defrost by lunchtime – without having announced its presence!

Indian Special

1 teaspoon chopped fresh ginger

1 tablespoon chopped fresh cilantro

½ cup tofu

1 teaspoon garam masala

2 teaspoons lemon juice

½ cup cooked diced potato

½ cup cooked cauliflower pieces

½ cup cooked green beans

½ cup diced red bell pepper

4 small pita breads

1 In blender, combine ginger, cilantro, tofu, garam masala and lemon juice. Process until smooth and thick.
2 Combine vegetables and tofu mixture.
3 Slit top of pita bread and use quarter of mixture to fill each one.

Nutritional information per serving: Protein 6 g; fat 1 g; carbohydrate 25 g; dietary fiber 3 g; 140 cals
Other features: An excellent source of vitamin C

Preparation time: 20 minutes
Cooking time: Nil

SERVES 2

Well-dressed Falafel

¼ cup yogurt

1 tablespoon tahini

2 teaspoons lemon juice

4–6 falafel (see recipe, page 116)

4 slices whole wheat or whole grain bread

fresh cilantro sprigs

1 Combine yogurt, tahini and lemon juice (mixture will thicken).
2 Spread two or three falafel onto each of two slices of bread. Dribble half the tahini dressing over each and add a few cilantro sprigs. Top with remaining slice of bread.

Nutritional information per sandwich: Protein 9 g; fat 7 g; carbohydrate 22 g; dietary fiber 5 g; 180 cals
Other features: Provides iron and B complex vitamins

Preparation time: 20 minutes
Cooking time: Nil

SERVES 2

HEALTH TIP

Chicken can contain salmonella bacteria. These are killed during cooking, but cooked chicken can be recontaminated if knives or cutting boards used for raw chicken are also used for cooked chicken.

Raisin and Nut Spread

2 cups raisins
1 cup water
½ cup walnuts

Combine raisins and water. Bring to the boil and simmer for 5 minutes. Cool, mash and add walnuts.

Nutritional information per 2 oz serving of spread: Protein 1 g; fat 3 g; carbohydrate 18 g; dietary fiber 2 g; 100 cals

Preparation time: 10 minutes
Cooking time: 8 minutes

MAKES 3 cups

Peanut, Carrot and Raisin Spread

Use this spread on hot toast, muffins and whole wheat scones as well as in sandwiches.

½ cup peanut butter
1 cup grated carrot
¼ cup raisins

Combine all ingredients, mixing well.

Nutritional information per 2 oz spread: Protein 7 g; fat 16 g; carbohydrate 9 g; dietary fiber 3 g; 210 cals

Preparation time: 10 minutes
Cooking time: Nil

MAKES 1 cup

Date and Apricot Spread

For a zesty date and apricot spread, add 2 teaspoons of finely grated lemon or lime rind.

1 cup dried apricots
1 cup dates, pitted
1 cup apple juice

Combine all ingredients in saucepan. Bring to the boil, stir well and simmer for 7–8 minutes. Cover and allow to stand until cool. Keep in refrigerator until needed.

Nutritional information per 2 oz spread: Protein 1 g; fat 0 g; carbohydrate 19 g; dietary fiber 5 g; 80 cals
Other features: Provides carotene (vitamin A)

Preparation time: 15 minutes
Cooking time: 10 minutes

MAKES 2½ cups

Herbed Cheese Spread

Herbed cheese spread is best used within three days of making. Use any fresh herbs.

1 cup low-fat ricotta cheese
1 tablespoon chopped chives
1 tablespoon chopped parsley
1 tablespoon chopped mint
1 teaspoon finely grated lemon rind

Combine all ingredients and mix until very smooth. Use as a sandwich spread or spread on hot toast. Also good tossed through hot pasta.

Nutritional information for spread: Protein 9 g; fat 6 g; carbohydrate 0 g; dietary fiber 2 g; 340 cals
Other features: Provides calcium

Preparation time: 10 minutes
Cooking time: Nil

MAKES 1 cup

Opposite, clockwise from top: Indian Special (page 51), Italian Special (page 50) in bread rolls and Spicy Apple (page 50) with Herbed Cheese Spread.

Nutty Spread

This delicious sandwich spread is also wonderful as a topping for potatoes in their jackets.

2 teaspoons ground cumin

1 teaspoon ground coriander

1 tablespoon chopped green onions

2 slices whole wheat bread

½ teaspoon cinnamon

2 tablespoons lemon juice

2 teaspoons olive oil

1 Gently cook cumin and coriander in a dry frying pan for 2–3 minutes, taking care spices do not burn.
2 Place all the ingredients in a food processor and blend them until smooth.
3 Pack into a small bowl and leave to stand for at least an hour before serving.

Nutritional information per tablespoon: Protein 3 g; fat 6 g; carbohydrate 4 g; some dietary fiber 2 g; low sodium 36 mg; 85 cals

SERVES 6

Preparation time: 15 minutes
+ 1 hour standing time
Cooking time: 3 minutes

Vegetables with Peanut Sauce.

Vegetables with Peanut Sauce

2 large potatoes, peeled

2 medium carrots, cut into thin strips

2 cups broccoli pieces

13 oz beans, trimmed

6½ oz snow peas

1 red bell pepper, seeded and sliced

1 green bell pepper, seeded and sliced

1 cucumber, cut into strips

1 cup mung bean sprouts

Sauce

2 tablespoons chicken stock

1 medium onion, chopped finely

2 cloves garlic, crushed

1 tablespoon tamarind purée (from Asian food stores)

1¾ oz crushed peanuts

1 tablespoon salt-reduced soy sauce

1 tablespoon lemon juice

1 tablespoon crunchy peanut butter, no added salt

1 teaspoon chopped ginger

1 teaspoon chopped chili

½ cup coconut milk

1 To make the sauce, heat chicken stock and gently cook onion and garlic for 3–4 minutes. Add remaining ingredients. Bring to the boil, cover and simmer for 20 minutes, stirring occasionally and adding a little water if necessary to produce a thick sauce. While sauce is cooking, prepare vegetables.
2 Steam or microwave potatoes until tender. Cut into thick slices. Place in the center of a large platter.
3 Individually steam or microwave carrots, broccoli, beans and snow peas until barely tender. Immediately place in colander and run cold water over vegetables so that they remain crisp. Drain and arrange on platter.
4 Arrange remaining vegetables on platter. Pour peanut sauce over vegetables.

Nutritional information per serving: Protein 11 g; fat 11 g; carbohydrate 19 g; excellent dietary fiber 8 g; sodium 140 mg; 215 cals
Other features: Excellent source of vitamin C, potassium and vitamin A; very good source of niacin (B3); good source of riboflavin (B2), iron and zinc. Has some calcium content

SERVES 6

Preparation time: 50 minutes
Cooking time: 35 minutes

Italian-style Sandwich

Full of flavor, this makes a simple and lovely lunch.

1 tablespoon virgin olive oil

1 large onion, sliced finely

4 baby eggplants (about 5 oz), sliced

1 red bell pepper, seeded and sliced

2 teaspoons dried oregano

12–15 black olives (about 2 oz)

1 piece focaccia (Italian flat bread), about 8 oz

1 Heat oil in a pan, add onion and cook with lid on over a gentle heat for 5 minutes.
2 Add eggplant and continue to cook, with lid on, for 10 minutes.
3 Add bell pepper, oregano and olives and stir well to combine.
4 Split focaccia through center. Pile filling onto bottom half, replace top of bread and bake on a foil-lined baking sheet at 375°F for 10 minutes. Slice and serve immediately.

Nutritional information per serving: Protein 6 g; fat 6 g; carbohydrate 26 g; good dietary fiber 3 g; sodium 485 mg; 185 cals
Other features: An excellent source of vitamin C and provides useful amounts of potassium.

Italian-style Sandwich.

MAKES 16 slices

Preparation time: 20 minutes
Cooking time: 25 minutes

Picnic Bread

Dough

2 packets dried yeast

½ cup warm water

1 teaspoon sugar

1½ cups warm water

3½ cups whole wheat flour

1 teaspoon chopped rosemary

Filling

6½ oz cottage cheese

½ cup chopped basil

2 tablespoons toasted pine nuts

10 black olives, pitted

2 medium tomatoes, sliced

2½ oz thinly sliced low-fat Cheddar cheese (7 per cent fat)

1 teaspoon olive oil

1 teaspoon chopped rosemary

SERVES 8

1 In a large bowl, combine yeast, ½ cup warm water and sugar. Leave for 10 minutes. Yeast mixture will be frothy.
2 Add remaining water, about 3¼ cups of the flour and the rosemary. Knead until well combined, using remaining flour if needed. Place ball of dough in a basin, cover with a plastic bag and leave to stand in a warm place until doubled in bulk (about 1 hour).
3 Punch dough down, cut into 2 pieces and roll each to a circle. Place one piece of dough on a greased baking sheet and leave to stand for 10 minutes.
4 Spread cottage cheese over dough. Sprinkle with basil, pine nuts and olives. Arrange tomatoes and cheese on top.
5 Place second piece of bread dough on top and seal edges by pressing gently together.
6 Warm oil (a microwave makes this easy) and brush over surface of dough. Sprinkle with rosemary. Bake at 400°F for 40 minutes. Serve warm, cut into wedges.

Nutritional information per serving: Protein 16 g; fat 5 g; carbohydrate 33 g; very good dietary fiber 6 g; sodium 18 mg; 240 cals
Other features: A good source of thiamin (B1), riboflavin (B2), niacin (B3) and iron. Provides useful amounts of calcium and potassium.

Preparation time: 30 minutes
+ 1 hour while dough rises
Cooking time: 40 minutes

> **TASTE TIP**
> To appreciate the true sweetness of red peppers, remove the skin by holding the pepper on a long fork over a gas flame, or broiling until blackened and slightly blistered. Place in a paper bag, secure top and leave for a few minutes before rubbing gently with a clean kitchen towel or cloth to remove the fine skin.

Tuna Lasagne

This fast and easy lasagne is a great store-cupboard standby for those times when you
have to entertain unexpected guests.

½ cup sliced green onions

1 clove garlic, crushed

2 cups diced tomatoes, fresh or canned

1 tablespoon tomato paste, no added salt

2 tablespoons chopped parsley

freshly ground pepper

14 oz tuna, no added salt

2 cups skim milk

2 tablespoons all-purpose flour

2 eggs, beaten

pinch nutmeg

12 sheets instant lasagne

1 tablespoon grated Parmesan cheese

½ cup grated low-fat cheese

½ teaspoon paprika

SERVES 6

1 Combine the green onions, garlic, tomatoes, tomato paste, parsley and pepper to taste. Gently mix in tuna.
2 Blend milk and flour and cook over a low heat until thick. Stir in beaten eggs and nutmeg.
3 Grease a casserole, dip lasagne sheets in hot water and spread four sheets over base of casserole. Top with half the tuna mixture. Repeat these layers and top with remaining lasagne noodles. Pour sauce over top. Sprinkle with combined cheese and paprika and bake at 350°F for 30 minutes.

Nutritional information per serving: Protein 28 g; fat 5 g; carbohydrate 28 g; good dietary fiber 3 g; sodium 400 mg; 260 cals
Other features: An excellent source of niacin (B3) and a very good source of riboflavin (B2). Also a good source of calcium, potassium, thiamin, iron and zinc and provides useful amounts of vitamins A, C and E

Preparation time: 20 minutes
Cooking time: 35 minutes

Risotto

If you don't have Arborio rice, use a short-grain rice and reduce the amount of chicken
stock to three cups.

1 tablespoon olive oil

1 medium-large onion, chopped

1¼ cups (8 oz) Arborio rice

4 bay leaves

rosemary sprig

7 or 8 saffron threads

4 cups hot chicken stock

½ cup white wine

1 cup peas

2 tablespoons almonds, chopped roughly

1 tablespoon grated Parmesan cheese

¼ cup sun-dried tomatoes

SERVES 6

1 Heat oil and gently cook onion, without browning, for 3–4 minutes. Add rice and stir for 1–2 minutes. Add bay leaves and rosemary.
2 Add saffron to chicken stock and pour about 1 cup of stock into rice. Simmer, stirring, until liquid is absorbed, then add another cup of stock. Repeat with a third cup of stock.
3 Add wine and peas and remaining stock. Continue cooking until all liquid is absorbed.
4 Add almonds, cheese and tomatoes and fold in gently with a fork. Cover and leave for about 3 minutes. Remove bay leaves and rosemary before serving.

Nutritional information per serving: Protein 8 g; fat 7 g; carbohydrate 44 g; very good dietary fiber 5 g; sodium 175 mg; 280 cals
Other features: Provides useful amounts of potassium and some vitamin C, niacin (B3), thiamin (B1), and iron

Preparation time: 10 minutes
Cooking time: 35 minutes

*Opposite: Risotto, top,
and Tuna Lasagne.*

Bulgur Tomatoes

You can substitute hollowed-out bell peppers in this recipe. Either way, they are delicious served hot or taken cold as a picnic food.

4 firm ripe tomatoes
⅓ cup bulgur
⅔ cup boiling water
2 teaspoons olive oil
1 medium onion, chopped finely
2 cups sliced mushrooms
2 tablespoons chopped mint
½ cup sliced celery
4 small cubes of low-fat Cheddar cheese

1 Cut a 'lid' from tomatoes and carefully remove seeds with a teaspoon.
2 Pour boiling water over bulgur. Cover tightly and leave to stand for 10 minutes (the water will be absorbed).
3 Heat olive oil, add onion, cover and leave to 'sweat' for 5 minutes, stirring once or twice. Add mushrooms and cook a further 3–4 minutes.
4 Add mushroom mixture, mint and celery to bulgur. Pile into tomatoes and place in a small casserole so that the tomatoes stay upright.
5 Push a cube of cheese into the center of each tomato. Replace 'lids' and bake at 350°F for 30 minutes.

Nutritional information per serving: Protein 9 g; fat 4 g (or 8 g if regular Cheddar is used); carbohydrate 15 g; good dietary fiber 4 g; 165 cals or 130 cals if low-fat cheese is used
Other features: Excellent source of vitamin C, a good source of potassium. Also a useful source of calcium, niacin and iron. Low sodium (120 mg)

SERVES 4

Preparation time: 20 minutes
Cooking time: 40 minutes

Pumpkin and Spinach Lasagne

This dish is popular with all age groups. It can be made and reheated in a microwave oven, or prepared up to the final stage and baked when ready to eat.

1 lb pumpkin, peeled and sliced
1 bunch spinach
1 lb low-fat ricotta cheese
½ cup sliced green onions
½ cup chopped parsley
12 instant lasagne sheets
2 cups skim milk
2 tablespoons all-purpose flour
2 eggs
¼ teaspoon nutmeg
1 cup grated Cheddar cheese, preferably low-fat

1 Steam pumpkin and spinach for 3 minutes each.
2 Combine spinach, ricotta, onions and parsley.
3 Dip lasagne sheets in hot water to soften slightly and arrange three sheets in a greased casserole. Top with one-third of the pumpkin slices and one-third of the spinach/ricotta mixture. Repeat twice. Top with remaining lasagne sheets.
4 Beat together milk, flour and eggs. Cook, stirring constantly until thick. Pour over lasagne, sprinkle with cheese and bake in a moderate oven (350°F) for 30 minutes.

Nutritional information per serving: Protein 25 g; fat 8 g (or 14 g if regular Cheddar is used); carbohydrate 32 g; very good dietary fiber 4 g; sodium 386 mg; 290 cals or 340 cals if regular Cheddar is used
Other features: Excellent source of vitamins A and C, very good source of potassium, good source of thiamin (B1), riboflavin (B2), zinc and iron. Rich in calcium

SERVES 6

Preparation time: 40 minutes
Cooking time: 30 minutes

Vegetarian Fettuccine

2 teaspoons olive oil

1 medium onion, sliced

1 clove garlic, crushed

1 teaspoon mixed
Italian herbs

1 medium eggplant, diced

1 lb tomatoes, chopped

2 cups sliced mushrooms

1 bell pepper,
seeded and sliced

1 cup red wine

11 oz fettuccine

2 tablespoons fresh
chopped basil

2 tablespoons
chopped parsley

1 tablespoon toasted
pine nuts

SERVES 4

1 In a large non-stick saucepan, heat oil and add onion, garlic and herbs. Cover and cook over a gentle heat for 3–4 minutes.
2 Add eggplant, cover and cook for 2–3 minutes more.
3 Add tomatoes, mushrooms, bell pepper and wine. Bring to the boil; cover and simmer for 10 minutes. Remove lid and cook until thick.
4 Cook fettuccine in large pan of boiling water until just tender.
5 Add basil, parsley and pine nuts to vegetable mix and serve over drained pasta.

Nutritional information per serving: Protein 15 g; fat 6 g; carbohydrate 75 g; excellent dietary fiber 10 g; 400 cals
Other features: An excellent source of vitamin C, a good source of the B-complex vitamins, vitamin A, potassium and iron and a useful source of zinc. Low sodium content (20 mg)

Preparation time: 15 minutes
Cooking time: 30 minutes

Vegetarian Fettuccine, left, and Cheese and Sage Damper (page 140).

Spinach and Salmon Roulade

This dish can be served warm or cold. Leftovers are great for the next day's lunch. (Do not use Swiss chard, as its flavor is too coarse for this delicate dish.)

Carefully fold beaten egg whites into spinach mixture with a metal spoon.

Pour mixture into greased, lined pan and sprinkle wheat germ evenly over the top.

Roll filled roulade from the short side, using the paper to help roll it evenly.

The finished Spinach and Salmon Roulade.

1 lb spinach
¼ cup all-purpose flour
2 tablespoons non-fat dry milk
¼ cup chopped green onions
3 eggs, separated
1 tablespoon wheat germ
3½ oz sliced mushrooms
8 oz cottage cheese
7 oz can red salmon, drained
1 tablespoon chopped fresh lemon thyme
1 teaspoon finely grated lemon rind
freshly ground black pepper

SERVES 6

1 Line a jelly roll pan with wax paper.
2 Steam or microwave shredded spinach. Purée spinach and add flour, dry milk, green onions and egg yolks.
3 Beat egg whites until stiff and gently fold through spinach mixture. Pour into prepared pan and sprinkle with wheat germ. Bake at 350°F for 20 minutes.
4 While roulade is baking, place mushrooms in a non-stick pan. Cook gently for 3–4 minutes.
5 Beat together cottage cheese, salmon, thyme, rind, pepper and mushrooms.
6 Turn roulade onto another piece of non-stick or greased wax paper. Gently spread filling over roulade and roll it up, using paper to help. Allow to stand for 5 minutes and serve warm, or refrigerate and serve cold.

Nutritional information per serving: Protein 20 g; fat 6 g; carbohydrate 6 g; good dietary fiber 3 g; sodium 285 mg; 155 cals

Other features: An excellent source of vitamin A, a good source of riboflavin (B2), vitamin C, calcium, potassium and niacin (B3). Also supplies iron and folic acid

Preparation time: 20 minutes
Cooking time: 20 minutes

Chive and Pumpkin Soufflé

3 tablespoons
all-purpose flour

1 cup skim milk

2 egg yolks

1 cup cooked, mashed
pumpkin

1 tablespoon Dijon mustard

1 tablespoon chopped chives

3 egg whites

1 In a saucepan, make a paste with the flour and a little of the milk. Gradually add the remaining milk. Cook over a low heat until thick, stirring constantly.
2 Add egg yolks to milk mixture, beating well after each one. Add pumpkin, mustard and chives.
3 Beat egg whites until stiff. Fold about one-quarter of the egg whites into the pumpkin mixture, then gently fold in remaining egg whites. Pour into four 1-cup capacity greased soufflé dishes and bake at 375°F for 15 minutes.

Nutritional information per serving: Protein 8 g; fat 3 g; carbohydrate 14 g; some dietary fiber 2 g; 110 cals
Other features: An excellent source of vitamin A and a good source of vitamin C and potassium. Useful amounts of calcium. Low sodium (80 mg)

Preparation time: 20 minutes
Cooking time: 20 minutes

SERVES 4

Spinach Pie

1 teaspoon butter or
margarine

3 tablespoons (1¼ oz)
wheat germ

1¼ lb spinach

13 oz low-fat ricotta cheese

4 eggs

pinch nutmeg

½ cup chopped green onions

2 tablespoons chopped mint

1 Use the butter or margarine to grease base of an 8 inch non-stick cake pan. Sprinkle with 2 tablespoons of the wheat germ and press down with back of spoon.
2 Steam or microwave spinach until just wilted (about 3–4 minutes). Drain and press out as much water as possible.
3 Beat together ricotta, eggs and nutmeg.
4 Add green onions, mint and spinach. Mix well and press on top of wheat germ. Sprinkle with remaining tablespoon of wheat germ. Bake at 350°F for 35 minutes.

Nutritional information per serving: Protein 18 g; fat 11 g; carbohydrate 5 g; very good dietary fiber 5 g; sodium 230 mg; 200 cals
Other features: An excellent source of vitamins A and C, a very good source of potassium and a good source of iron and zinc. Rich in calcium.

Preparation time: 20 minutes
Cooking time: 40 minutes

SERVES 8

Healthy Quiche

8 sheets filo pastry

1 cup diced cooked turkey

½ cup grated low-fat cheese

1 tablespoon chopped chives

12 oz can evaporated
skim milk

2 eggs

1 Grease a 9 inch quiche dish and line with pastry sheets.
2 Sprinkle turkey, cheese and chives over pastry.
3 Beat milk and eggs together and pour over mixture. Bake at 350°F for 40 minutes.

Nutritional information per serving: Protein 35 g; fat 6 g; carbohydrate 24 g; dietary fiber 1 g; sodium 386 mg; 295 cals
Other features: An excellent source of riboflavin (B2), a very good source of niacin (B3). Also a good source of potassium

Preparation time: 10 minutes
Cooking time: 40 minutes

SERVES 4

Mushroom Rice Pie

A delightful lunch dish which can be served hot or cold with a tossed salad.

Pie crust

1½ tablespoons sesame seeds

1½ cups cooked brown rice
(½ cup raw)

1 egg, beaten

1 teaspoon dried
parsley flakes

Filling

2 tablespoons chicken stock

1 medium onion, sliced

1 medium bell pepper,
seeded and sliced

8 oz mushrooms, sliced

2 eggs

¾ cup evaporated skim milk

1 tablespoon grated
Parmesan cheese

¼ teaspoon paprika

1 Toast sesame seeds in a dry frying pan over a moderate heat until golden brown.
2 Mix all pie crust ingredients together and press firmly into a greased 8 inch pie dish.
3 Heat chicken stock; add onion, cover and cook for 2–3 minutes. Add pepper and mushrooms and cook without lid for a further 2–3 minutes, mixing gently. Spoon mushroom mixture into rice crust.
4 Beat eggs and milk and pour over mushrooms. Sprinkle with cheese and paprika and bake at 350°F for 30 minutes.

Nutritional information per serving: Protein 16 g; fat 8 g; carbohydrate 27 g; good dietary fiber 4 g; sodium 180 mg; 235 cals
Other features: An excellent source of vitamin C and a good source of calcium, potassium, thiamin (B1) and niacin (B3)

SERVES 6

Preparation time: 20 minutes
Cooking time: 40 minutes

Carrot and Lentil Patties

Serve these nutritious patties with herbed tomato sauce.

1 cup red lentils

2 bay leaves

2 cups chicken stock

6 medium carrots

1 tablespoon chopped chives

2 tablespoons
chopped almonds

1 egg

2 slices whole wheat bread,
made into crumbs

Sauce

14 oz can tomatoes,
chopped roughly

1 teaspoon dried oregano

1 clove garlic, crushed

¼ cup red wine

1 Add lentils and bay leaves to the chicken stock. Bring to the boil, cover and cook over a low heat for 20 minutes. Discard the bay leaves.
2 While lentils are cooking, grate carrots and mix with chives, almonds, egg and bread crumbs.
3 To make sauce, place all ingredients in saucepan. Bring to the boil and simmer, uncovered, for 5 minutes. Stir mixture occasionally.
4 Add lentils to carrot mixture and form into six patties.
5 Cook patties in a non-stick pan for 3–4 minutes on each side. Serve with sauce.

Nutritional information per serving: Protein 13 g; fat 4 g; carbohydrate 28 g; excellent dietary fiber 8 g; sodium 150 mg; 200 cals
Other features: An excellent source of vitamin A. Also a very good source of iron, B-complex vitamins, potassium and vitamin C

SERVES 6

Preparation time: 5 minutes
Cooking time: 35 minutes

HEALTH TIP

Margarine has as many calories as butter: both have a massive 145 cals in a tablespoon. Low-fat butters and margarines have about half this amount. Low-fat margarines and low-fat butter cannot be used for frying as they contain either gelatin or maltodextrin – both will cause the food to stick firmly to the frying pan.

Opposite, clockwise from top left: Mushroom Rice Pie, Healthy Quiche (page 61) and Carrot and Lentil Patties with Tomato Sauce.

Vegetable Crisp

This dish can change to fit the seasons and is an ideal way to use up small quantities of different vegetables.

2 teaspoons olive oil

1 medium onion, sliced

1 clove garlic

6 cups diced, mixed vegetables

14 oz can tomatoes, roughly chopped

Topping

1 tablespoon butter or margarine

1 cup rolled oats

1 slice whole wheat bread, made into crumbs

1 tablespoon toasted sunflower seeds

1 teaspoon dried basil

½ cup grated low-fat cheese

1 Heat oil, add onion and garlic, cover and cook over a gentle heat for 3–4 minutes.
2 Add vegetables (any combination of broccoli, cauliflower, zucchini, carrot, asparagus, whole button mushrooms, green beans) and tomatoes. Bring to the boil, simmer 3–4 minutes. Pour into six 1-cup capacity ovenproof, individual casseroles.
3 Cut the fat into the oats, then combine all ingredients for crumble topping and sprinkle over vegetables. Bake at 350°F for 20 minutes until golden.

Nutritional information per serving: Protein 14 g; fat 11 g; carbohydrate 26 g; excellent dietary fiber 8 g; sodium 175 mg; 265 cals

Other features: An excellent source of vitamins A and C, a good source of iron, zinc, calcium, potassium and the B-complex vitamins.

Preparation time: 10 minutes
Cooking time: 30 minutes

Vegetable Crisp.

SERVES 6

Creamy Salmon Pasta.

Creamy Salmon Pasta

A fast, delicious meal. Tastes so creamy, but without any cream!

8 oz fusilli or shell noodles or fettuccine

½ cup chicken stock

½ cup sliced green onions

2 cups sliced mushrooms

1 red bell pepper, seeded and sliced

½ cup chopped fresh basil

7 oz can salmon, drained

1 cup evaporated skim milk

1 tablespoon grated Parmesan cheese

freshly ground black pepper

1 Cook pasta in a large pan of boiling water until just tender.
2 While pasta is cooking, heat chicken stock and add green onions, mushrooms and pepper. Cook 2 minutes, tossing ingredients gently.
3 Add basil, salmon, milk, Parmesan cheese and pepper to mushroom mixture.
4 Drain pasta and add to the salmon sauce. Serve at once, accompanied by a tossed green salad.

Nutritional information per serving: Protein 28 g; fat 6 g; carbohydrate 58 g; very good dietary fiber 6 g; sodium 445 mg; 390 cals
Other features: An excellent source of vitamin C, a very good source of niacin (B3), riboflavin (B2) and a good source of iron, zinc, vitamin A, potassium and thiamin (B1). A rich source of calcium.

HEALTH TIP

There are only eight genuine members of the vitamin B complex. These are thiamin (B1), riboflavin (B2), niacin (B3), pantothenic acid (B5), pyridoxine (B6), folate, biotin and cyanocobalarnin (B12).

Preparation time: 15 minutes
Cooking time: 20 minutes

SERVES 4

Triticale Vegetable Loaf

This loaf is delicious served hot, or cold as a sandwich filling or with salads.

1 cup brown rice

2½ cups water

¾ cup triticale flakes

¼ cup sliced shallots

½ cup chopped unsalted peanuts

2 tablespoons peanut butter (no added salt)

1 bell pepper, seeded and diced

2 eggs

1 tablespoon salt-reduced soy sauce

1 teaspoon chopped ginger

SERVES 6

1 Place rice and water in a saucepan and bring to the boil. Cover and cook over a low heat for 30 minutes. Add triticale flakes and cook, uncovered, for a further 5 minutes.
2 Combine shallots, peanuts, peanut butter, bell pepper, eggs, soy sauce and ginger. Add rice and triticale and mix thoroughly. Press mixture firmly into a greased loaf pan and bake at 350°F for 45 minutes.
3 Stand for 5 minutes before serving.

Nutritional information per serving: Protein 12 g; fat 13 g; carbohydrate 37 g; dietary fiber 5 g; 305 cals
Other features: An excellent source of vitamin C; good source of niacin (B3); provides iron

Preparation time: 20 minutes
Cooking time: 1 hour 20 minutes

Middle Eastern Kibbi

Serve Middle Eastern Kibbi with tabbouleh and pita bread.

1 cup boiling water

1 cup bulgur (cracked wheat)

½ cup pine nuts

1 lb ground, lean lamb

1 medium onion, chopped

1 teaspoon ground allspice

2 teaspoons coarsely ground black pepper

¼ cup iced water

1 teaspoon warm olive oil

1 Pour boiling water over cracked wheat, cover tightly and leave to stand for 10 minutes (water will be absorbed).
2 Toast pine nuts in a dry frying pan until golden brown. Set to one side.
3 Combine lamb, onion, allspice, pepper and cracked wheat and mix thoroughly, adding the iced water little by little (a food processor makes this easy).
4 Spread half the meat mixture over the base of a greased 7 inch-square shallow pan or non-stick cake pan. Top with pine nuts (reserve 1 tablespoon) and then remaining meat. Press mixture firmly into dish.
5 Mark top into diamond shapes, using a sharp knife. Brush with olive oil and place a pine nut in each diamond. Bake in a moderate oven (350°F) for 45 minutes.

Nutritional information per serving: Protein 30 g; fat 16 g; carbohydrate 25 g; dietary fiber 3 g; 350 cals
Other features: An excellent source of niacin (B3), zinc and iron

Middle Eastern Kibbi.

SERVES 6

Preparation time: 40 minutes
Cooking time: 50 minutes

Millet-stuffed Peppers

Serve bell peppers with vegetables or salad.

Millet-stuffed Peppers, left, and Triticale Vegetable Loaf.

½ cup millet

1 cup water

4 bell peppers

½ cup sliced shallots

1 cup diced mushrooms

1 teaspoon chopped fresh ginger

1 teaspoon dried basil

1 egg, beaten

½ cup cottage cheese

1 medium tomato, diced finely

½ cup reduced-fat Cheddar cheese

1 Put millet and water into a saucepan, bring to the boil, cover and simmer 20 minutes.
2 Remove tops from bell peppers and scoop out seeds.
3 Preheat oven to 350°F. Combine shallots, mushrooms, ginger, basil, egg, cottage cheese and millet. Use to fill bell peppers. Bake for 15 minutes.
4 Combine tomato and cheese and sprinkle on top of each bell pepper. Bake for a further 5 minutes. Serve piping hot.

Nutritional information per serving: Protein 15 g; fat 6 g; carbohydrate 13 g; dietary fiber 3 g; 170 cals
Other features: An excellent source of vitamin C; good source of niacin (B3); provides calcium and carotene (vitamin A)

Preparation time: 35 minutes

SERVES 4

Cooking time: 40 minutes

Tacos with Beans

- 1 tablespoon olive oil
- 1 large onion, chopped finely
- 1 clove garlic, crushed
- 1–2 teaspoons chopped fresh chili
- 2 cups diced tomatoes, fresh or canned
- 2 cups cooked kidney beans (home-cooked or canned)
- 2 tablespoons red wine vinegar
- 1 teaspoon dark brown sugar
- taco shells
- shredded lettuce, diced tomato, grated Cheddar cheese and yogurt to serve

1 Heat oil and gently cook onion, garlic and chili for 3–4 minutes.
2 Add remaining ingredients, bring to the boil and simmer, stirring frequently, for 10 minutes (mixture should be thick).
3 Heat taco shells in oven. (To prevent them from closing while they are being heated, hang them upside down over the rungs of the oven racks.)
4 To serve, place a spoonful of the bean mixture into each hot taco shell and top with lettuce, tomato, grated cheese and a dollop of yogurt.

Nutritional information per serving (bean mix only): Protein 16 g; fat 4 g; carbohydrate 14 g; dietary fiber 7 g; 125 cals

SERVES 4

Preparation time: 25 minutes
Cooking time: 20 minutes

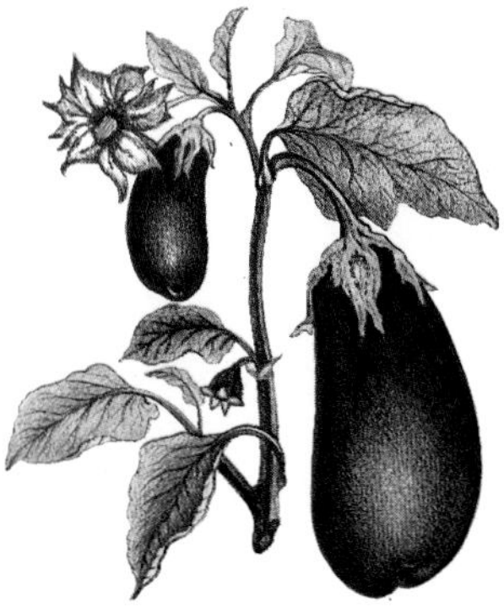

Soy Burgers

These may also be barbecued on a lightly oiled grill.

- 1 cup (6½ oz) soybeans
- 3 cups water
- 1 small onion, chopped
- ½ cup ground almonds
- 1 red bell pepper, seeded and finely chopped
- 1 teaspoon dried marjoram
- 2 eggs
- freshly ground pepper

1 Put beans, water and onion in a saucepan. Bring to the boil. Cover, turn off heat and leave to stand for an hour (if leaving longer, place in refrigerator).
2 Bring beans to the boil and simmer, covered, for 1½ hours. Drain and discard liquid.
3 Combine drained beans with remaining ingredients in food processor and mix until well combined.
4 Form mixture into four large or eight small patties. Broil until golden brown on both sides. Serve in pita bread with shredded lettuce, sliced tomato and bean sprouts.

Nutritional information per serving: Protein 16 g; fat 12 g; carbohydrate 25 g; dietary fiber 13 g; 270 cals
Other features: An excellent source of vitamin C; good source of iron; provides thiamin (B1), niacin (B3), riboflavin (B2), potassium, zinc and calcium

SERVES 4

Preparation time: 20 minutes
+ 1 hour standing time
Cooking time: 1 hour 40 minutes

HEALTH TIP

Muscle cramps may be caused by a failure to warm up properly, a lack of regular exercise, or hormonal changes. However, the most common cause is a lack of water.

Opposite: Tacos with Beans, top, and Soy Burgers.

MAIN DISHES

MANY PEOPLE ARE UNDER THE IMPRESSION THAT 'healthy' eating is synonymous with 'boring' eating. If you have the idea that dreary broiled meat or baked fish without a vestige of sauce are what constitute healthy food, think again. Imaginative, tasty food that isn't wicked and off-limits can be yours, as the recipes in this section prove. Stir-fried dishes, pasta and savory loaves can taste wonderful – and be very good for you. Cook Cashew Nut Rice Mold, or Chicken with Prunes and Nuts for your family and you'll soon discover what healthy eating is really all about. If you like to entertain, try Thai-style Fish. And if the children are proving hard to please, you won't go wrong with Tortillas, Seafood Pizza or Pasta with Chicken and Spring Vegetables. Adults love them, too.

Pasta with Chicken and Spring Vegetables ♨

Any pasta shapes – farfalle (bow ties), fettuccine or penne – can be used for this recipe. The chicken can be omitted if you like.

8 oz pasta

¾ cup chicken stock

½ cup sliced green onions

1 bunch fresh asparagus, cut into 1½ inch pieces

1 cup snow peas, ends removed

1 cup shredded cooked chicken

¾ cup low-fat ricotta cheese

½ cup low-fat yogurt

2 tablespoons lemon juice

1 teaspoon prepared mild mustard

¼ teaspoon dried chilies

1 Cook pasta in a large pan of boiling water until just tender. Drain.

2 While pasta is cooking, heat ¼ cup of the chicken stock, add green onions, asparagus and snow peas and simmer for 2 minutes. Add chicken and stir lightly.

3 Blend ricotta, yogurt, lemon juice, mustard and remaining ½ cup of chicken stock. Add to vegetables, stir until boiling. Serve over hot pasta. Garnish with dried chilies.

Nutritional information per serving: Protein 25 g; fat 6 g; carbohydrate 53 g; very good dietary fiber 6 g; sodium 143 mg; calcium 225 mg; 370 cals

Other features: Good source of calcium, vitamin C, niacin (B3) and potassium, and supplies some iron

SERVES 4

Preparation time: 5 minutes
Cooking time: 25 minutes

Barbecued Seafood ♨

Served with a tossed salad and some crusty bread, this meal is hard to beat. The octopus must be cooked on a very hot plate or pan. Do not overcook or it will be tough.

½ cup red wine

1 tablespoon olive oil

2 cloves garlic, crushed

2 tablespoons chopped parsley

8 baby octopus (remove heads and 'beaks' in center of tentacles; cut tentacles in halves)

12 large raw shrimp

8 scallops

freshly ground pepper

1 Combine wine, oil, garlic and parsley and marinate octopus for an hour or more (in refrigerator).

2 Have barbecue plate very hot (if indoors, heat a large pan until very hot). Remove octopus from marinade, dry on paper towels and cook for 4–5 minutes.

3 Add shrimp and cook for 3–4 minutes. Add scallops and cook for 1–2 minutes (they toughen if overcooked). Serve seafood immediately with ground pepper.

Nutritional information per serving: Protein 31 g; fat 4 g; no carbohydrate; no dietary fiber; sodium 510 mg; 160 cals

Other features: An excellent source of iodine, a good source of potassium, niacin (B3), thiamin (B1), iron and zinc. Also provides useful amounts of calcium

Previous page: Barbecued Seafood, top, and Pasta with Chicken and Spring Vegetables.

SERVES 4

Preparation time: 20 minutes
+ 1 hour marinating time
Cooking time: 10 minutes

Chicken Breasts with Flaming Sauce

4 boneless, skinless chicken breasts

chives, for garnish

Sauce

3 medium-sized tomatoes, very ripe

2 teaspoons olive oil

1 small onion, chopped roughly

1 clove garlic, crushed

1 tablespoon paprika

½ teaspoon dried thyme

1 large red bell pepper, seeded and sliced

1 For the suace, pour boiling water over tomatoes and leave them for 1 minute, then plunge into cold water and peel. Dice the flesh.

2 Heat oil and cook chopped onion, covered, for 2–3 minutes. Add garlic, paprika and thyme and cook a further 1 minute. Add bell pepper and tomatoes and cook for 10 minutes or until soft. Purée mixture until smooth.

3 While sauce is cooking, broil or barbecue chicken breasts for 6–8 minutes, turning once (do not overcook). Serve the chicken breasts on top of the sauce and garnish each serving with several whole chives.

Nutritional information per serving: Protein 30 g; fat 5 g; carbohydrate 5 g; good dietary fiber 3 g; 190 cals

Other features: An excellent source of niacin (B3), a good source of potassium, thiamin (B1), riboflavin (B2) and vitamin C. Also provides some iron, zinc and vitamin A. Low sodium (75 mg)

SERVES 4

Preparation time: 15 minutes

Cooking time: 12 minutes

Seafood Pizza

Chicken Breasts with Flaming Sauce.

Crust

1 tablespoon dried yeast

2 tablespoons lukewarm water

1 teaspoon sugar

¾ cup whole wheat flour

¾ cup all-purpose flour

½ cup lukewarm water

1 teaspoon dried Italian herbs

2 teaspoons olive oil

Topping

½ cup tomato paste

2 teaspoons dried oregano

1 large onion, sliced

8 oz mixed seafood (small shrimp, scallops, mussels)

1 red bell pepper, seeded and cut into thin strips

½ cup grated low-fat Cheddar cheese

2 tablespoons grated Parmesan cheese

12 black olives

1 Combine the yeast, 2 tablespoons water and sugar and leave for 10–15 minutes until bubbles appear.

2 Sift flours. Add remaining water, herbs, yeast mixture and oil and mix well. Knead well until smooth and shiny, adding a little more flour if necessary. Place in a greased bowl, place bowl in a large plastic bag and leave in a warm place until doubled in bulk (approximately 1 hour).

3 Punch dough down, knead well and roll out to a 12 inch circle. Place on a greased pizza pan.

4 Spread tomato paste over pizza dough. Sprinkle with oregano, sliced onion, seafood, bell pepper and cheeses and arrange olives on top. Bake at 400°F for 20 minutes.

Nutritional information per serving: Protein 20 g; fat 6 g; carbohydrate 24 g; dietary fiber 3 g; sodium 410 mg; 230 cals

Other features: An excellent source of thiamin (B1), a good source of calcium, potassium, iron, vitamin C and niacin (B3)

Preparation time: 30 minutes

+ 1 hour standing time

Cooking time: 20 minutes

SERVES 6

Chicken and Oat Loaf

This is delicious served with red bell pepper sauce.

1 lb ground chicken

1 cup rolled oats

¼ cup evaporated skim milk

1 egg, beaten

1 cup grated carrot

1 cup chopped mushrooms

½ cup sliced green onions

1 teaspoon dried rosemary

½ cup chopped parsley

2 tablespoons toasted sesame seeds

Sauce

1 red bell pepper, seeded and chopped roughly

¾ cup chicken stock

freshly ground pepper

1 Combine all ingredients for the loaf except sesame seeds.
2 Grease a loaf pan and sprinkle 1 tablespoon sesame seeds over the base. Press chicken mixture into pan and sprinkle with remaining sesame seeds. Bake at 350°F for 45–50 minutes. Allow to stand 5 minutes before turning out. If serving loaf cold, allow to cool in pan.
3 To make the sauce, place bell pepper and stock into a small saucepan, bring to the boil, cover and simmer for 6–7 minutes. Purée in blender, adding pepper to taste. Serve warm.

Nutritional information per serving: Protein 26 g; fat 6 g; carbohydrate 16 g; good dietary fiber 3 g; 225 cals
Other features: Very good source of vitamin A, a good source of riboflavin (B2), potassium and niacin (B3). Some iron, calcium and zinc. Low sodium (110 mg)

Preparation time: 15 minutes
Cooking time: 50 minutes

SERVES 6

Veal and Wheat Loaf

Serve this loaf with apricot sauce – the sweetness of the apricots makes it a popular dish with children.

1 cup bulgur (cracked wheat)

½ cup chopped dried apricots

1¼ cups boiling water

1 medium onion, chopped finely

1 lb ground veal

1 teaspoon ground allspice

½ teaspoon coarsely ground black pepper

1 tablespoon chopped mint

2 teaspoons finely grated orange rind

1 tablespoon pine nuts

Sauce

½ cup orange juice

½ cup chicken stock

¼ cup dried apricots

1 Combine the bulgur and apricots in a bowl. Pour boiling water over, cover bowl tightly and then leave for 15–20 minutes (water will be absorbed).
2 Add all the loaf ingredients to the wheat, except the pine nuts. Mix thoroughly and pack into a greased loaf pan. Press pine nuts into top of loaf. Bake in a moderate (350°F) oven for 1 hour. Leave for 5 minutes before turning out. Serve hot with apricot sauce or cold with a spicy chutney.
3 To make the sauce, combine all the ingredients in small saucepan. Bring to the boil, cover and simmer for 15 minutes. Purée until smooth.

Nutritional information per serving (with sauce): Protein 23 g; fat 3 g; carbohydrate 26 g; very good dietary fiber 7 g; 215 cals
Other features: A good source of potassium, iron, zinc and niacin (B3). Low sodium (100 mg)

Preparation time: 30 minutes
Cooking time: 1 hour

SERVES 6

HEALTH TIP

If you think a weight loss of 1 lb a week isn't much, just imagine losing the equivalent amount of fat as in a tub of margarine!

Opposite: Chicken and Oat Loaf with Pepper Sauce and, below, Beef, Beans and Beer Casserole (page 77).

Using wet hands, roll tablespoons of the fish mixture into even balls.

Roll fish balls in drained rice to coat each one evenly.

Place fish balls on lightly oiled paper in a steamer.

Fish and Rice Balls

Serve steamed fish balls as a first course or with stir-fried vegetables as a main dish.

1 cup rice

2 cups water

13 oz boneless white fish

1 small can water chestnuts, drained and chopped

½ cup sliced green onions

1 cup chopped fresh cilantro

1 teaspoon chopped fresh ginger

1 tablespoon fish sauce

2 egg whites

1 Soak rice in water for at least 2 hours. Drain and tip into a shallow bowl.

2 Place fish in a food processor and mince. Add remaining ingredients and mix well.

3 Using wet hands, take out a tablespoonful of the fish mixture and roll it in the rice. Continue in this way – mixture should make 16–18 balls.

4 Place the fish balls on lightly oiled wax paper in a steamer (bamboo or stainless steel – or use a metal rack, or tiny non-stick muffin pans on a rack in a frying pan). Place water in base of steamer, cover and steam fish balls for 15 minutes.

Nutritional information per fish ball: Protein 6 g; fat less than 1 g; carbohydrate 9 g; dietary fiber 0.5 g; 65 cals
Other features: Provides some B-complex vitamins and iron. Has a low sodium content (70 mg)

SERVES 6

Preparation time: 30 minutes
+ 2 hours for soaking rice
Cooking time: 15 minutes

Fish and Rice Balls.

Beef, Beans and Beer Casserole

The alcohol in the beer evaporates during cooking but leaves a great taste.

1 lb boneless, lean stewing beef (e.g. chuck or rump), trimmed of all fat, cubed

1 large onion, cut into eighths

1 medium eggplant, diced

½ teaspoon dry mustard

1 teaspoon dried basil leaves

1 cup low-alcohol beer

14 oz can red kidney beans

1 Using a non-stick pan, brown meat. Place in casserole.
2 In the same pan, brown onion. Place on top of meat.
3 Add eggplant, mustard, basil, beer and beans plus their liquid to meat. Stir well. Bake, covered, at 300°F for 2 hours, or until beef is very tender.

Nutritional information per serving: Protein 29 g; fat 4 g; carbohydrate 12 g; excellent dietary fiber 8 g; sodium 145 mg; 205 cals
Other features: Good source of B-complex vitamins, iron, zinc and potassium

SERVES 6

Preparation time: 20 minutes
Cooking time: 2 hours

Lamb Steaks in Whiskey Sauce

2 tablespoons whiskey

2 tablespoons mango chutney

8 boneless lamb steaks (about 2¼ oz each)

¾ cup evaporated skim milk

2 teaspoons cornstarch

1 tablespoon water

1 Combine whiskey and chutney in a shallow dish. Add lamb steaks, turn them and leave for 30 minutes to marinate.
2 Remove lamb from marinade and place in a hot non-stick pan. Reserve marinade. Cook lamb for no more than 5–6 minutes, turning once.
3 While lamb is cooking, heat milk. Add combined cornstarch and water and the remaining marinade. Stir constantly until boiling. Serve with lamb.

Nutritional information per serving: Protein 36 g; fat 5 g; carbohydrate 15 g; no dietary fiber; sodium 235 mg; 250 cals
Other features: Good source of iron, zinc, niacin (B3), calcium and potassium

SERVES 4

Preparation time: 30 minutes
Cooking time: 6 minutes

Chicken with Prunes and Nuts

½ cup pitted prunes

2 tablespoons blanched almonds

½ cup dry sherry

¼ cup orange juice

1 teaspoon ground cinnamon

1 teaspoon finely grated orange rind

1¼ lb boneless, skinless chicken thighs

freshly ground black pepper

1 tablespoon chopped fresh cilantro

1 Place prunes, almonds, sherry, juice, cinnamon and orange rind in a saucepan and bring to the boil.
2 Slice chicken and add to saucepan with pepper. Cover and simmer for 20 minutes, or until chicken is tender. Sprinkle with cilantro. Serve with rice.

Nutritional information per serving: Protein 31 g; fat 9 g; carbohydrate 13 g; very good dietary fiber 5 g; 255 cals
Other features: A very good source of riboflavin (B2) and niacin (B3) and good source of potassium, zinc and iron. Low sodium (120 mg)

Chicken with Prunes and Nuts.

SERVES 4

Preparation time: 5 minutes
Cooking time: 25 minutes

HEALTH TIP

Look for canned tuna, salmon and sardines in a water pack. They are lower in fat than the oil-packed varieties and have less salt than those that are packed in brine.

Barbecued Cod

This is an easy way to cook fish. A barbecue is ideal, or use a broiler pan lined with foil.

- ½ cup white wine
- 2 tablespoons lemon juice
- 1 teaspoon coarsely cracked pepper
- 2 tablespoons chopped fresh herbs (use thyme, parsley, rosemary, oregano or a mixture of any of these)
- 4 cod steaks, about 1½ lb (or any other white fish)

1 Combine wine, juice, pepper and herbs in a shallow dish. Place fish in mixture, turn each steak over and leave for at least 30 minutes (or cover and place in refrigerator all day).
2 Remove fish from marinade and place on a hot barbecue or under a pre-heated broiler. Cook for no more than 8–10 minutes, turning once. When fish flakes easily it is cooked. Do not overcook.
3 While fish is cooking, heat remaining marinade and cook until reduced slightly. Pour over cooked fish.

Nutritional information per serving: Protein 29 g; fat 6 g*; no carbohydrate; no dietary fiber; sodium 225 mg; 165 cals
Other features: A good source of iodine, potassium and the B-complex vitamins, provides some iron, calcium and zinc
* Fat content will vary with the fish used.

SERVES 4

Preparation time: 5 minutes
\+ 30 minutes for marinating
Cooking time: 8–10 minutes

TASTE TIP

Many people dislike fish because they overcook it. Most fish take only a few minutes for their flesh to become opaque and cooked. When fish flakes easily it is cooked.

Veal with Noodles

An all-in-one dish which is great served in deep bowls. If fresh noodles are unavailable, use dried spaghetti or fettuccine.

- 8 oz fresh egg noodles
- 2 teaspoons sesame oil
- 1 large onion, sliced
- 1 clove garlic, crushed
- 1 teaspoon chopped chili
- 1 lb veal steak, cut into strips
- ½ cup chicken stock
- ½ cup sliced green onions
- 1 red bell pepper, seeded and sliced
- 1 cup sliced broccoli
- 1 cup sliced green beans
- ½ cup chopped fresh cilantro
- 2 teaspoons cornstarch
- 2 tablespoons water

1 Drop noodles into a large saucepan of boiling water. Cook until just tender (about 3 minutes) and drain well.
2 In a large non-stick wok or frying pan, heat oil and gently cook onion, garlic and chili for 3–4 minutes. Remove onion.
3 Make sure pan is hot, then add veal. Stir-fry for 3–4 minutes or until just beginning to brown. Add to onion.
4 Add chicken stock to pan, heat and stir in any 'bits' from pan. Add vegetables and cilantro. Cover and simmer for 3–4 minutes.
5 Add veal, onions and noodles and stir until hot. Stir in combined cornstarch and water, cook 1 minute and serve.

Nutritional information per serving: Protein 39 g; fat 5 g; carbohydrate 41 g; very good dietary fiber 5 g; 365 cals
Other features: A very good source of iron, vitamins A and C and the B-complex vitamins, and a good source of potassium. Low sodium (100 mg)

SERVES 4

Preparation time: 10 minutes
Cooking time: 20 minutes

Opposite: Veal with Noodles and, bottom, Barbecued Cod.

HEALTH TIP

When used in cooking, the alcohol in wines and spirits evaporates but leaves behind delicious flavors. You do not need to count the calories from wines used in foods which have been boiled or heated.

Green Curry

This simple dish fills the kitchen with wonderful aromas. It takes only a few minutes to make, and even non-vegetarians will love it.

- 1 tablespoon unsalted butter or oil
- 2 medium-large onions, each cut into quarters
- 1 teaspoon ground cumin
- 1 teaspoon ground fenugreek
- 1 tablespoon ground coriander
- 1 teaspoon chopped ginger
- 1 teaspoon chopped chili
- 4 medium tomatoes, chopped roughly
- 13 oz green beans, ends removed
- 8 oz defrosted frozen spinach
- ¾ cup water

1 Heat butter or oil and gently cook onion and spices for 4–5 minutes, stirring several times.
2 Add remaining ingredients and bring to the boil. Cover and simmer, stirring occasionally, for 10–15 minutes. Serve with boiled rice and pappadams.

Nutritional information per serving: Protein 6 g; fat 4 g; carbohydrate 8 g; excellent dietary fiber 9 g; 100 cals
Other features: An excellent source of vitamin C, a very good source of iron and potassium, a good source of vitamin A. Also provides useful amounts of calcium. Low sodium (30 mg)

SERVES 4

Preparation time: 10 minutes
Cooking time: 20 minutes

HEALTH TIP

Always make sure a pan or barbecue plate is hot before cooking meat. When hot, brush on a little oil and then add meat. A hot surface 'seals' the meat. Olive oil can be taken to a much higher temperature than other cooking oils before the fat changes structure.

Pork with Pears and Juniper Berries

Place juniper berries in a plastic bag and hit with a rolling pin to crush.

- 1 tablespoon honey
- 1 tablespoon salt-reduced soy sauce
- 2 tablespoons gin (or use orange juice)
- 1 ¼ lb boneless lean pork cutlets
- 1 ½ tablespoons juniper berries, crushed
- 2 teaspoons olive oil
- 2 pears, peeled, cored and cut in halves
- ¼ teaspoon cinnamon

1 In a shallow dish, mix together honey, soy sauce and gin (or juice). Dip pork cutlets into this mixture and then into juniper berries, pressing berries into pork.
2 Heat a non-stick pan, add oil and cook pork for 8–10 minutes, turning once.
3 While pork is cooking, slice each pear half without cutting right through (so slices can fan out). Push pork to one side of pan. Add pears to pan and sprinkle with cinnamon. Cook for a further 2–3 minutes until pears are hot but still firm. Serve with steamed vegetables and new potatoes.

Nutritional information per serving: Protein 35 g; fat 5 g; carbohydrate 16 g; some dietary fiber 2 g; sodium 245 mg; 245 cals
Other features: An excellent source of thiamin, a very good source of other B-complex vitamins and a good source of potassium, iron and zinc.

SERVES 4

Preparation time: 25 minutes
Cooking time: 15 minutes

Herbed Chicken

4 boneless, skinless chicken breasts

2 teaspoons oil

2 medium onions, sliced

¼ cup white vinegar

½ cup mint leaves

¼ cup fresh cilantro

1 clove garlic

1 teaspoon chopped ginger

1 teaspoon chopped chili

1 Trim breasts of fat and make criss-cross cuts across one side of each cutlet. Combine oil, onions, vinegar, mint, cilantro, garlic, ginger and chili in food processor and process until finely chopped.
2 Brush a little herb mixture evenly over each chicken breast. Place under a medium hot broiler and cook for 3–4 minutes on each side until just tender.
3 Serve with the remaining herb mixture and a salad.

Nutritional information per serving: Protein 17 g; fat 7 g; carbohydrate 3 g; dietary fiber 1 g; 140 cals
Other features: A good source of niacin (B3) and riboflavin (B2) and provides some potassium, iron and zinc. Low sodium (70 mg)

Herbed Chicken.

Preparation time: 10 minutes
Cooking time: 8 minutes

SERVES 4

Thai-style Fish

1 teaspoon oil

4 green onions, sliced

1 clove garlic, crushed

½ teaspoon chopped chili

3 mint sprigs, chopped finely

3 lemon grass stalks, sliced finely

4 fish steaks or fillets

½ cup chopped fresh cilantro

1 tablespoon lemon juice

1 teaspoon fish sauce

2 tomatoes, cut into eighths

1 Using a non-stick pan, heat oil. Add green onions, garlic, chili, mint and lemon grass. Stir over a gentle heat for 2–3 minutes.
2 Add fish to pan and cook for 5–7 minutes, turning once. Remove the fish steaks and keep them warm.
3 Add remaining ingredients to pan and cook for 3–4 minutes (tomatoes should be hot but not mushy). Pour over fish steaks.

Nutritional information per serving: Protein 32 g; fat 3 g; carbohydrate 4 g; no dietary fiber; sodium 280 mg; 180 cals
Other features: An excellent source of niacin (B3), iodine, a very good source of potassium, a good source of vitamin C and provides some vitamin A and calcium

Preparation time: 15 minutes
Cooking time: 15 minutes

Thai-style Fish.

SERVES 4

Mustard Beef Kebabs

With a few minutes' preparation in the morning, it takes very little time to cook this dish when you get home from work.

2 tablespoons grainy mustard

1 teaspoon prepared horseradish

2 teaspoons brown sugar

2 tablespoons brandy (or orange juice)

½ cup low-fat yogurt

1 lb lean rump steak, cut into 1 inch cubes

2 medium onions, cut into wedges

1 Combine mustard, horseradish, sugar, brandy or juice and yogurt. Toss beef in yogurt mixture. Leave, covered, in the refrigerator for at least 30 minutes (or all day).
2 Thread meat and onion onto eight skewers (soaked in water to prevent burning) and broil or barbecue for 5–10 minutes, brushing several times with yogurt mixture. Serve with steamed new potatoes and a green vegetable or salad.

Nutritional information per serving: Protein 32 g; fat 4 g; carbohydrate 6 g; dietary fiber 1 g; 195 cals
Other features: A very good source of zinc, niacin (B3) and riboflavin (B2), a good source of potassium, thiamin (B1) and iron. Low sodium (95 mg)

SERVES 4

Preparation time: 10 minutes + 30 minutes marinating
Cooking time: 10 minutes

Pork Cutlets with Mango Sauce

This is one of those wonderfully easy dishes that seems very special. If fresh mangoes are out of season, drained, canned mangoes can be used.

flesh of 1 large mango

2 tablespoons mango chutney

2 teaspoons Dijon mustard

2 tablespoons port

2 tablespoons lemon juice

2 teaspoons oil

1 lb boneless pork cutlets, sliced

1 medium onion, cut into wedges

1 In blender combine mango, chutney, mustard, port and lemon juice. Blend only briefly, so that the mixture retains some texture.
2 In a non-stick pan, heat oil and stir-fry pork cutlets for 2–3 minutes. Add onion and continue stir-frying for a further 2–3 minutes.
3 Pour mango sauce over pork and heat until just boiling. Serve at once with steamed potatoes, noodles or steamed rice and vegetables or salad.

Nutritional information per serving: Protein 23 g; fat 4 g; carbohydrate 9 g; dietary fiber 1 g; 165 cals
Other features: An excellent source of thiamin (B1) and niacin (B3), a very good source of riboflavin (B2) and zinc and provides some iron, potassium, vitamin A and vitamin C. Low sodium (80 mg)

Opposite: Mustard Beef Kebabs, top, and Pork Cutlets with Mango Sauce.

SERVES 4

Preparation time: 15 minutes
Cooking time: 10 minutes

Tuna and Pasta

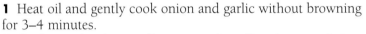

12 oz fusilli
1 cup low-fat ricotta cheese
2 tablespoons grated Parmesan cheese
½ cup fresh basil leaves (or 2 teaspoons dried)
½ cup dry white wine
1 cup snow or sugar snap peas, ends trimmed
½ cup sliced green onions
½ cup sliced celery
1 cup drained corn kernels
13 oz can tuna in water, drained

1 Cook pasta according to packet directions until just tender (do not overcook).

2 While pasta is cooking, place ricotta, Parmesan and basil in blender or food processor and beat until smooth.

3 Heat wine in a saucepan and add peas. Cover and simmer for 2–3 minutes. Add green onions, celery, corn and tuna and heat through. Add ricotta mixture and stir well.

4 Drain pasta and add to vegetable mixture. Stir well and serve at once.

Nutritional information per serving: Protein 42 g; fat 10 g; carbohydrate 80 g; dietary fiber 8 g; 570 cals

Other features: Excellent source of niacin (B3); provides thiamin (B1), iron, vitamin C, zinc, calcium and carotene (vitamin A)

SERVES 4

Preparation time: 25 minutes
Cooking time: 20 minutes

Spaghetti Marinara

If you like, vary the proportions of fish and seafood according to preference.

1 tablespoon olive oil
1 medium onion, sliced
1 clove garlic, crushed
12 oz spaghetti
2 tablespoons tomato paste (no added salt)
13 oz can tomatoes (no added salt), chopped roughly
½ cup dry white wine
10 oz boneless white fish
5 oz peeled raw shrimp
8 oysters
5 oz scallops
2 tablespoons chopped parsley

1 Heat oil and gently cook onion and garlic without browning for 3–4 minutes.

2 Cook spaghetti according to packet directions until just tender (do not overcook).

3 While spaghetti is cooking, add tomato paste, tomatoes and wine to onions. Bring to the boil and simmer 2 minutes. Add fish and shrimp and simmer a further 5–6 minutes. Add oysters and scallops and cook a further 2 minutes.

4 Drain spaghetti, return to saucepan and pour sauce over. Toss well and serve sprinkled with parsley.

Nutritional information per serving: Protein 41 g; fat 8 g; carbohydrate 65 g; dietary fiber 6 g; 485 cals

Other features: An excellent source of niacin (B3), vitamin C, zinc and thiamin (B1); a good source of iron; provides calcium, potassium and vitamin A

SERVES 4

Preparation time: 30 minutes
Cooking time: 20 minutes

Pasta with Low-fat Basil Sauce

12 oz pasta

1 large bunch basil

2 cloves garlic

2 tablespoons lemon juice

2 tablespoons olive oil

2 tablespoons pine nuts

1 cup low-fat ricotta cheese

2 tablespoons grated Parmesan

SERVES 4

1 Cook pasta, according to directions, while making sauce.
2 Place basil leaves in food processor and chop finely.
3 Add garlic, lemon juice, oil, pine nuts and ricotta. Blend well. Add Parmesan.
4 To serve, stir through hot cooked, drained pasta.

Nutritional information per serving: Protein 20 g; fat 20 g; carbohydrate 72 g; dietary fiber 7 g; 525 cals
Other features: An excellent source of vitamin C, a good source of B-complex vitamins; provides iron, calcium , carotene (vitamin A) and zinc

Preparation time: 25 minutes
Cooking time: 15 minutes

HEALTH TIP

Herbs are not usually eaten in sufficient amounts to provide many nutrients. However, dishes such as tabbouleh or pesto sauce use so much parsley and basil that they are significant sources of vitamins and minerals.

Pasta with Meat Sauce

1 lb very lean ground beef

1 medium onion, chopped

1 tablespoon paprika

2 teaspoons dried oregano

¾ cup red wine

13 oz can tomatoes (no added salt), chopped

1 cup grated carrot

1 cup grated zucchini

1 cup peeled diced eggplant

1 lb pasta

SERVES 6

1 In a non-stick pan, cook beef and onion until meat browns.
2 Add paprika and oregano and cook for a further 2–3 minutes, stirring well.
3 Add remaining ingredients, bring to the boil, cover and simmer for 30 minutes.
4 To serve, stir through hot cooked, drained pasta. Sprinkle with freshly grated Parmesan.

Nutritional information per serving: Protein 29 g; fat 4 g; carbohydrate 65 g; dietary fiber 6 g; 400 cals. Sauce only: 120 cals
Other features: An excellent source of niacin (B3) and vitamin C; good source of carotene (vitamin A); provides thiamin (B1), iron and zinc

Preparation time: 30 minutes
Cooking time: 40 minutes

RECIPE TIP

An Italian legend maintains that the shape of tortellini copies that of the navel of the goddess Venus.

Pasta Carbonara

This dish is usually high in fat. This low-fat version tastes surprisingly good.

12 oz penne (or other noodles)

1 tablespoon olive oil

1 medium onion, chopped

1 cup diced turkey salami

2 eggs

1 cup evaporated skim milk

1 tablespoon chopped fresh basil

freshly ground black pepper

SERVES 4

1 Cook pasta according to packet directions until just tender (do not overcook). Drain and return to saucepan.
2 While pasta is cooking, heat oil and gently cook onion until soft. Add turkey salami and stir for 3–4 minutes. Add to pasta.
3 Beat eggs and milk. Add basil and pepper. Pour into pasta and stir until mixture is hot and thickens. Serve at once.

Nutritional information per serving: Protein 34 g; fat 11 g; carbohydrate 83 g; dietary fiber 5 g; 550 cals
Other features: An excellent source of niacin (B3); a good source of riboflavin (B2); provides thiamin (B1), zinc, calcium, iron and potassium.

Preparation time: 20 minutes
Cooking time: 15 minutes

Cashew Nut Rice Mold

1½ cups brown rice

few saffron strands soaked in
2 tablespoons boiling water

3 cups chicken stock

½ cup chopped cashews

1 tablespoon olive oil

1 tablespoon lemon juice

¼ cup chopped
fresh cilantro

½ cup cooked peas

freshly ground black pepper

1 Put rice, saffron liquid and stock into a saucepan and bring to the boil. Reduce heat, cover and simmer for 25 minutes.
2 While rice is cooking, toast cashew nuts in a dry frying pan until brown. Set aside.
3 Add remaining ingredients to cooked rice in saucepan. Spoon rice into an oiled pudding basin or ring mold, pressing rice down well. Cover and allow to stand for 5 minutes before turning out. Decorate with cashew nuts.
4 Serve with salad and bread or with fish, chicken or lean meat.

Nutritional information per serving: Protein 11 g; fat 14 g; carbohydrate 56 g; dietary fiber 4 g; 390 cals
Other features: A good source of niacin (B3); provides some thiamin (B1)

SERVES 6

Preparation time: 30 minutes
Cooking time: 25 minutes

Pasta with Tomato and Mushroom Sauce

2 tablespoons olive oil

1 large onion, sliced finely

2 cloves garlic, crushed

2 lb ripe tomatoes, diced

1 cup red wine

2 tablespoons tomato paste

2 teaspoons dried oregano

1 teaspoon dried basil

8 oz mushrooms, sliced

12 oz pasta

1 Heat oil and cook onion and garlic without browning. Add tomatoes and stir thoroughly.
2 Add red wine, tomato paste and herbs. Bring to the boil, cover and simmer for 10 minutes.
3 Add mushrooms, stir well and cook for a further 5 minutes.
4 To serve, stir through hot cooked, drained pasta. Sprinkle with freshly grated Parmesan.

Nutritional information per serving, including pasta: Protein 17 g; fat 11 g; carbohydrate 80 g; dietary fiber 11 g; 475 cals. Sauce only: 150 cals
Other features: An excellent source of vitamin C; good source of B-complex vitamins; provides potassium, iron and carotene (vitamin A) plus some zinc.

SERVES 4

Preparation time: 30 minutes
Cooking time: 20 minutes

All-in-one Rice Pie

3 cups cooked brown rice

¾ cup chopped walnuts

1 cup cooked cubed chicken

1 large tomato, diced

1 cup corn kernels

½ cup sliced green onions

½ cup diced bell pepper

2 tablespoons chopped basil

2 eggs, beaten

½ cup yogurt

½ cup grated cheese

1 Combine all ingredients except cheese. Press mixture into a greased 8 inch pie dish and sprinkle with cheese.
2 Bake at 350°F for 25–30 minutes. Stand for 5 minutes. Cut into wedges to serve.

Nutritional information per serving: Protein 16 g; fat 16 g; carbohydrate 31 g; dietary fiber 3 g; 320 cals
Other features: A good source of vitamin C; provides niacin (B3), thiamin (B1) and riboflavin (B2)

SERVES 6

Preparation time: 35 minutes
Cooking time: 30 minutes

Opposite, clockwise from top: Shrimp and Citrus Fettuccine (page 88), All-in-one Rice Pie and Pasta with Tomato and Mushroom Sauce.

Shrimp and Citrus Fettuccine

12 oz spinach fettuccine
10 oz green beans
1 tablespoon olive oil
1 lb shrimp, shelled and de-veined
1 bunch fresh asparagus, cut into 1¼–1½ inch lengths
1 red bell pepper, seeded and sliced
1 cup orange juice
1 tablespoon lemon juice
1 can mandarins, drained
1 tablespoon chopped lemon thyme (or use parsley)

1 Cook fettuccine according to packet directions until just tender (do not overcook).
2 While fettuccine is cooking, steam green beans for 4–5 minutes.
3 In a non-stick pan, heat oil and gently stir-fry shrimp for 3 minutes, turning frequently until flesh is pink (do not overcook).
4 Add beans, asparagus, bell pepper and juices and bring to the boil. Simmer, uncovered, for 2 minutes. Add mandarins and lemon thyme.
5 Drain fettuccine and add sauce. Toss well together and serve at once.

Nutritional information per serving: Protein 37 g; fat 8 g; carbohydrate 87 g; dietary fiber 8 g; 560 cals
Other features: Excellent source of vitamin C and niacin (B3); good source of thiamin (B1) and iron; provides zinc, calcium and carotene (vitamin A)

SERVES 4

Preparation time: 20 minutes
Cooking time: 20 minutes

Pasta and Vegetable Bake.

Pasta and Vegetable Bake

12 oz fusilli
1 tablespoon olive oil
1 onion, finely chopped
1 small eggplant, diced
3 small zucchini, cut into 1¼ inch lengths
1 red bell pepper, seeded and sliced
2 medium tomatoes, diced
1 tablespoon tomato paste
½ teaspoon dried oregano
½ cup grated Parmesan cheese
¼ cup packaged dry bread crumbs
2 tablespoons grated cheese
2 teaspoons whole grain mustard

1 Cook pasta until just tender (do not overcook). Drain well.
2 Heat oil in pan and gently cook onion for 1 minute. Add eggplant, zucchini, pepper and tomatoes and cook, turning often, until just tender. Stir in tomato paste and oregano.
3 In a large bowl combine pasta, vegetable mixture and Parmesan cheese.
4 Lightly oil a deep 8 inch-round cake pan and coat base and sides with 2 tablespoons bread crumbs. Spoon pasta mixture into pan and press down well. Bake at 350°F for 30–35 minutes. Stand 5 minutes; turn onto serving plate.
5 Combine remaining bread crumbs, cheese and mustard and sprinkle over the Bake. Place under hot broiler for 1 minute.

Nutritional information per serving: Protein 15 g; fat 9 g; carbohydrate 55 g; dietary fiber 6 g; 355 cals
Other features: Excellent source of vitamin C; good source of protein and dietary fiber; provides iron, B vitamins and zinc

SERVES 6

Preparation time: 40 minutes
Cooking time: 40 minutes

Chicken and Rice Cake

Serve with lemon wedges or a crisp garden salad.

1¼ lb boneless chicken thighs, cut into 1 inch cubes

2½ cups yogurt

½ teaspoon cinnamon

½ teaspoon coarsely ground black pepper

2 teaspoons paprika

1 teaspoon turmeric

1 lb long-grain rice

6 cups water

2 egg yolks

2 teaspoons olive oil

1 Combine the chicken, two cups of the yogurt and the spices. Cover and refrigerate for at least 2 hours (or overnight).
2 Bring rice and water to the boil and cook for 5 minutes (rice will not be fully cooked). Drain.
3 Take out 1½ cups of the rice and mix with the egg yolks and remaining ½ cup yogurt. Grease a 2.6 quart heavy casserole with the oil. Press the egg yolk mixture over the base of the casserole.
4 Remove ½ cup of the yogurt marinade from the chicken and set aside. Place half the chicken and yogurt mixture in the casserole, followed by half the plain rice. Repeat the chicken and rice layers and top with the reserved yogurt marinade.
5 Cover and bake in a moderate (350°F) oven for 1¼ hours. Stand on a cold surface for 10 minutes, then invert onto a large serving platter. Cut into wedges to serve.

Nutritional information per serving: Protein 30 g; fat 10 g; carbohydrate 71 g; dietary fiber 2 g; 510 cals
Other features: Excellent source of niacin (B3); good source of riboflavin (B2); provides some zinc and calcium

Chicken and Rice Cake.

SERVES 6

Preparation time: 40 minutes
+ 2 hours standing time
Cooking time: 1¼ hours

> **HEALTH TIP**
>
> Many Asian foods are healthy choices. One exception is deep-fried dishes, which are high in fat.

Spinach Risotto

1 bunch spinach, stalks removed

1 tablespoon olive oil

1 medium onion, chopped

1 clove garlic, crushed

1 lb Arborio rice

5½ cups chicken stock

2 teaspoons finely grated lemon rind

½ cup dry white wine

freshly ground black pepper

2 tablespoons grated Parmesan cheese

1 Wash spinach and place in a saucepan. Cover and cook over a gentle heat for 2–3 minutes. Drain and chop finely.
2 Heat oil and cook onion and garlic until soft but not brown. Add rice and stir for 3–4 minutes.
3 Combine chicken stock, lemon rind and wine. Pour half the stock mixture over rice, bring to the boil, cover and simmer until stock has been absorbed.
4 Add spinach and remaining stock mixture, cover and simmer until all liquid has been absorbed.
5 Sprinkle with pepper and Parmesan cheese.

Nutritional information per serving: Protein 13 g; fat 6 g; carbohydrate 67 g; dietary fiber 4 g; 390 cals
Other features: Good source of niacin (B3); provides iron and some zinc

SERVES 6

Preparation time: 30 minutes
Cooking time: 30 minutes

Spinach Risotto.

Fruity Barley Pilaf

As an alternative, use long-grain brown rice instead of barley and reduce cooking time to 30–35 minutes.

2 tablespoons olive oil
1 medium onion, chopped
1½ cups (8 oz) pearl barley
¼ cup raisins
¼ cup chopped dried apricots
¼ cup chopped almonds
4 inch cinnamon stick
1 teaspoon ground cardamom
3¼ cups chicken stock

1 Heat oil and gently cook onion until lightly browned. Add barley and stir for 3–4 minutes.

2 Add remaining ingredients and bring to the boil. Cover tightly and simmer for 1 hour. (All liquid should be absorbed and barley should be chewy-tender.)

Nutritional information per serving: Protein 12 g; fat 17 g; carbohydrate 63 g; dietary fiber 8 g; 440 cals
Other features: A good source of niacin (B3); provides iron

SERVES 4

Preparation time: 20 minutes
Cooking time: 1 hour

Salmon Cornmeal Pie

Cornmeal is bland and most people's palates will need salt. Tuna can be used instead of salmon, if you prefer.

¾ cup cornmeal
3 cups boiling water (or chicken stock)
¼ teaspoon garlic salt (optional)
1 teaspoon dried thyme
13 oz can salmon, drained and flaked
½ cup sliced shallots
1 teaspoon chopped chili
1½ cups low-fat evaporated milk
3 eggs, beaten
freshly ground black pepper
1 cup corn kernels
1 bell pepper, seeded and diced

1 Gradually add cornmeal to boiling water or chicken stock, stirring constantly. Turn heat to low and simmer for 10 minutes or until thick (stir regularly and take care not to burn yourself as the mixture bubbles). Add salt (if used) and thyme. Allow to cool slightly.

2 Mix remaining ingredients together.

3 Spread cornmeal mixture on bottom and up sides of a greased pie dish. Pour salmon mixture into dish. Bake in a moderate oven (350°F) for 30–40 minutes or until set.

Nutritional information per serving: Protein 28 g; fat 10 g; carbohydrate 35 g; dietary fiber 2 g; 335 cals
Other features: An excellent source of vitamin C; good source of riboflavin (B2), niacin (B3) and calcium; provides iron and vitamin A

Opposite from top left: Barley Soup (page 42), Salmon Cornmeal Pie and Fruity Barley Pilaf.

SERVES 6

Preparation time: 30 minutes
Cooking time: 50 minutes

Barley Burgers

Serve these burgers with lettuce, tomato, beets and alfalfa in a toasted whole wheat hamburger bun.

1 tablespoon olive oil

1 medium onion, chopped

1 clove garlic, crushed

1 cup pearl barley

1 cup tomato juice

1 cup water

1 cup grated carrot

2 tablespoons chopped parsley

1 egg, lightly beaten

1 teaspoon dried basil

½ cup whole wheat flour

2 tablespoons sesame seeds

1 Heat oil and cook onion and garlic until soft.
2 Add barley, tomato juice and water. Bring to the boil, cover and simmer 20 minutes.
3 Combine barley with remaining ingredients except seeds (a food processor makes it easier).
4 Using wet hands, form into six patties. Roll in sesame seeds and cook in a non-stick pan for about 5 minutes on each side or until brown.

Nutritional information for patty only: Protein 6 g; fat 7 g; carbohydrate 32 g; dietary fiber 4 g; 210 cals
Other features: A good source of vitamin C and carotene (vitamin A); provides some iron

SERVES 6

Preparation time: 20 minutes
Cooking time: 30 minutes

Moroccan-style Chickpeas

1 tablespoon oil

1 lb lean lamb, cut into cubes

1 large onion, cut into eighths

1 clove garlic, crushed

2 teaspoons ground coriander

1 teaspoon ground allspice

¼ teaspoon ground black pepper

2 cups chicken stock

½ cup dried apricots

½ cup prunes

½ cup raisins

3 cups cooked chickpeas (1 cup raw)

1 tablespoon slivered almonds, toasted

1 Heat oil and cook lamb and onion until brown. Add garlic and spices and cook a further 2 minutes.
2 Add stock and fruits. Place in an ovenproof dish, cover and bake in a moderate oven for 45 minutes.
3 Add cooked chickpeas, stir well and bake, uncovered, for a further 10 minutes. Sprinkle almonds on top just before serving.

Nutritional information per serving: Protein 41 g; fat 18 g; carbohydrate 31 g; dietary fiber 10 g; 440 cals
Other features: An excellent source of niacin (B3); good source of iron and zinc; provides potassium, B-complex vitamins and some carotene (vitamin A)

SERVES 6

Preparation time: 20 minutes
Cooking time: 1 hour

Tortillas

Delicious fillings and a fresh salad make tortillas a favorite with the children.

8 oz cornmeal

1 cup water

2 teaspoons salt

1 Combine all ingredients, working quickly to mix. Using hands, form mixture into a soft dough, adding a little more cornmeal if necessary.
2 Divide dough into 12 portions and roll each into a ball, then flatten until it forms a thin round.
3 Cook tortillas in a hot non-stick pan until speckled and brown on each side. Keep warm.
4 Serve with Mouth-watering Beans (page 120) or the sauce in Tacos with Beans (page 69).

Nutritional information per tortilla: Protein 2 g; fat 1 g; carbohydrate 15 g; dietary fiber 1 g; 75 cals

Preparation time: 15 minutes

MAKES 12 Tortillas

Cooking time: 2–3 minutes each

RECIPE TIP

Cornmeal, also known as maize meal, is a finely-ground yellow flour, similar to whole wheat flour in texture, and is readily available. Polenta, the classic accompaniment to Italian foods, is a coarsely-ground yellow cornmeal.

Barley and Mushrooms

1 tablespoon butter or margarine

1 medium onion, chopped

1 cup pearl barley

8 oz sliced mushrooms

2 cups chicken stock

¼ cup white wine

1 tablespoon fresh lemon thyme (or ½ teaspoon dried)

8 oz whole baby button mushrooms

½ cup chopped cashew nuts

SERVES 4

1 Heat butter or margarine and gently cook onion until soft but not brown. Add barley and cook for 2–3 minutes, stirring well.
2 Add sliced mushrooms, stock, wine and thyme. Bring to the boil; cover tightly and simmer for 50 minutes.
3 Add whole mushrooms and cook a further 10 minutes.
4 Add cashews and fork through barley mixture (all water should be absorbed).

Nutritional information per serving: Protein 12 g; fat 13 g; carbohydrate 42 g; dietary fiber 6 g; 320 cals
Other features: A good source of niacin (B3) and riboflavin (B2); provides iron

Preparation time: 20 minutes

Cooking time: 65 minutes

HEALTH TIP

These foods all supply the same amount of vitamin C:

1 medium orange;
4 pounds of lettuce;
2 large tomatoes;
18 medium apples.

Barley Casserole

This dish is delicious served as a main course or with lean broiled lamb leg chops.

1 tablespoon olive oil

1 medium onion, chopped

1 clove garlic, crushed

1½ cups (8 oz) pearl barley

2 medium zucchini, diced

1 red bell pepper, diced

1 cup diced mushrooms

3 cups chicken stock

1 teaspoon dried oregano

SERVES 4

1 Heat oil and cook onion and garlic until soft. Add barley and cook, stirring constantly, for 3–4 minutes.
2 Add remaining ingredients and turn into a greased casserole. Cover and cook for 1 hour.

Nutritional information per serving: Protein 11 g; fat 7 g; carbohydrate 56 g; dietary fiber 6 g; 325 cals
Other features: An excellent source of vitamin C, good source of niacin (B3); provides iron

Preparation time: 30 minutes

Cooking time: 1 hour

Cornmeal Soufflés

2 cups low-fat milk

½ cup cornmeal

½ teaspoon baking powder

2 teaspoons Dijon mustard

pinch nutmeg

1 tablespoon butter
or margarine

2 eggs, separated

1 tablespoon finely grated
Parmesan cheese

SERVES 4

1 Heat 1¼ cups of the milk and, when hot, add cornmeal. Cook for 2 minutes, stirring constantly. Remove from heat.
2 Add baking powder, mustard, nutmeg, butter or margarine and remaining ¾ cup milk. Stir in egg yolks.
3 Beat egg whites until stiff and fold into cornmeal mixture. Spoon into four well-greased soufflé dishes, sprinkle cheese on top and bake at 350°F for about 40 minutes. Serve at once.

Nutritional information per serving: Protein 10 g; fat 8 g; carbohydrate 22 g; dietary fiber 1 g; 200 cals
Other features: Provides some calcium

Preparation time: 40 minutes
Cooking time: 40 minutes

Chicken and Wheat Loaf

1 cup bulgur (cracked wheat)

½ cup chopped dried apricots

1¼ cups boiling water

1 medium onion,
chopped finely

1 lb ground chicken

1 teaspoon allspice

½ teaspoon coarsely ground
black pepper

1 tablespoon chopped mint

2 teaspoons finely grated
orange rind

1 tablespoon pine nuts

SERVES 6

1 Combine bulgur and apricots in a bowl. Pour boiling water over, cover tightly and leave to stand for 15–20 minutes (water will be absorbed).
2 Add all ingredients except pine nuts to bulgur. Mix thoroughly and pack into a greased loaf pan. Press pine nuts into top of loaf. Bake in a moderate (350°F) oven for 1 hour. Leave for 5 minutes before turning out. Serve hot or cold with a spicy chutney or relish.

Nutritional information per serving: Protein 23 g; fat 3 g; carbohydrate 29 g; dietary fiber 6 g; 235 cals
Other features: A good source of niacin (B3); provides iron

Preparation time: 20 minutes
+ 20 minutes standing time
Cooking time: 1 hour

Millet Patties

1 cup millet

2½ cups water

1 cup mashed pumpkin
(or mashed potato)

½ cup rolled oats

½ cup sliced shallots

1 egg, beaten

2 teaspoons grainy mustard

Sauce

1 cup yogurt

2 teaspoons grainy mustard

1 tablespoon chopped mint

SERVES 6

1 Put millet and water into saucepan. Bring to the boil, cover and simmer over very low heat for 35 minutes (millet will absorb water and become sticky).
2 Add remaining ingredients to millet. Mix well and form into six patties. Cook in a non-stick pan for about 10 minutes, or until brown on both sides.
3 To make sauce: Combine yogurt, mustard and mint thoroughly.

Nutritional information per serving: Protein 7 g; fat 4 g; carbohydrate 22 g; dietary fiber 3 g; 155 cals

Preparation time: 15 minutes
Cooking time: 45 minutes

Lentil Burgers

1 cup (6 oz) red lentils

2¼ cups water

1 medium onion, chopped

1 teaspoon chopped
fresh ginger

2 slices whole wheat bread,
made into crumbs

½ cup unprocessed oat bran

2 tablespoons chopped
cilantro (or mint or parsley)

1 egg

2 tablespoons sesame seeds

4 flat whole wheat
hamburger rolls

½ cup yogurt

2 tablespoons mango chutney

shredded lettuce, sliced
tomato and cucumber

SERVES 4

1 Place lentils, water, onion and ginger in a saucepan; bring to the boil. Cover and simmer for 20–25 minutes (lentils should be quite dry but check to see they do not burn). Set aside.
2 In food processor, combine bread crumbs, oat bran, cilantro and egg. Blend well. Add lentil mixture.
3 Form mixture into four large patties. Press sesame seeds into the surface.
4 Using a non-stick pan, cook burgers for about 4–5 minutes on each side or until brown.
5 Split and toast buns.
6 Combine yogurt and chutney and spread on toasted buns.
7 Arrange salad ingredients on one half of each bun. Top with lentil patty and remaining bun.

Nutritional information per burger (including bun and salad): Protein 25 g; fat 5 g; carbohydrate 66 g; dietary fiber 11 g; 410 cals
Other features: A good source of iron, thiamin (B1), and niacin (B3); provides zinc, riboflavin (B2) and calcium

Preparation time: 20 minutes
Cooking time: 30 minutes

Lentil Lasagne

If ready-made pasta sauce is not available, use two cups tomato purée.

1 cup (6 oz) red
or brown lentils

2¼ cups water

1 tablespoon olive oil

1 large onion, sliced

1 tablespoon chopped
garlic chives (or 1 clove
crushed garlic)

2 cups ready-made tomato
pasta sauce

1 cup sliced mushrooms

1 cup sliced zucchini

1 cup grated carrot

2 teaspoons dried oregano

7½ oz instant lasagne sheets

1 lb low-fat ricotta cheese

½ cup reduced-fat
grated cheese

1 teaspoon paprika

SERVES 6

1 Cook lentils in water, covered, for 25 minutes or until water has been absorbed.
2 Heat oil and gently cook onion until soft. Add garlic chives, sauce, vegetables and oregano. Bring to the boil and simmer for 15 minutes. Add lentils and stir well.
3 In a greased shallow casserole, place one-third of vegetable mixture. Top with a layer of lasagne and one-third of the ricotta. Repeat layers twice. Sprinkle with cheeses and paprika. Bake in a moderate oven for 25 minutes.

Nutritional information per serving: Protein 27 g; fat 19 g; carbohydrate 57 g; dietary fiber 9 g; 500 cals
Other features: An excellent source of vitamin A; good source of vitamin C, niacin (B3), thiamin (B1) and calcium; provides iron, riboflavin (B2), zinc and potassium

Preparation time: 15 minutes
Cooking time: 1 hour

SALADS & VEGETABLES

THE VARIETY OF VEGETABLES AND SALAD INGREDIENTS readily available to us is quite astonishing. Yet many people, lacking a sense of adventure, still stick to a few old faithfuls. Don't miss out on some wonderful tastes and textures; resolve to try something new next time you visit the supermarket, farmers' market or ethnic market. With each season, a bountiful supply of vegetables, salad greens and fruits awaits. Check farmers' markets for the best seasonal buys and choose your recipe accordingly. Many of the dishes in this section need only fresh bread and a juicy fruit dessert to make a complete meal. Some, such as Stuffed Tomatoes or Roasted Red Pepper Salad, make perfect appetizers. Others – Parsley Potatoes or Gingered Snow Peas – are ideal accompaniments to meat or fish courses.

Potato Cakes.

*Previous page, clockwise from top:
Carrot and Hazelnut Salad
(page 110), Bean Salad (page 102)
and Italian-style Fennel (page 106).*

Potatoes Anna

1 clove garlic, peeled
and cut in half

1 teaspoon olive oil

1¼ lb potatoes (about
4 medium-sized), peeled
and sliced finely

2 medium onions, sliced finely

2 teaspoons finely grated
orange rind

1 teaspoon coarsely
ground pepper

1¼ cups low-fat milk

pinch nutmeg

SERVES 4

1 Rub a shallow ovenproof casserole with the cut garlic clove. Discard garlic. Use oil to grease casserole.
2 Layer potatoes and onions in casserole, sprinkling each layer with a little of the orange rind and pepper and finishing with a layer of potato.
3 Pour milk over potatoes. Bake, uncovered, at 350°F for about 40 minutes or until potatoes are tender and top is browned. Sprinkle with nutmeg and serve at once.

Nutritional information per serving: Protein 7 g; fat 3 g; carbohydrate 27 g; dietary fiber 3 g; 150 cals
Other features: Excellent source of vitamin C

Preparation time: 30 minutes
Cooking time: 40 minutes

Potato Cake

2 slices whole wheat bread

6 medium-sized
potatoes, peeled

1 large onion

2 medium carrots

2 eggs, beaten

1 cup instant non-fat dry milk

2 teaspoons grainy mustard

2 tablespoons olive oil

½ cup grated
reduced-fat cheese

1 tablespoon sesame seeds

SERVES 6

1 Using food processor, make bread into crumbs and set aside.
2 Grate potatoes, onion and carrots.
3 Combine all ingredients except cheese and sesame seeds and mix well. Press into a greased 8 inch-square cake pan or ovenproof casserole and bake, uncovered, in a moderate oven (350°F) for 45–50 minutes.
4 Sprinkle cheese and seeds on top and bake a further 5 minutes. Serve hot or cold.

Nutritional information per serving: Protein 28 g; fat 19 g; carbohydrate 62 g; dietary fiber 8 g; 510 cals
Other features: Excellent source of vitamin C and carotene (vitamin A) and potassium; good source of niacin (B3), calcium, iron and zinc

Preparation time: 30 minutes
Cooking time: 55 minutes

Cheese-stuffed Potatoes

4 large potatoes

½ cup cottage cheese

2 teaspoons grainy mustard

1 tablespoon chopped herbs

4 cubes (about 1 inch) Cheddar or reduced-fat Swiss cheese

1 Prick potatoes and bake at 350°F for 1–1½ hours.
2 Cut a lid from each potato, scoop out flesh.
3 Combine potato flesh with cottage cheese, mustard and herbs. Pile filling in shells and press a cube of cheese into each. Replace lids and bake a further 10–15 minutes.

Nutritional information per serving: Protein 15 g; fat 5 g; carbohydrate 28 g; dietary fiber 4 g; 210 cals
Other features: Excellent source of vitamin C; good source of calcium and potassium

SERVES 4

Preparation time: 15 minutes
Cooking time: 1 hour 45 minutes

Chicken and Corn Potatoes

4 large potatoes

2 teaspoons chopped chives

2 tablespoons nonfat yogurt

½ cup drained corn kernels

3 cups cubed cooked chicken

1 Prick potatoes and bake at 350°F for 1–1½ hours.
2 Cut a lid from each potato, scoop out flesh.
3 Mash flesh with chives and yogurt. Mix in corn and chicken; pile into shells. Replace lids and bake a further 10–15 minutes.

Nutritional information per serving: Protein 12 g; fat 2 g; carbohydrate 32 g; dietary fiber 5 g; 185 cals
Other features: Excellent source of vitamin C; good source of niacin (B3) and potassium

SERVES 4

Preparation time: 20 minutes
Cooking time: 1 hour 45 minutes

HEALTH TIP

Frozen vegetables are almost as nutritious as fresh. Freezing slows down loss of vitamins.

HEALTH TIP

The best way to retain vitamins in vegetables is to microwave them, without water, until just cooked. Steaming is the next best method.

From left: Mushroom and Onion-stuffed Potatoes (page 100), Avocado-stuffed Potatoes (page 100) and Chicken and Corn Potatoes.

A certain amount
of confusion exists
over the term shallot –
a true shallot looks
like a small
brown onion.

Avocado-stuffed Potatoes

For spicy avocado potatoes, add 1 teaspoon chili powder to potato flesh with avocado.

4 large potatoes

⅓ cup cottage cheese

1 tablespoon chopped fresh
herbs (chives, parsley, mint,
thyme or tarragon)

1 small avocado, peeled

1 teaspoon grated lemon rind

1 Prick potatoes and bake at 350°F for 1–1½ hours.
2 Cut a lid from each potato and scoop out flesh.
3 Combine potato flesh with remaining ingredients and mash until smooth and creamy. Pile mixture back into potato shells, replace lids and bake for a further 10–15 minutes.

Nutritional information per serving: Protein 8 g; fat 9 g; carbohydrate 28 g; dietary fiber 4 g; 215 cals
Other features: Excellent source of vitamin C; good source of potassium

SERVES 4

Preparation time: 20 minutes
Cooking time: 1 hour 45 minutes

Mushroom and Onion-stuffed Potatoes

4 large potatoes

2 teaspoons olive oil

1 small onion, chopped

1 cup sliced mushrooms

½ teaspoon dried tarragon

2 teaspoons grainy mustard

1 tablespoon non-fat yogurt

1 Prick potatoes and bake at 350°F for 1–1½ hours.
2 Cut a lid from each potato and scoop out flesh.
3 Heat oil and gently cook onion for 2 minutes. Add mushrooms and tarragon and cook for 3–4 minutes.
4 Mash potato flesh with mustard and yogurt. Fold in mushrooms and onions and pile filling back into potato shells. Replace lids and bake for a further 10–15 minutes.

Nutritional information per serving: Protein 5 g; fat 3 g; carbohydrate 28 g; dietary fiber 4 g; 145 cals
Other features: Excellent source of vitamin C; good source of potassium

SERVES 4

Preparation time: 20 minutes
Cooking time: 1 hour 45 minutes

To reduce the fat in the
dressing for a potato
salad, use half light
mayonnaise and half
yogurt. Flavor with
fresh chopped herbs.

German Potato Salad

1½ lb small new
potatoes, scrubbed

1 tablespoon olive oil

1 medium onion, chopped

2 teaspoons sugar

½ cup cider vinegar

2 teaspoons dry
mustard powder

1 teaspoon caraway seeds

3 hard-boiled eggs,
peeled and chopped

2 tablespoons
chopped parsley

1 Steam potatoes (or microwave) until just tender. While still hot, cut in halves and place in a bowl.
2 While potatoes are cooking, heat oil and gently cook onion, without browning, for 2–3 minutes. Add vinegar, sugar, mustard and caraway seeds and bring to the boil.
3 Pour hot dressing mixture over the hot potatoes.
4 Add hard-boiled eggs and parsley and toss gently. Serve while warm.

Nutritional information per serving: Protein 8 g; fat 8 g; carbohydrate 32 g; dietary fiber 5 g; 215 cals
Other features: Excellent source of vitamin C; good source of iron and potassium

SERVES 4

Preparation time: 30 minutes
Cooking time: 15 minutes

Opposite: Potato and Leek Soup (page 42) and, bottom, Hot Orange Beets (page 103).

Crunchy-topped Vegetables

An ideal accompaniment to broiled fish, chicken or lean meat.

1¼ lb vegetables (Brussels sprouts, broccoli, cauliflower pieces, green beans, carrots or pumpkin)

1 tablespoon grainy mustard

1 tablespoon chopped parsley

2 slices whole wheat bread, made into crumbs

1 tablespoon grated Parmesan cheese

1 teaspoon paprika

1 Steam or microwave the vegetables until just tender. Place in an ovenproof dish. Toss with mustard and parsley.
2 Combine crumbs, Parmesan and paprika. Sprinkle over vegetables and place under broiler for about 2 minutes, until crumbs are brown. (Alternatively, place dish in a moderate oven for 10 minutes.)

Nutritional information per serving: Protein 6 g; fat 2 g; carbohydrate 10 g; dietary fiber 5 g; 80 cals
Other features: Excellent source of vitamin C and carotene (vitamin A); provides iron

SERVES 4

Preparation time: 20 minutes
Cooking time: 20 minutes

Bean Salad.

Bean Salad

Served with some crisp lettuce, sun-ripened tomatoes and a chunk of fresh whole wheat bread, this salad makes a perfect lunch or summer meal. It is just as good the following day, providing the bean sprouts are fresh. Use pre-cooked, canned kidney and lima beans that have been drained and rinsed, if you prefer.

2 cups green beans, cut in halves

1 cup cooked red kidney beans

1 cup cooked lima beans

3½ oz mushrooms, sliced

1 red and 1 green bell pepper, seeded and sliced

1 cup mung bean sprouts

½ cup parsley

Dressing

1 clove garlic, crushed

1 teaspoon dried tarragon

1 teaspoon crumbled dried rosemary

2 tablespoons lemon juice

1 tablespoon olive oil

freshly ground black pepper

1 Steam or microwave beans until barely tender. Rinse immediately under cold water and drain.
2 Combine all salad ingredients.
3 Mix all dressing ingredients and pour over salad. Allow to stand for at least 10 minutes before serving.

Nutritional information per serving: Protein 7 g; fat 3 g; carbohydrate 8 g; very good dietary fiber 6 g; 90 cals
Other features: Excellent source of vitamin C and provides useful amounts of potassium and some vitamin A, niacin (B3) and iron. Negligible sodium

SERVES 4

Preparation time: 20 minutes
Cooking time: 5 minutes

Hot Orange Beets

4 medium-sized beets
1 cup orange juice
2 tablespoons wine vinegar
1 teaspoon brown sugar
2 teaspoons cornstarch
extra 2 tablespoons orange juice
½ cup non-fat yogurt
2 teaspoons finely shredded orange rind
freshly ground black pepper

1 Cut stalks from beets. Place in a saucepan with orange juice. Bring to the boil, cover tightly and simmer for about 40 minutes, or until just tender. Remove beets, cool slightly and slip skins off. Quarter beets.
2 Return beets to saucepan. Add vinegar and sugar and cook for 1 minute.
3 Combine cornstarch with extra orange juice and add to beets, stirring constantly until mixture thickens.
4 Serve with a side dish of the yogurt sprinkled with the orange rind and pepper.

Nutritional information per serving: Protein 4 g; fat 0 g; carbohydrate 20 g; dietary fiber 3 g; 100 cals
Other features: Excellent source of vitamin C

Preparation time: 10 minutes

SERVES 4

Cooking time: 45 minutes

Greek-style Beans

2 tablespoons olive oil
1 large onion, sliced thinly
1 clove garlic, crushed
13 oz can tomatoes, chopped roughly
2 tablespoons cider vinegar
½ cup white wine
2 bay leaves
1 teaspoon dried oregano
1 lb green beans
2 tablespoons chopped parsley

1 Heat oil and gently cook onion and garlic, without browning, for 3–4 minutes. Add tomatoes, vinegar, wine, bay leaves and oregano. Bring to the boil and simmer, uncovered, for 5 minutes, stirring occasionally.
2 Add beans; cover and simmer for 5 minutes. Remove bay leaves. Serve hot or cold, sprinkled with the parsley.

Nutritional information per serving: Protein 5 g; fat 10 g; carbohydrate 7 g; dietary fiber 5 g; 130 cals
Other features: Excellent source of vitamin C; source of iron

Preparation time: 20 minutes

SERVES 4

Cooking time: 20 minutes

Greek-style Beans.

Cabbage, Sweet Potato and Apple

1 teaspoon cinnamon

1 teaspoon caraway seeds

1 teaspoon brown sugar

2 cups shredded cabbage

1 lb sweet potato, peeled and sliced thinly

2 cooking apples, peeled, cored and sliced thinly

freshly ground pepper

1 cup apple juice

1 Combine cinnamon, caraway seeds and sugar.
2 In a greased casserole, place layers of cabbage, sweet potato and apple, sprinkling cinnamon mixture over each apple layer and pepper on each layer of sweet potato.
3 Pour on apple juice and bake, uncovered, at 350°F for 25–30 minutes. Serve hot.

Nutritional information per serving: Protein 3 g; fat 0 g; carbohydrate 28 g; dietary fiber 6 g; 125 cals
Other features: Excellent source of vitamin C and carotene (vitamin A)

SERVES 4

Preparation time: 30 minutes
Cooking time: 30 minutes

Nutty Broccoli

1 lb broccoli pieces

1 cup chicken stock

¼ cup almonds

1 clove garlic

1 teaspoon grated lemon rind

freshly ground black pepper

1 tablespoon fresh lemon thyme

1 Steam or microwave broccoli until barely tender. Place in an ovenproof dish.
2 While broccoli is cooking, heat chicken stock. Place in blender with remaining ingredients and purée to a smooth paste. Pour over broccoli and place in a moderate (350°F) oven for a few minutes to heat through.

Nutritional information per serving: Protein 8 g; fat 6 g; carbohydrate 1 g; dietary fiber 7 g; 85 cals
Other features: Excellent source of vitamin C; provides some iron

SERVES 4

Preparation time: 15 minutes
Cooking time: 20 minutes

Golden Puffed Eggplant

2 medium-sized eggplants

½ cup sliced green onion

2 slices bread, made into crumbs

½ cup low-fat ricotta cheese

2 eggs, separated

2 tablespoons grated cheese

2 teaspoons sesame seeds

2 teaspoons slivered almonds

1 Place eggplants on oven shelf and bake at 350°F for 20 minutes. When cool enough to handle, cut in halves and carefully scoop out the flesh, leaving the shells about ¼ inch thick. Chop flesh finely.
2 Combine eggplant flesh, green onion, crumbs, ricotta cheese and egg yolks. Mix well.
3 Beat egg whites until stiff and fold into the eggplant mixture. Spoon mixture into eggplant shells.
4 Combine cheese, seeds and almonds. Sprinkle over top of eggplant halves. Bake in a moderate (350°F) oven for 30 minutes until golden brown.

Nutritional information per serving: Protein 9 g; fat 8 g; carbohydrate 9 g; dietary fiber 4 g; 140 cals
Other features: Provides some calcium

Opposite: Cabbage, Sweet Potato and Apple and, bottom, Golden Puffed Eggplant, served with Crunchy-topped Vegetables (page 102).

SERVES 4

Preparation time: 30 minutes
Cooking time: 50 minutes

Stuffed Tomatoes

4 large tomatoes

¾ cup cooked green peas

½ cup chopped green onions

½ cup cottage cheese

1 teaspoon grainy mustard

2 tablespoons chopped fresh mint

freshly ground pepper

1 tablespoon grated Parmesan cheese

1 Cut a 'lid' from top of each tomato and carefully scoop out contents. Turn tomatoes upside down to drain.
2 Chop the flesh from the tomatoes roughly and place in a small non-stick pan. Boil until thick.
3 Combine cooked tomato flesh with peas, green onions, cottage cheese, mustard, mint and pepper. Spoon back into tomato shells. Top with Parmesan and bake at 350°F for 10 minutes.

Nutritional information per serving: Protein 10 g; fat 1 g; carbohydrate 8 g; very good dietary fiber 5 g; 85 cals
Other features: An excellent source of vitamin C, a good source of vitamin A, potassium, riboflavin (B2) and thiamin (B1), provides useful amounts of niacin (B3) and some calcium, iron and zinc. Low sodium (80 mg)

SERVES 4

Preparation time: 10 minutes
Cooking time: 25 minutes

Italian-style Fennel.

Italian-style Fennel

2 teaspoons olive oil

1 medium onion, chopped

1 clove garlic, crushed

14 oz can tomatoes

2 large fennel bulbs, cut lengthwise into quarters

1 teaspoon dried basil

2 bay leaves

2 tablespoons chopped parsley

1 Heat oil, add onion and garlic. Cover and allow to sweat gently for 2–3 minutes.
2 Add tomatoes, fennel, basil and bay leaves. Cover and simmer for 15 minutes. Remove bay leaves and sprinkle with parsley.

Nutritional information per serving: Protein 3 g; fat 2 g; carbohydrate 8 g; very good dietary fiber 7 g; 65 cals
Other features: An excellent source of vitamin C, a good source of potassium and provides some iron and vitamin A. Low sodium (80 mg)

SERVES 4

Preparation time: 5 minutes
Cooking time: 20 minutes

Cauliflower Salad with Tahini Dressing

1 small cauliflower, left whole

¾ cup low-fat yogurt

1 tablespoon orange juice

1 tablespoon tahini

1 small onion, sliced finely

1 teaspoon finely grated orange rind

fresh cilantro sprigs

1 Remove outer leaves and trim stalk on cauliflower. Steam for 10 minutes (cauliflower should remain crisp). Immediately rinse under cold water. Drain well.
2 Combine yogurt, orange juice and tahini (if mixture is too thick, add a little more orange juice).
3 Arrange onion rings over cauliflower. Top with yogurt mixture and sprinkle with orange rind. Garnish with cilantro.

Nutritional information per serving: Protein 5 g; fat 3 g; carbohydrate 6 g; good dietary fiber 3 g; 75 cals
Other features: An excellent source of vitamin C and a good source of potassium, riboflavin (B2) and thiamin (B1). Also provides some calcium. Low in sodium (45 mg)

SERVES 6

Preparation time: 15 minutes
Cooking time: 10 minutes

Cauliflower Cheese Soufflés

Remember – to enjoy soufflés at their best, have your guests waiting for the soufflés rather than the soufflés waiting for them.

1 small cauliflower, broken into pieces

¼ cup cottage cheese

pinch nutmeg

freshly ground pepper

1 teaspoon Dijon mustard

2 tablespoons finely grated Parmesan cheese

2 eggs, separated

1 slice whole wheat bread, made into bread crumbs

1 tablespoon chopped fresh thyme (or 1 teaspoon dried thyme)

1 Steam or microwave cauliflower until tender. Place in blender or food processor and process until broken but not puréed.

2 Add cottage cheese, nutmeg, pepper, mustard, half the cheese and the egg yolks. Mix well.

3 Beat egg whites until stiff and carefully fold into the cauliflower mixture. Spoon into four ½-cup capacity soufflé dishes and sprinkle with remaining cheese. Combine breadcrumbs and thyme and sprinkle on top of cheese.

4 Bake at 350°F for 20 minutes until puffed and golden. Serve at once.

Nutritional information per serving: Protein 12 g; fat 5 g; carbohydrate 7 g; dietary fiber 5 g; 120 cals

Other features: Excellent source of vitamin C; good source of iron; provides some calcium

SERVES 4

Preparation time: 20 minutes
Cooking time: 30 minutes

Sesame Broccoli Salad

This is ideal to serve with broiled chicken, beef, lamb or fish. It can be made ahead if necessary, and refrigerated for an hour or so.

1 tablespoon sesame seeds

1 lb broccoli

3½ oz snow peas, ends removed

10 oz can baby corn, drained

½ cup sliced green onions

1 teaspoon sesame oil

2 teaspoons peanut oil

1 tablespoon lemon juice

2 teaspoons salt-reduced soy sauce

1 Toast sesame seeds in a dry frying pan, using a moderate heat and taking care that seeds do not burn. Set aside.

2 Trim broccoli; steam 3–4 minutes. Immediately run cold water over broccoli. Drain well.

3 Steam snow peas for 1–2 minutes. Run cold water over snow peas and drain well.

4 On serving dish, toss together broccoli, snow peas, baby corn and green onions.

5 Combine oils, lemon juice and soy sauce. Pour over salad and sprinkle with sesame seeds.

Sesame Broccoli Salad.

Nutritional information per serving: Protein 7 g; fat 5 g; carbohydrate 9 g; very good dietary fiber 7 g; 110 cals

Other features: Good source of thiamin (B1), riboflavin (B2) and potassium and provides some iron, zinc and niacin (B3). Low sodium (80 mg)

SERVES 4

Preparation time: 15 minutes
Cooking time: 10 minutes

Braised Leeks

These are wonderful served hot or cold.

¾ cup chicken stock
3 leeks, washed
2 bay leaves
few sprigs of thyme
1 tablespoon olive oil
1 tablespoon wine vinegar
½ teaspoon brown sugar
1 tablespoon chopped parsley

SERVES 4

1 Heat chicken stock and boil, uncovered, until reduced by half.
2 Add remaining ingredients, except parsley, to stock. Bring to the boil. Cover tightly, turn heat low and simmer for 10 minutes. Remove bay leaves and thyme. Sprinkle with parsley. Serve hot or cold.

Nutritional information per serving: Protein 2 g; fat 5 g; carbohydrate 4 g; good dietary fiber 3 g; 65 cals
Other features: Excellent source of vitamin C; provides some iron and potassium. Low sodium (25 mg)

Preparation time: 5 minutes
Cooking time: 15 minutes

Potato Bake

Traditionally made brimming with butter, this low-fat version tastes delectable, too.

½ cup white wine
11 oz pumpkin pieces
11 oz potatoes, peeled
2 medium green apples, peeled and cored
½ cup low-fat yogurt
pinch nutmeg
freshly ground black pepper
2 egg whites
1 tablespoon chopped mint

SERVES 6

1 Heat wine, add pumpkin, potatoes and apples and cook, covered, until vegetables are tender.
2 Mash vegetables, adding yogurt, nutmeg and pepper.
3 Beat egg whites until stiff and gently fold through vegetable mixture with mint. Pour into a greased ovenproof dish. Bake at 350°F for 15 minutes.

Nutritional information per serving: Protein 7 g; fat 1 g; carbohydrate 28 g; very good dietary fiber 5 g; 135 cals
Other features: An excellent source of vitamin C, a very good source of vitamin A and potassium and a good source of riboflavin (B2). Provides some calcium. Low sodium (60 mg)

Preparation time: 20 minutes
Cooking time: 30 minutes

Parsley Potatoes

Few foods are as comforting as hot creamy mashed potato.

1 lb potatoes, peeled
1 cup chopped parsley
½ cup low-fat yogurt
1 teaspoon Dijon mustard
freshly ground black pepper

SERVES 4

1 Steam potatoes until tender.
2 Drain potatoes and add parsley. Whip potato/parsley mixture with yogurt and mustard until very smooth and fluffy. Reheat in microwave for 1 minute. Sprinkle with freshly ground pepper.

Nutritional information per serving: Protein 5 g; no fat; carbohydrate 18 g; good dietary fiber 3 g; 95 cals
Other features: An excellent source of vitamin C, a good source of potassium and provides useful amounts of iron and vitamin A. Also has some calcium and niacin (B3). Low sodium (35 mg)

Preparation time: 5 minutes
Cooking time: 20 minutes

Legumes – the collective name for beans and peas – are wonderful foods. They are rich in complex carbohydrate and a great source of valuable types of dietary fiber. Legumes are also low in fat, high in protein and provide high quantities of many vitamins of the B complex as well as being good sources of iron and other minerals. As a bonus, dried legumes are cheap. On the negative side, many need to be soaked before cooking. All this really means is a little planning. If you have never cooked dried legumes before, you might like to start with lentils which do not need soaking and cook relatively quickly.

Opposite, clockwise from top: Gingered Snow Peas (page 110), Braised Leeks, and Potato Bake.

Carrot and Hazelnut Salad.

Gingered Snow Peas

A simple and superbly flavored vegetable dish. Serve it with steamed rice.

¾ cup chicken stock

1 clove garlic

2 teaspoons sliced fresh ginger

10 oz snow peas, trimmed

2 cups sliced mushrooms

½ cup sliced green onions

2 tablespoons dry sherry

1 tablespoon salt-reduced soy sauce

SERVES 4

1 Heat chicken stock and garlic and boil until reduced to ¼ cup. Remove garlic.
2 In a wok or large frypan, place reduced chicken stock, ginger, vegetables and the sherry. Stir-fry for 3–4 minutes, tossing frequently. Add soy sauce. Serve with steamed rice.

Nutritional information per serving: Protein 6 g; no fat; carbohydrate 8 g; very good dietary fiber 5 g; sodium 155 mg; 55 cals
Other features: Very good source of vitamin C, good source of niacin (B3) and provides some iron and potassium

Preparation time: 5 minutes
Cooking time: 15 minutes

Carrot and Hazelnut Salad

¼ cup chopped hazelnuts

1 lb carrots, peeled

½ cup sliced green onions

1 cup sunflower sprouts

1 tablespoon sunflower seeds

¼ cup orange juice

1 tablespoon extra virgin olive oil

coarsely ground pepper

SERVES 4

1 Toast hazelnuts in a dry frying pan over a moderate heat until they are golden brown (be careful they do not burn).
2 Grate carrots, preferably using a food-processor blade to achieve the best texture and appearance. Toss lightly with green onions, sprouts, sunflower seeds and half the hazelnuts.
3 In blender, combine remaining hazelnuts, orange juice and olive oil. Pour over salad and sprinkle with pepper.

Nutritional information per serving: Protein 3 g; fat 10 g; carbohydrate 10 g; very good dietary fiber 5 g; 135 cals
Other features: Excellent source of vitamin A, very good source of vitamin C and provides useful amounts of potassium. Low sodium (60 mg)

Preparation time: 15 minutes
Cooking time: 5 minutes

Chickpea and Avocado Salad

3 cups cooked chickpeas

1 cup cooked green peas

1 red bell pepper, seeded and diced

1 avocado, peeled, seeded and diced

selection of lettuce leaves

Dressing

1 tablespoon virgin olive oil

2 tablespoons wine vinegar

1 teaspoon Dijon mustard

1 tablespoon chopped fresh tarragon

SERVES 6

1 Combine chickpeas, green peas and pepper.
2 Mix all dressing ingredients together and pour over peas. Let stand for 15 minutes.
3 Add avocado and serve with lettuce leaves.

Nutritional information per serving: Protein 10 g; fat 14 g; carbohydrate 21 g; excellent dietary fiber 8 g; 240 cals
Other features: Excellent source of vitamin C, good source of iron, potassium, thiamin (B1), niacin (B3). Low sodium (15 mg)

Preparation time: 20 minutes
Cooking time: Nil

Roasted Red Pepper Salad

A great salad to make when red bell peppers are cheap, plentiful and full-flavored. Serve it on its own as an appetizer or with broiled fish, steak or chicken.

4 red bell peppers
1 tablespoon pine nuts
2 cups watercress
4 medium tomatoes, very ripe, cut into wedges
1 tablespoon extra virgin olive oil
1 tablespoon balsamic vinegar
1 tablespoon fresh shredded basil

1 To remove skin from peppers, cut in half, remove seeds and place cut side down under a hot broiler until skins blister. Place peppers in a paper bag or wrap in a clean, damp kitchen towel for 10 minutes. Gently rub off skins. Slice peppers into strips.

2 Toast pine nuts in a dry frying pan over a low/moderate heat until golden brown. Set aside.

3 Arrange watercress on each serving dish. Arrange tomatoes on half the watercress and peppers on the other.

4 Combine oil and vinegar and drizzle a little over each plate. Top with basil and pine nuts.

Nutritional information per serving: Protein 4 g; fat 5 g; carbohydrate 7 g; good dietary fiber 3 g; 85 cals

Other features: Excellent source of vitamin C, good source of potassium and vitamin A and provides some iron and niacin (B3). Negligible sodium (60 mg)

Preparation time: 30 minutes
Cooking time: 10 minutes

SERVES 4

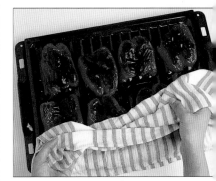

Cover blackened peppers with a clean, damp kitchen towel.

Peel away the skin from each pepper and discard.

Cut peeled pepper into thick strips.

Roasted Red Pepper Salad with watercress, tomato, basil and pine nuts.

Crunchy Mushroom Salad

Crunchy Mushroom Salad.

3 slices whole wheat bread, crusts removed

2 tablespoons extra virgin olive oil

1 clove garlic, crushed

1 tablespoon chopped fresh basil

1 tablespoon chopped fresh parsley

freshly ground black pepper

¼ cup lemon juice

1 teaspoon Dijon mustard

13 oz button mushrooms, sliced

1 red bell pepper, seeded and cut into thin strips

SERVES 6

1 Preheat oven to 400°F. Cut bread into ½ inch cubes and place on baking sheet. Bake for 10 minutes. Reduce oven to 375°F and bake for 5–10 minutes, or until crisp and golden. Allow to cool.

2 Mix together oil, garlic, herbs, pepper, lemon juice and mustard in a bowl.

3 Pour over mushrooms and toss gently. Refrigerate for an hour before serving. When ready to serve, sprinkle bread cubes and pepper strips on top and serve at once.

Nutritional information per serving: Protein 4 g; fat 7 g; carbohydrate 7 g; good dietary fiber 3 g; 100 cals
Other features: Good source of riboflavin (B2) and niacin (B3) and supplies some potassium. Low sodium (75 mg)

Preparation time: 15 minutes
Cooking time: 20 minutes

Spicy Green Beans and Walnuts

1 tablespoon walnut pieces

1 lb green beans,
ends removed

2 teaspoons walnut oil

1 small onion, chopped finely

¼ teaspoon coarsely ground
black pepper

1 teaspoon hot mustard

2 teaspoons paprika

2 tablespoons wine vinegar

SERVES 4

1 Toast walnuts in a dry frying pan over a moderate heat until golden brown. Set aside.
2 Steam beans for 5–6 minutes.
3 While beans are cooking, heat oil and add onion. Cover and allow to cook over a gentle heat for 3–4 minutes. Add pepper, mustard, paprika, vinegar and drained beans. Toss gently and top with walnuts.

Nutritional information per serving: Protein 3 g; fat 4 g; carbohydrate 4 g; good dietary fiber 4 g; 70 cals
Other features: An excellent source of vitamin A and also provides some iron and potassium. Negligible sodium

Preparation time: 5 minutes
Cooking time: 15 minutes

HEALTH TIP

Use the minimum amount of water when cooking vegetables so that less flavor is lost and less salt is needed.

Hot Baby Mushrooms

2 teaspoons olive oil

1 medium onion, sliced

1 clove garlic, crushed

1 teaspoon chopped chili

2 tablespoons lemon juice

½ cup chicken stock

13 oz baby mushrooms

1 tablespoon chopped chives

SERVES 4

1 Heat oil, add onion, garlic and chili, cover and leave to 'sweat' for 3–4 minutes.
2 Add lemon juice, stock and mushrooms. Cover and simmer for 5 minutes. Sprinkle mushrooms with chives. Serve hot or cold.

Nutritional information per serving: Protein 4 g; fat 3 g; carbohydrate 4 g; good dietary fiber 3 g; 55 cals
Other features: A good source of niacin (B3) and riboflavin (B2). Useful amounts of potassium. Low sodium (15 mg)

Preparation time: 5 minutes
Cooking time: 10 minutes

Hot Baby Mushrooms, top, and Spicy Green Beans and Walnuts.

Tomato Pie

3 slices whole wheat bread, made into crumbs

4 or 5 large ripe tomatoes, sliced

1 large onion, sliced

3 medium zucchini, sliced

freshly ground black pepper

¼ cup chopped fresh basil

2 teaspoons butter or margarine

SERVES 4

1 Grease an ovenproof pie dish. Sprinkle with 1 tablespoon of the bread crumbs.
2 Arrange vegetables in layers in dish, sprinkle with pepper.
3 Combine remaining bread crumbs with basil. Sprinkle over vegetables. Dot with butter or margarine and bake at 350°F for 35 minutes. Serve hot.

Nutritional information per serving: Protein 5 g; fat 3 g; carbohydrate 15 g; very good dietary fiber 6 g; 90 cals
Other features: Excellent source of vitamin C; good source of potassium and also provides useful amounts of iron, riboflavin (B2), niacin (B3) and vitamin A. Low sodium (120 mg)

Preparation time: 15 minutes
Cooking time: 35 minutes

Greek-style Zucchini

¾ cup white wine

½ cup tomato juice

1 tablespoon lemon juice

1 tablespoon tomato paste

1 teaspoon coriander seeds

⅓ cup raisins

1 bunch brown shallots

1¼ lb small zucchini

SERVES 4

1 Combine white wine, tomato juice, lemon juice, tomato paste and coriander seeds. Heat gently, cover and simmer 5 minutes.
2 Add raisins, shallots and zucchini, cover and simmer gently for 12 minutes.

Nutritional information per serving: Protein 4 g; no fat; carbohydrate 15 g; very good dietary fiber 5 g; sodium 130 mg; 80 cals
Other features: An excellent source of vitamin C, a good source of vitamin A and potassium and provides useful amounts of iron, riboflavin (B2) and niacin (B3)

Preparation time: 5 minutes
Cooking time: 20 minutes

Greek-style Zucchini, left, and Tomato Pie.

Celeriac With Honey Dressing

The flavor of celeriac resembles celery but the texture is quite different

1 bulb celeriac (about 13 oz)
2 tablespoons lemon juice
1 butterhead lettuce
8 oz cherry tomatoes

Dressing

2 tablespoons orange juice
2 teaspoons honey
1 teaspoon Dijon mustard
½ teaspoon finely grated orange rind
1 tablespoon tarragon vinegar
1 tablespoon olive oil

1 Peel celeriac and cut into fine strips. Toss with lemon juice to prevent it turning brown.
2 Combine all dressing ingredients and pour over celeriac.
3 Line a shallow bowl with lettuce leaves, pile celeriac in the center and decorate with cherry tomatoes.

Nutritional information per serving: Protein 3 g; fat 5 g; carbohydrate 11 g; very good dietary fiber 7 g; 100 cals
Other features: An excellent source of vitamin C, a good source of potassium and provides some riboflavin (B2) and niacin (B3). Low sodium (40 mg)

SERVES 4

Preparation time: 20 minutes
Cooking time: Nil

Thai-style Cabbage

This delightfully fresh dish makes a superb accompaniment to steamed rice and fish or chicken. Use prepared chopped ginger and chili to save time.

1 teaspoon oil
1 clove garlic, crushed
2 teaspoons finely chopped lemon grass
1 teaspoon fresh chopped ginger
½ teaspoon chopped chili
2 tablespoons chicken stock
10 oz shredded cabbage
1 red bell pepper, seeded and sliced
1 cup sliced mushrooms
1 cup snow pea shoots (or use bean sprouts)
1 tablespoon chopped mint

1 Heat oil and gently cook garlic, lemon grass, ginger and chili for 2–3 minutes. Add chicken stock and bring to the boil.
2 Add cabbage, pepper, mushrooms, shoots and mint. Toss gently together for 4–5 minutes until thoroughly heated. Serve at once.

Nutritional information per serving: Protein 3 g; fat 1 g; carbohydrate 4 g; very good dietary fiber 4 g; 35 cals
Other features: An excellent source of vitamin C and provides useful amounts of potassium as well as some iron and B vitamins. Low sodium (15 mg)

SERVES 4

Preparation time: 15 minutes
Cooking time: 10 minutes

Thai-style Cabbage.

115

Barbecued Vegetable Kebabs

These vegetable kebabs combine well with barbecued fish or chicken.

Barbecued Vegetable Kebabs.

8 small Spanish onions, peeled and cut in half

1 red bell pepper, seeded and cut into 16 squares

1 green bell pepper, seeded and cut into 16 squares

16 button mushrooms

2 leeks, cut into 1 inch pieces

4 thin eggplants, cut into 1 inch pieces

8 oz cherry tomatoes

2 tablespoons low-calorie dressing

2 tablespoons chopped fresh herbs (parsley, chives, rosemary or other combinations)

SERVES 4

1 Arrange vegetables on skewers (soaked in water to prevent burning).
2 Combine dressing with herbs and brush it over vegetables. Barbecue for about 10 minutes, turning skewers several times and brushing with remaining dressing.

Nutritional information per serving: Protein 7 g; no fat; carbohydrate 11 g; very good dietary fiber 6 g; sodium 185 mg; 75 cals
Other features: Excellent source of vitamin C, good source of potassium, niacin (B3) and riboflavin (B2) and provides useful amounts of iron and vitamin A

Preparation time: 15 minutes
Cooking time: 10 minutes

Falafel

Serve two or three falafel in pita bread, with chopped tomato and shredded lettuce, topped with one dollop of tahini and one of low-fat yogurt.

1½ cups (9 oz) chickpeas (or 4 cups drained, cooked or canned chickpeas)

6 cups water

1 large onion

1 clove garlic

½ cup tightly-packed parsley sprigs

½ cup tightly-packed cilantro sprigs (or 2 teaspoons ground coriander seed)

1 teaspoon ground cumin

2 tablespoons lemon juice

1 egg

SERVES 6

1 Bring chickpeas and water to the boil, cover tightly, turn off heat and leave to stand for 1 hour (or longer, in refrigerator).
2 Bring chickpeas back to the boil and simmer for about 40 minutes. Drain.
3 In food processor, chop onion. Add all other ingredients and process until well mixed.
4 Form mixture into about 20 small balls. Place on a greased baking sheet and bake in a moderate (350°F) oven for 20 minutes, turning once.

Nutritional information per serving: Protein 8 g; fat 3 g; carbohydrate 19 g; very good dietary fiber 6 g; 130 cals
Other features: Provides iron

Preparation time: 20 minutes
+ 1 hour standing time
Cooking time: 1 hour

Lentil Loaf

2 cups (12 oz) red lentils

4 cups water

1 tablespoon olive oil

1 large onion, finely chopped

1 teaspoon dried thyme

2 tablespoons chopped parsley (or 1 teaspoon parsley flakes)

½ cup rolled oats

1 egg, beaten

freshly ground black pepper

SERVES 4

1 Cook lentils in water, covered, for 25 minutes. Remove lid from saucepan and cook uncovered for about 5 minutes or until mixture is quite dry (take care it does not burn).
2 Heat oil and gently cook onion until golden brown.
3 Combine lentils, onion and remaining ingredients. Mix well.
4 Bake in a greased loaf dish, uncovered, in a moderate oven (350°F) for 45 minutes.

Nutritional information per serving: Protein 21 g; fat 6 g; carbohydrate 47 g; dietary fiber 10 g; 320 cals
Other features: A good source of iron and thiamin (B1); provides niacin (B3) and zinc

Preparation time: 20 minutes
Cooking time: 1 hour 15 minutes

RECIPE TIP

Always cook dried legumes (dried peas or beans) in unsalted water. Salt hinders the uptake of water into the beans and extends the cooking times.

Dhal

1 cup (6 oz) lentils

2 medium potatoes, peeled and sliced roughly

1 cup canned tomatoes, chopped roughly

½ teaspoon turmeric

1 teaspoon ground cumin

2 teaspoons ground coriander

1 clove garlic, crushed

3 cups water

2 teaspoons garam masala

SERVES 4

1 Put all ingredients except garam masala in a saucepan. Bring to the boil; cover and simmer for 20 minutes.
2 Stir in garam masala, cover and leave for 2–3 minutes for flavors to blend.

Nutritional information per serving: Protein 9 g; fat 0 g; carbohydrate 22 g; excellent dietary fiber 4 g; 125 cals
Other features: A good source of vitamin C; provides iron

Preparation time: 15 minutes
Cooking time: 20 minutes

Herbed Beans

½ cup (3½ oz) dried cranberry (borlotti) beans

½ cup (3½ oz) dried kidney beans

½ cup (3½ oz) dried navy beans

5 cups water

½ cup chopped parsley

¼ cup chopped mint

¼ cup chopped cilantro

¾ cup yogurt

freshly ground black pepper

SERVES 4

1 Bring beans and water to the boil. Cover, turn heat off and leave to stand for 1 hour (or soak overnight).
2 Bring beans to the boil and simmer gently, covered, for 40 minutes. Drain.
3 Add remaining ingredients to drained beans and toss well. Serve at once with broiled fish, chicken or lamb chops.

Nutritional information per serving: Protein 17 g; fat 3 g; carbohydrate 36 g; excellent dietary fiber 18 g; 240 cals
Other features: A good source of thiamin (B1) and iron; provides niacin (B3), potassium and zinc

Preparation time: 30 minutes
+ 1 hour standing time
Cooking time: 40 minutes

HEALTH TIP

Dried legumes have about 20 per cent protein – a similar level to that in meat. They are also rich in iron and other minerals and are an excellent source of vitamins.

Hummus

1 cup (6 oz) dry chickpeas (or 3 cups drained, cooked or canned chickpeas)

4 cups water

1 teaspoon cumin seeds

2 bay leaves

⅓ cup lemon juice

½ cup tahini

2 cloves garlic

1 tablespoon sesame seeds

MAKES 1¾ cups

1 Bring chickpeas and water to the boil. Cover tightly; turn off heat and leave to stand for 1 hour (or longer, in refrigerator).
2 Bring chickpeas back to the boil and add cumin seeds and bay leaves. Simmer for about 40 minutes. Remove bay leaves.
3 Purée chickpeas with lemon juice, tahini and garlic, adding enough cooking liquid to make a smooth paste. Tip into dish.
4 Toast sesame seeds in a dry pan. Sprinkle on chickpea mixture.

Nutritional information per serving: Protein 9 g; fat 14 g; carbohydrate 17 g; excellent dietary fiber 7 g; 220 cals
Other features: A good source of thiamin (B1); provides zinc and iron

Preparation time: 15 minutes + 1 hour standing time
Cooking time: 40 minutes

Lentils and Rice

2 slices lean bacon, chopped

1 small onion, chopped finely

1 teaspoon chopped chili

1 teaspoon chopped fresh ginger

1 teaspoon ground cumin

1 tablespoon ground coriander

½ teaspoon cinnamon

1 clove garlic, crushed

1½ cups (9 oz) lentils

1½ cups (8 oz) brown rice

6 cups boiling water

2 tablespoons slivered almonds

SERVES 4

1 Cook bacon, onion, spices and garlic over a low heat together for 3–4 minutes.
2 Add lentils, rice and water, bring to the boil, cover and simmer for 35 minutes. (You may need to add a little more water; it should be dry but not mushy.)
3 Toast almonds in a dry pan until golden brown. Serve on top of lentils and rice.

Nutritional information per serving: Protein 17 g; fat 5 g; carbohydrate 59 g; excellent dietary fiber 8 g; 340 cals
Other features: A good source of thiamin (B1) and niacin (B3); provides iron

Preparation time: 20 minutes
Cooking time: 40 minutes

Black-eyed Peas with Chicken.

Black-eyed Peas with Chicken

1 cup (6½ oz) black-eyed peas

3 cups water

1 tablespoon olive oil

1 lb boneless chicken thighs, sliced

2 medium onions, sliced

13 oz can tomatoes (no added salt), crushed

4 slices French bread

2 tablespoons grainy mustard

SERVES 4

1 Bring peas and water to the boil. Cover and simmer 35 minutes. Drain, saving liquid. Place in greased ovenproof dish.
2 Heat oil and cook chicken and onions until lightly browned. Place on top of peas.
3 Pour tomatoes, their liquid and ½ cup reserved pea liquid over chicken. Cover and bake in a moderate oven for 30 minutes.
4 Spread bread with mustard and place, mustard-side up, on top. Cook, uncovered, for 20 minutes or until bread is crisp and brown.

Nutritional information per serving: Protein 37 g; fat 13 g; carbohydrate 36 g; excellent dietary fiber 13 g; 410 cals
Other features: An excellent source of niacin (B3) and vitamin C; good source of thiamin (B1) and iron; also provides potassium, zinc and riboflavin (B2)

Preparation time: 45 minutes
Cooking time: 1 hour

Spicy Chickpeas

1½ cups (9 oz) chickpeas (or 4 cups drained, cooked or canned chickpeas)

5 cups water

1 tablespoon olive oil

1 medium onion, finely chopped

2 teaspoons ground coriander seed

freshly ground black pepper

8 oz button mushrooms, sliced

¾ cup white wine

1 cup diced tomatoes (fresh or canned)

2 tablespoons chopped fresh cilantro or parsley

1 Bring chickpeas and water to the boil. Cover tightly, turn off heat and leave to stand for 1 hour (or longer, in refrigerator).
2 Bring chickpeas back to the boil and simmer for about 40 minutes. Drain.
3 Heat oil and gently cook onion until golden brown. Add coriander and pepper and stir to combine.
4 Add mushrooms, drained chickpeas, wine and tomatoes, bring to the boil and simmer, uncovered, for 5 minutes.
5 Serve sprinkled with cilantro or parsley.

Nutritional information per serving: Protein 17 g; fat 9 g; carbohydrate 37 g; dietary fiber 13 g; 285 cals
Other features: A good source of iron, thiamin (B1) and niacin (B3); provides riboflavin (B2), potassium, zinc and some calcium

SERVES 4

Preparation time: 20 minutes + 1 hour standing time
Cooking time: 45 minutes

Spicy Chickpeas.

Navy Bean Stew

2 cups (12 oz) navy or small white beans

6 cups water

1 tablespoon olive oil

1 large onion, sliced

1 clove garlic

1 cup sliced celery

1 cup sliced mushrooms

1 cup tomato purée

1 teaspoon finely grated lemon rind

1 teaspoon dark brown sugar

1 teaspoon chopped chili (optional)

SERVES 6

1 Bring beans and water to the boil. Cover; turn heat off and leave to stand for 1 hour.
2 Bring beans to the boil and simmer, covered, for 20–30 minutes.
3 While beans are cooking, heat oil and gently cook onion and garlic until onion is soft. Add remaining ingredients to onion and garlic and stir well.
4 Add onion mixture to beans, cover tightly and simmer for 1 hour, adding a little more water if necessary. Serve sprinkled with finely chopped mint.

Nutritional information per serving: Protein 14 g; fat 4 g; carbohydrate 32 g; dietary fiber 14 g; 220 cals
Other features: A good source of vitamin C and iron; also provides potassium, calcium and some B-complex vitamins

Preparation time: 20 minutes
+ 1 hour standing time
Cooking time: 1 hour 30 minutes

Black-eyed Peas with Rice and Shrimp

1 cup (6½ oz) black-eyed peas
3 cups water
1 tablespoon olive oil
1 medium onion, sliced
1 bell pepper, seeded and sliced
1 lb tomatoes, diced
1 lb raw shrimp, shelled and deveined
freshly ground black pepper
1 tablespoon chopped fresh thyme (or 1 teaspoon dried thyme)
2 cups hot cooked rice
¾ cup dry white wine

1 Bring peas and water to the boil. Cover and simmer for 35 minutes. Drain and reserve liquid.
2 While peas are cooking, heat oil and gently cook onion for 3–4 minutes. Add bell pepper and tomatoes and cook, stirring occasionally, for 8–10 minutes.
3 Add shrimp, pepper and thyme and cook for 2 minutes.
4 Add rice, drained peas and wine. Bring to the boil, stirring gently and adding a little of the reserved pea liquid if necessary. Serve when thoroughly hot.

Nutritional information per serving: Protein 24 g; fat 5 g; carbohydrate 32 g; dietary fiber 10 g; 270 cals
Other features: An excellent source of vitamin C; good source of niacin (B3); provides iron and calcium

SERVES 6

Preparation time: 45 minutes
Cooking time: 35 minutes

Mouth-watering Beans

Serve Mouth-watering Beans with tortillas or steamed rice and a green vegetable.

2 cups (12 oz) kidney beans
5 cups water
5 oz turkey ham, diced
1 large onion, chopped finely
8 oz sliced Portobello mushrooms
1 celery stalk, sliced
4 large tomatoes, diced
2 tablespoons tomato paste
1 cup red wine
freshly ground pepper

1 Place beans and water in saucepan, bring to the boil, cover, turn heat off and leave to stand for 1 hour. Drain.
2 Add all other ingredients to beans. Turn into a casserole, cover and cook in a moderate oven for 1½ hours. (If using canned beans, omit step 1 and cook for 30 minutes.)

Nutritional information per serving: Protein 24 g; fat 2 g; carbohydrate 34 g; dietary fiber 19 g; 245 cals
Other features: An excellent source of vitamin C; good source of niacin (B3), thiamin (B1) and iron; provides riboflavin (B2), potassium and zinc

SERVES 4

Preparation time: 30 minutes
+ 1 hour standing time
Cooking time: 1½ hours

Buckwheat Bengali

Buckwheat Bengali can also be served hot with roast lamb or chicken.

- 1 tablespoon olive oil
- 1 medium onion, sliced
- 1 clove garlic, crushed
- 1 cup buckwheat groats
- 1 tablespoon ground coriander
- 2 teaspoons ground cumin
- ½ teaspoon chili powder
- 1 cup orange juice
- 1 cup chicken stock (or water)
- ½ cup raisins
- ¼ cup slivered almonds, toasted
- 2 tablespoons chopped fresh cilantro

1 Heat oil and gently cook onion and garlic together until soft and lightly brown. Add buckwheat groats and spices and stir for 3–4 minutes.
2 Add juice, stock and raisins. Bring to the boil, cover and simmer for 15–20 minutes.
3 Top with slivered almonds and chopped fresh cilantro.

Nutritional information per serving: Protein 4 g; fat 6 g; carbohydrate 34 g; dietary fiber 2 g; 200 cals
Other features: A good source of vitamin C

SERVES 6

Preparation time: 30 minutes
Cooking time: 20 minutes

HEALTH TIP

Moderate exercise throughout life is best. Studies have shown that exercising beyond a weekly level of 3,500 cals may do more harm than good. Most people will expend about 3,500 cals in a daily exercise period of an hour of strenuous activity.

Tabbouleh

Crushed garlic and a quarter cup of toasted pine nuts may be added for extra flavor.

- 1 cup bulgur (cracked wheat)
- 1¼ cups boiling water
- 2 cups chopped parsley
- ½ cup chopped mint
- ½ cup sliced shallots
- 2 tablespoons olive oil
- 2 tablespoons lemon juice
- freshly ground black pepper
- 1 lb tomatoes, diced

1 Place bulgur in a bowl. Pour boiling water over; cover tightly and leave to cool (water will be absorbed and wheat will be quite dry).
2 Add parsley, mint and shallots to wheat and use a fork to mix.
3 Combine oil, lemon juice and pepper and pour over wheat. Add tomatoes and mix gently with fork.

Nutritional information per serving: Protein 4 g; fat 7 g; carbohydrate 24 g; dietary fiber 5 g; 170 cals
Other features: An excellent source of vitamin C; provides carotene (vitamin A), niacin (B3) and iron

HEALTH TIP

Exercise increases HDL cholesterol – the 'good' kind.

Tabbouleh.

SERVES 6

Preparation time: 35 minutes
Cooking time: Nil

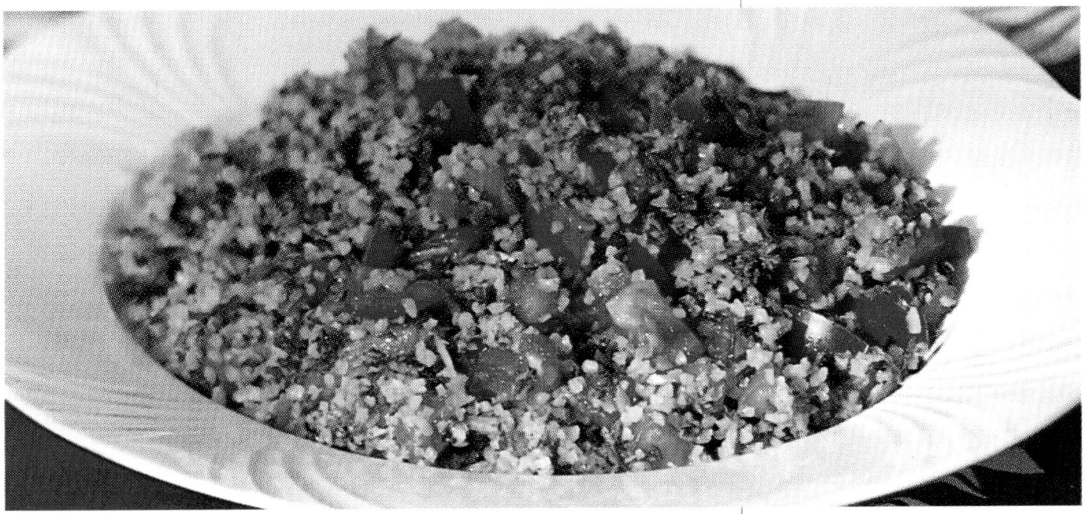

DESSERTS & CAKES

HERE LIES THE DOWNFALL OF MANY A HEALTHY EATER!
But don't despair if you love cakes and desserts. You
don't have to live your life without them. There are
many recipes which fall into the category of healthy
as well as delectable, that use only a fraction of the
fat, sugar and calories needed in traditional recipes.
Indulge family and friends (and yourself, of course)
with Ricotta Cheesecake or Raspberry Ice-cream.
Lovers of comfort food, please note – there's plenty
for you, too. Try Steamed Peach Pudding with Orange
Sauce or home-style Fruit Crisp and discover that
sweet treats can do you a power of good!

Lemon Heart with Berries

This is a light dessert which can be served at any time of the year. Vary the type of berries according to the seasons and your taste.

2 teaspoons gelatin

1 tablespoon water

1 tablespoon lemon juice

8 oz low-fat ricotta cheese

1 cup low-fat yogurt

1 egg white

2 tablespoons sugar, or use artificial sweetener

Fruit Topping

8 oz strawberries

8 oz raspberries

1 tablespoon rum (optional)

1 Soften gelatin in water. Add lemon juice and heat gently until gelatin dissolves.
2 Beat together ricotta, yogurt and gelatin mixture.
3 Beat egg white until stiff, adding sugar or sweetener. Gently fold into ricotta mixture. Rinse a heart-shaped pan with cold water. Pour ricotta mixture into pan and refrigerate for 2–3 hours.
4 Hull strawberries and slice. Mix with raspberries and rum and allow to stand, covered, for at least 30 minutes.
5 Turn heart out of pan and top with the strawberries and raspberries.

Nutritional information per serving: Protein 9 g; fat 3 g; carbohydrate 10 g (or 16 g if sugar is used); some dietary fiber 2 g; 110 cals or 135 cals if sugar is used
Other features: A good source of vitamin C and calcium. Useful amounts of potassium. Low sodium (120 mg)

SERVES 6

Preparation time: 20 minutes
+ 3 hours setting time
Cooking time: Nil

Ricotta Cheesecake

This cake is half way between a moist cake and a baked cheesecake in texture. It is delicious served with puréed raspberries or puréed apricots (fresh or canned).

2 egg whites

2 tablespoons sugar

1 lb low-fat ricotta cheese

1 tablespoon honey

2 tablespoons all-purpose flour

1 teaspoon finely grated lime or lemon rind

1 tablespoon lime or lemon juice

½ cup low-fat yogurt

2 egg yolks

½ teaspoon angostura bitters

1 Beat egg whites until peaks form. Add sugar and continue beating until stiff. Gently tip egg whites onto a plate.
2 Using the same bowl (no need to wash), combine remaining ingredients and beat until smooth.
3 Fold in egg white mixture. Place in a paper-lined 8 inch cake pan and bake at 350°F for 40 minutes.

Nutritional information per serving: Protein 9 g; fat 6 g; carbohydrate 11 g; no dietary fiber; sodium 145 mg; 130 cals
Other features: A good source of calcium

Previous page: Lemon Heart with Berries, bottom, and Ricotta Cheesecake.

SERVES 8

Preparation time: 15 minutes
Cooking time: 40 minutes

Grecian Oranges

4 oranges

1 cup water

½ cup sugar, or use powdered artificial sweetener

2 tablespoons brandy

1 Using a potato peeler or a very sharp knife, cut the peel thinly from two of the oranges. Slice into fine strips.
2 Cover orange-peel strips with water. Bring to the boil and simmer gently for 10 minutes. Drain and rinse well.
3 Combine water and sugar, if used, and bring to the boil. Add peel and simmer for about 5 minutes or until peel looks clear. Using a slotted spoon, remove peel from syrup and reserve. Sprinkle with sweetener, if used.
4 Peel and remove pith from remaining oranges. Add oranges to syrup and simmer for 2 minutes. Add brandy (and extra sweetener to taste). Cool, then chill well. Serve each orange in a glass dish and top with orange shreds.

Nutritional information per serving: Protein 2 g; no fat; carbohydrate 43 g (or 18 g if artificial sweetener used); good dietary fiber 4 g; 190 cals or 90 cals if sweetener is used
Other features: An excellent source of vitamin C. Also provides some vitamin A and potassium. Negligible sodium

Preparation time: 20 minutes + chilling time
Cooking time: 15–20 minutes

SERVES 4

Banana Whip

6 bananas

1 Peel bananas and place on a tray lined with plastic wrap. Freeze for several hours.
2 Break frozen bananas into chunks and place in a food processor. Process until thick, creamy and fluffy (this may take 5 minutes). Either serve immediately, or return to freezer. Keeps for about two days but is best eaten on the day it is made.

Nutritional information per serving: Protein 2 g; no fat; carbohydrate 23 g; good dietary fiber 3 g; 100 cals
Other features: Good source of vitamin C

Preparation time: 10 minutes + freezing time
Cooking time: Nil

SERVES 6–8

Coffee Cream Pots

1 lb low-fat ricotta cheese

2 tablespoons strong coffee

¼ cup sugar or use powdered artificial sweetener

pinch cinnamon

1 tablespoon brandy

1 tablespoon finely shredded orange rind

¼ cup water

1 Using an electric mixer, combine all ingredients except orange rind and water. Whip until very smooth. Place in six small individual dishes and refrigerate for at least an hour.
2 Place orange rind in a small saucepan with ¼ cup water. Boil for 2 minutes. Drain. Use to decorate the dessert.

Nutritional information per serving: Protein 10 g; fat 6 g; carbohydrate 11 g (or 2 g if using sweetener); no dietary fiber; sodium 165 mg; 155 cals or 120 cals if sweetener is used
Other features: A good source of calcium

Preparation time: 10 minutes
+ at least 1 hour refrigeration
Cooking time: 5 minutes

SERVES 6

Almond Bread

4 egg whites

½ cup sugar

1 cup all-purpose flour

1 cup almonds

½ teaspoon vanilla extract

1 Beat egg whites until stiff. Fold in sugar and continue beating until shiny.

2 Gently fold in the flour, almonds and vanilla. Spoon mixture into a well-greased loaf pan. (If pan is not a non-stick variety, line with wax paper.) Bake at 350°F for 25–30 minutes until pale brown.

3 Tip loaf out. Allow to cool completely. Store in an airtight container for at least 12 hours.

4 Using a very sharp knife, cut loaf into very thin slices. Place on ungreased baking sheets and bake at 300°F for about 10 minutes or until lightly browned (be careful not to burn).

Nutritional information per slice: Protein 1 g; fat 2 g; carbohydrate 5 g; small amount of dietary fiber 1 g; 42 cals
Other features: Negligible sodium (6 mg)

MAKES 40 slices

Preparation time: 20 minutes
Cooking time: 40 minutes

Champagne Mangoes

4 medium mangoes

1 tablespoon Cointreau or Grand Marnier

1 cup Champagne

sprigs mint

1 Peel mangoes and cut into slices.

2 Combine Cointreau and Champagne. Pour over mango slices and leave for 10 minutes. Decorate each serve with a sprig of mint and serve with Almond Bread.

Nutritional information per serving: Protein 1 g; no fat; carbohydrate 17 g; some dietary fiber 2 g; 125 cals
Other features: An excellent source of vitamins C and A and a useful source of potassium. Sodium negligible

SERVES 4

Preparation time: 15 minutes
Cooking time: Nil

Raspberry Ice-cream

2 cups skim milk

½ cup evaporated skim milk

1 cup non-fat dry milk

1 tablespoon cornstarch

1 teaspoon vanilla extract

⅓ cup sugar or use powdered artificial sweetener

8 oz raspberries (or strawberries)

1 In blender or food processor, combine all ingredients except raspberries.

2 Place in saucepan and heat gently, stirring continuously until mixture boils and thickens. Cool slightly.

3 Add raspberries and freeze in an ice-cream churn, following the manufacturer's directions. Or freeze until edges are solid, beat in an electric mixer and re-freeze until mixture is solid.

Nutritional information per serving: Protein 13 g; no fat; carbohydrate 33 g (or 21 g if sweetener used); good dietary fiber 3 g; sodium 200 mg; 185 cals or 140 cals if sweetener used
Other features: A very good source of riboflavin (B2) and a good source of potassium. Rich in calcium

SERVES 6

Preparation time: 15 minutes + 1–4 hours freezing, depending on equipment
Cooking time: 5 minutes

Opposite: Champagne Mangoes, top, Raspberry Ice-cream and Almond Bread.

Lemon Mousse with Strawberry Sauce

1 tablespoon gelatin

2 tablespoons lemon juice

¼ cup boiling water

1 tablespoon honey

1 lb low-fat yogurt

1½ cups evaporated skim milk

1 teaspoon very finely grated lemon rind

Strawberry sauce

8 oz strawberries

1 tablespoon rum

2 tablespoons low-sugar strawberry preserve

SERVES 6

1 Soften gelatin in lemon juice. Dissolve in boiling water. Add honey.

2 Combine yogurt, milk and rind. Add gelatin mixture and stir thoroughly. Pour into a mold which has been lightly oiled and leave to set for 2 hours.

3 To make sauce, place all ingredients in a blender and process until smooth. If preferred, sieve to remove 'seeds'.

Nutritional information per serving: Protein 13 g; no fat; carbohydrate 21 g; sodium 175 mg; 145 cals

Other features: An excellent source of riboflavin (B2), a good source of potassium, niacin (B3) and vitamin C. Rich in calcium

Preparation time: 20 minutes
+ 2 hours setting time
Cooking time: Nil

Fresh Fruit with Fruit Salad Dip

This refreshing dip can also be served as a sauce with low-fat ice-cream.

selection of seasonal fruits

Dip

¼ cantaloupe melon

1 mango

4 apricots

1 kiwi fruit, peeled

½ cup orange juice

3 passion fruit

SERVES 4

1 Arrange fresh fruit on a serving plate.

2 Peel and seed cantaloupe, mango and apricots and place fruit flesh in blender with kiwi fruit and juice. Process until smooth. Stir in passion fruit pulp. Serve with prepared fruit.

Nutritional information per serving (dip): Protein 2 g; no fat; carbohydrate 14 g; very good dietary fiber 5 g; 65 cals

Other features: An excellent source of vitamin C, very good source of vitamin A and provides useful amounts of potassium. Sodium negligible (10 mg)

Preparation time: 10 minutes
Cooking time: Nil

Strawberry Shortcake

3 tablespoons sliced almonds

½ cup whole wheat flour

½ cup self-rising flour

⅓ cup cornstarch

½ cup dark brown sugar

1 egg, beaten

1 teaspoon finely grated lemon rind

1 cup low-fat yogurt

8 oz strawberries

1 tablespoon brandy

SERVES 8

1 Grease an 8 inch non-stick cake pan and sprinkle the almonds over the base.

2 Combine all ingredients except strawberries and brandy. Spoon mixture over almonds. Bake at 375°F for 25 minutes.

3 While shortcake is cooking, slice strawberries and sprinkle with brandy. Serve with wedges of the cake turned upside down.

Nutritional information per serving: Protein 5 g; fat 3 g; carbohydrate 23 g; good dietary fiber 3 g; sodium 170 mg; 150 cals

Other features: Provides some potassium

Preparation time: 15 minutes
Cooking time: 25 minutes

Coconut and Almond Kulfi

2 cups skim milk

1 cup non-fat dry milk

½ cup evaporated skim milk

1 tablespoon custard powder

⅓ cup shredded coconut

⅓ cup sugar (or use equivalent in powdered sweetener)

⅓ cup almonds, chopped roughly

2 teaspoons finely grated orange rind

1 teaspoon vanilla extract

SERVES 6

1 In a saucepan, combine milks, custard powder and coconut. Stir continuously over a low heat until mixture boils and thickens.

2 Add sugar (or sweetener), almonds, rind and vanilla. Place mixture into an ice-cream maker or churn and follow manufacturer's directions. Alternatively, freeze in a shallow dish until completely frozen, beat and re-freeze. Serve in small portions with sliced mango or other fresh fruit.

Nutritional information per serving: Protein 14 g; fat 6 g; carbohydrate 32 g (or 20 g if sweetener used); some dietary fiber 2 g; sodium 195 mg; 225 cals or 190 cals if sweetener is used
Other features: An excellent source of riboflavin (B2) and a good source of potassium. Rich in calcium

Preparation time: 15 minutes + 1–3 hours freezing time, depending on equipment
Cooking time: 5 minutes

Coconut and Almond Kulfi, left, and Strawberry Shortcake.

Steamed Peach Pudding and Orange Sauce 🍲

A steamed pudding with minimum fat but a surprisingly good flavor and texture.

1 teaspoon butter or margarine

4 slices smooth whole wheat bread, without crusts

½ cup chopped dried peaches

1 cup skim milk

1 tablespoon honey

2 eggs

1 teaspoon finely grated orange rind

½ teaspoon vanilla extract

Sauce

1 cup orange juice

1 tablespoon cornstarch

1 tablespoon orange juice, extra

1 tablespoon brandy

SERVES 4

1 Butter a small pudding basin.
2 Cut each slice of bread into cubes (do not cut through all slices at once, or bread will be doughy). Combine with peaches.
3 Beat together milk, honey, eggs, rind and vanilla. Pour over bread and leave for 20 minutes.
4 Pour pudding mixture into greased basin, cover with buttered foil and secure with string. Place in a saucepan with enough water to come half way up sides of pudding basin. Steam pudding for 1 hour. Turn out and serve with sauce.
5 To make the sauce, heat juice until almost boiling.
6 Blend cornstarch with extra juice and brandy. Stir into hot juice and cook for 1–2 minutes.

Nutritional information per serving (with sauce): Protein 8 g; fat 4 g; carbohydrate 33 g; good dietary fiber 4 g; sodium 190 mg; potassium 420 mg; 205 cals

Other features: Good source of vitamin C; a good source of riboflavin (B2) and of iron. Provides useful amounts of calcium and potassium.

Preparation time: 10 minutes
+ 30 minutes standing
Cooking time: 1 hour

Pour pudding mixture over bread cubes and peaches.

Place the pudding mixture into a greased pudding basin.

Place a layer of greased foil over basin and tie securely with string.

Stir blended cornstarch, extra juice and brandy into hot juice.

Steamed Peach Pudding and Orange Sauce.

Fruit Rounds

1 cup dates

1 cup golden raisins

1 cup raisins

½ cup currants

¾ cup (3½ oz) chopped nuts

¼ cup sunflower seeds

½ cup shredded coconut

2 tablespoons lemon juice

1 tablespoon extra coconut, toasted in dry pan until brown

1 Grind fruits and nuts together in food processor. Add remaining ingredients and mix well.
2 Using wet hands, shape mixture into two logs. Roll them in extra coconut. Wrap in plastic wrap and refrigerate for several hours before cutting into slices to serve.

Nutritional information per round: Protein 1 g; fat 1 g; carbohydrate 7 g; small amounts of dietary fiber 1 g; 40 cals
Other features: Negligible sodium

Preparation time: 20 minutes
+ refrigeration time
Cooking time: Nil

MAKES about 48 rounds

Apricot Squares

1 cup chopped dried apricots

¾ cup golden raisins

½ cup chopped prunes, pitted

½ cup orange juice

1 cup non-fat dry milk

½ cup fresh whole wheat bread crumbs

½ cup chopped almonds

¼ cup shredded coconut

1 Combine apricots, golden raisins, prunes and orange juice. Bring to the boil, cover and leave to stand for 15 minutes.
2 Add dry milk, bread crumbs and almonds and mix thoroughly.
3 Sprinkle half the coconut over the base of a non-stick shallow pan about 10 x 7 inch. Press mixture into pan and sprinkle with remaining coconut, pressing it in well. Cover and leave in refrigerator for several hours. Cut into small squares to serve.

Nutritional information per square: Protein 2 g; fat 1 g; carbohydrate 5 g; small amounts of dietary fiber 1 g; 35 cals
Other features: Low sodium (20 mg)

Preparation time: 25 minutes + refrigeration
Cooking time: Nil

MAKES about 48

Fruit Crisp

1¾ oz butter or margarine

½ cup brown sugar

1 teaspoon cinnamon

1 cup rolled oats

½ cup unprocessed oat bran

1 tablespoon sunflower seeds

1 tablespoon sesame seeds

13 oz canned apples or peaches, in pear juice, drained and chopped

1 In a food processor, combine all ingredients except fruit.
2 Place fruit in a casserole and pour crumble mixture on top. Press down with your fingers or the back of a spoon. Bake at 350°F for 20 minutes.

Nutritional information per serving: Protein 5 g; fat 14 g; carbohydrate 38 g; good dietary fiber 4 g; 295 cals
Other features: Useful source of iron. Low in sodium (16 mg)

Fruit Crisp.

Preparation time: 10 minutes
Cooking time: 20 minutes

SERVES 4

Strawberry Soufflé

8 oz strawberries, washed and hulled

3 egg whites

¼ cup sugar

1 Purée strawberries.
2 Beat egg whites until stiff; add sugar gradually and continue beating until sugar is dissolved.
3 Gently fold in strawberry purée. Pour into four individual greased 1-cup capacity soufflé dishes and bake at 350°F for 20 minutes. Serve at once.

Nutritional information per serving: Protein 5 g; fat 0 g; carbohydrate 39 g; dietary fiber 3 g; 180 cals
Other features: An excellent source of vitamin C

SERVES 4

Preparation time: 30 minutes
Cooking time: 20 minutes

Fresh Blueberry Gelatin Dessert

Replace the port with two teaspoons of honey and a tablespoon of apple juice if you like.

8 oz blueberries

2 tablespoons sugar

2⅓ cups water

3 teaspoons gelatin

2 tablespoons apple juice

2 tablespoons port

1 Put blueberries, sugar and ⅓ cup water into a saucepan and cook over a gentle heat for about 5 minutes.
2 Dissolve gelatin in the apple juice.
3 Stir gelatin into blueberry mixture. Add remaining water and port and pour into a jelly mold or into individual glasses. Place in refrigerator for at least 4 hours to set. Serve with yogurt.

Nutritional information per serving: Protein 2 g; fat 0 g; carbohydrate 19 g; dietary fiber 2 g; 95 cals
Other features: A good source of vitamin C

SERVES 4

Preparation time: 20 minutes
+ 4 hours setting time
Cooking time: 5 minutes

Passion Fruit Lime Mousse.

Passion Fruit Lime Mousse

2 teaspoons gelatin

½ cup boiling water

8–10 passion fruit

2 tablespoons lime or lemon juice

3 egg whites

½ cup sugar

1 Dissolve the gelatin in water. Stir in the passion fruit flesh and lime juice.
2 Beat egg whites until stiff and fold in sugar. Combine with passion fruit mixture and pour into a soufflé dish (or individual soufflé dishes). Chill for 2–4 hours until set.

Nutritional information per serving: Protein 3 g; fat 0 g; carbohydrate 23 g; excellent dietary fiber 6 g; 110 cals
Other features: A good source of vitamin C

SERVES 6

Preparation time: 30 minutes
+ 4 hours setting time
Cooking time: Nil

Winter Fruit Salad

Three peeled and chopped kiwi fruit can be added to the fruit salad just before serving.

4 bananas, peeled and
cut into chunks

2 oranges, peeled and diced

2 apples, peeled,
cored and diced

1 pear, peeled, cored and
cut into 8 pieces

1 teaspoon finely grated
orange rind

¼ cup orange juice

1 tablespoon brandy

1 Combine all ingredients in an ovenproof dish.
2 Bake in a moderate oven (350°F) for 10 minutes. Serve hot.

Nutritional information per serving: Protein 2 g; fat 0 g; carbohydrate 28 g; excellent dietary fiber 5 g; 120 cals
Other features: An excellent source of vitamin C

SERVES 4

Preparation time: 20 minutes
Cooking time: 10 minutes

Apricot Yogurt

You can flavor apricots with a cinnamon stick if you like. Remove before you purée.

1 cup dried apricots

1 cup orange juice

½ cup white wine (or use
extra orange juice)

1 lb non-fat yogurt

1 Soak apricots in orange juice and wine for at least an hour. Bring to the boil, cover and simmer for 20–25 minutes. Purée and chill.
2 Swirl apricot mixture and yogurt together.

Nutritional information per serving: Protein 8 g; fat 1 g; carbohydrate 30 g; excellent dietary fiber 9 g; 160 cals
Other features: An excellent source of vitamin C; provides calcium, iron and potassium

Preparation time: 15 minutes + 1 hour standing time
Cooking time: 25 minutes

SERVES 4

Healthy Peach Crisp

You can also use fresh peaches, plums or nectarines, peeled and blanched, in this recipe.

2 x 13 oz cans peaches in
pear juice, drained, chopped

1 teaspoon cinnamon

1 cup rolled oats

½ cup barley flakes (or use
extra oats)

½ cup processed oat bran

¼ cup shredded coconut

¼ cup dark brown sugar

2 tablespoons softened butter

¼ cup toasted pecan nuts
or walnuts

1 Place peaches in an ovenproof dish.
2 Combine remaining ingredients except nuts. Sprinkle over peaches. Top with nuts and bake in a moderate oven (350°F) for 25 minutes.

Nutritional information per serving: Protein 7 g; fat 13 g; carbohydrate 49 g; excellent dietary fiber 6 g; 350 cals
Other features: Provides some vitamin A and iron

Preparation time: 20 minutes
Cooking time: 25 minutes

SERVES 4

HEALTH TIP

There's little wonder the Scots head the heart disease death statistics. As well as having a high rate of smoking, 20 per cent of men and 10 per cent of women eat no fresh fruit – and 12 per cent of men and 7 per cent of women eat no green vegetables.

Summer Berry Pudding

- about 8 slices of white or smooth whole wheat bread, crusts removed
- 3 tablespoons apple juice
- 2 tablespoons sugar
- 3 cups mixed berries (strawberries, blueberries, mulberries, blackberries)

1 Line the base and side of a 4-cup capacity pudding basin with bread, cutting the bread to fit. Do not leave gaps.
2 Heat apple juice and sugar and stir for a minute or two until sugar dissolves. Add berries and squash slightly until some juice comes from a few berries.
3 Pour berries into bread-lined basin, reserving a tablespoon or two of the juice. Top with more crustless bread and pour reserved juice over bread. Cover with plastic wrap or foil and place a heavy can or other weight on top. Leave in refrigerator for at least 12 hours. Unmold to serve.

Nutritional information per serving: Protein 3 g; fat 1 g; carbohydrate 23 g; dietary fiber 3 g; 115 cals
Other features: A good source of vitamin C

SERVES 6

Preparation time: 40 minutes + overnight standing time
Cooking time: Nil

Baked Stuffed Apples

- 4 green apples, cored
- 12 prunes, pits removed
- ¼ teaspoon cinnamon
- 1 tablespoon slivered almonds
- 1 cup apple juice

1 Using a sharp knife, make a tiny slit around the center of each apple so that skin will not burst.
2 Combine prunes, cinnamon and almonds and use to stuff centers of apples. Place apples in a shallow ovenproof dish just large enough to hold them. Pour apple juice over apples. Bake in a moderate oven (350°F) for 25 minutes. Serve hot.

Nutritional information per serving: Protein 1 g; fat 1 g; carbohydrate 32 g; excellent dietary fiber 7 g; 140 cals
Other features: Provides vitamin C

SERVES 4

Preparation time: 15 minutes
Cooking time: 25 minutes

HEALTH TIP

A nip (1 fl oz) spirits, 2 fl oz fortified wine (such as sherry), 4 fl oz wine or an 8 fl oz glass of beer all pack the same alcoholic punch.

Apricot Pancakes

- 1 tablespoon slivered almonds
- ½ cup self-rising flour
- ½ cup apricot yogurt
- 1 egg
- 1 tablespoon lemon juice
- 1 can apricot halves (no added sugar)
- extra ½ cup apricot yogurt

1 Toast almonds in a dry frying pan over a moderate heat, shaking frequently until golden brown. Set aside.
2 Blend together flour, yogurt, egg and lemon juice.
3 Using a non-stick frying pan, pour about one-quarter of pancake mixture into pan and cook until brown on both sides. Repeat with remaining mixture, keeping pancakes warm.
4 Reserve four apricot halves. Purée remaining apricot halves and any liquid with the extra yogurt to make a sauce.
5 To serve, pour a little sauce over each pancake and top with apricot half. Sprinkle with almonds.

Nutritional information per serving: Protein 8 g; fat 5 g; carbohydrate 21 g; dietary fiber 3 g; 165 cals
Other features: Provides some carotene (vitamin A)

SERVES 4

Preparation time: 40 minutes
Cooking time: 6 minutes each pancake

Opposite, clockwise from front: Summer Berry Pudding, Baked Stuffed Apples and Apricot Pancakes.

BREADS, SHAKES & SAUCES

THERE ARE ALL SORTS OF RECIPES THAT MAKE healthy eating a pleasure – and that make excellent substitutes for the sugary, less-nutritious foods that we often crave during a 'snack attack'. Delicious fruit loaves and muffins – such as Banana Bread or Whole Wheat Date Scones – are ideal for filling up hungry teenagers after school. And if breakfast times are so rushed they tend to be overlooked, try whipping up a creamy-tasting low-fat drink for your morning meal. These health shakes are also ideal between meals for active, growing children – but Banana Smoothie or Peach Cooler will prove irresistible to adults as well.

Carrot Muffins

1 cup whole wheat flour

1 cup self-rising flour

1 teaspoon baking powder

2 teaspoons cinnamon

1 cup quick-cooking oats

⅓ cup honey

2 eggs

1 cup low-fat evaporated milk

1 tablespoon lemon juice

1 cup grated carrot

1 large apple, peeled, cored and grated

1 Sift flours, baking powder and cinnamon, stirring. Add oats.
2 In blender, combine honey, eggs, milk, lemon juice, carrot and apple. Pour over dry ingredients and mix lightly.
3 Fill greased non-stick muffin pans two-thirds full with mixture and bake in a moderately hot (400°F) oven for 20–25 minutes. Serve warm.

Nutritional information per muffin: Protein 5 g; fat 1 g; carbohydrate 20 g; dietary fiber 2 g; 110 cals
Other features: Provides some carotene (vitamin A)

MAKES 18 muffins

Preparation time: 20 minutes
Cooking time: 25 minutes

Date and Apple Loaf

1 cup dates, pitted

¼ cup honey

1 teaspoon baking soda

1 cup apple juice

1 cup grated apple

½ cup pecans or walnuts

¾ cup whole wheat flour

¾ cup self-rising flour

1 In a saucepan place dates, honey, baking soda and apple juice. Bring to the boil, simmer 2 minutes, cover and leave to cool.
2 Stir in remaining ingredients and spoon into a greased non-stick 5½ x 8½ inch loaf pan. Bake in a moderate (350°F) oven for 40 minutes. Turn out and cool.

Nutritional information per slice: Protein 2 g; fat 2 g; carbohydrate 16 g; dietary fiber 2 g; 90 cals

MAKES 1 loaf
(about 18 slices)

Preparation time: 20 minutes
Cooking time: 40 minutes

RECIPE TIP

When using banana, avocado or apple slices on sandwiches, brush with a little lemon juice to prevent browning.

Banana Bread

2 oz butter or margarine

¼ cup brown sugar

2 eggs

1 cup mashed banana

1 teaspoon vanilla extract

½ cup low-fat milk

½ cup whole wheat flour

1½ cups self-rising flour

1 teaspoon baking soda

⅓ cup chopped walnuts

1 Cream butter or margarine and sugar until well mixed. Add eggs, banana, vanilla and milk.
2 Sift together flours and baking soda. Add to banana mixture and mix lightly. Add nuts.
3 Spoon mixture into a paper-lined non-stick 5½ x 8½ inch loaf pan and bake in a moderate (350°F) oven for 50 minutes or until a wooden skewer inserted into loaf comes out clean. Turn out and cool before serving.

Nutritional information per slice: Protein 3 g; fat 4 g; carbohydrate 13 g; dietary fiber 1 g; 100 cals

Previous page, from top: Banana Bread, Date and Apple Loaf, and Carrot Muffins.

MAKES 1 loaf
(about 20 slices)

Preparation time: 30 minutes
Cooking time: 50 minutes

Seeded Apricot Loaf

1 cup processed bran cereal

½ cup wheat germ

1½ cups skim milk

½ cup dried apricots, chopped

½ cup golden raisins

1 teaspoon vanilla extract

2 tablespoons brown sugar

¼ cup sunflower seeds

¼ cup poppy seeds

½ cup whole wheat flour

½ cup self-rising flour

MAKES 1 loaf
(about 18 slices)

1 Place all ingredients except 1 tablespoon of the poppy seeds and the flours in a bowl and leave for 30 minutes.
2 Add sifted flours and mix well. Pour into a greased non-stick 5½ x 8½ inch loaf pan. Top with remaining poppy seeds and bake in a moderate (350°F) oven for 45 minutes. Turn out and cool.

Nutritional information per slice: Protein 4 g; fat 2 g; carbohydrate 14 g; dietary fiber 4 g; 90 cals

Preparation time: 20 minutes
+ 30 minutes standing time
Cooking time: 45 minutes

Fruit and Nut Loaf

1 cup oat bran

1 cup raisins

¾ cup currants

½ cup dried peaches, chopped

2½ cups skim milk

1 cup whole wheat flour

½ cup all-purpose flour

3 teaspoons baking powder

½ cup walnut pieces

MAKES 1 loaf
(about 18 slices)

1 Combine bran, fruits and milk. Cover and leave to stand for 1 hour.
2 Add sifted dry ingredients and nuts to bran mixture. Mix well and spoon into a non-stick 5½ x 8½ inch loaf pan. Bake in a moderate (350°F) oven for 1 hour or until a skewer comes out clean. Turn out and leave until thoroughly cold before slicing.

Nutritional information per slice: Protein 4 g; fat 2 g; carbohydrate 21 g; dietary fiber 3 g; 120 cals

Preparation time: 30 minutes
+ 1 hour standing time
Cooking time: 1 hour

Whole Wheat Date Scones

2 teaspoons lemon juice

¾ cup low-fat milk

1 cup whole wheat flour

1 cup self-rising flour

1 teaspoon baking powder

1 tablespoon softened butter or margarine

½ cup chopped dates

MAKES 12 scones

1 Add lemon juice to milk and set aside for 5 minutes until milk thickens.
2 Sift flour and baking powder. Rub in butter.
3 Add dates and milk and mix quickly to a soft dough. Turn out onto a floured surface, knead lightly and pat to 1 inch thickness. Using a sharp cutter, cut into 12 scones.
4 Place scones on a non-stick baking sheet, leaving about ½ inch between them. Brush tops with a little milk (so they will brown) and bake in a hot (425°F) oven for 10–12 minutes. Cool on a rack, for scones with crisp edges, or wrap in a clean kitchen towel to make soft-edged scones.

Nutritional information per scone: Protein 4 g; fat 2 g; carbohydrate 19 g; dietary fiber 3 g; 115 cals

Preparation time: 30 minutes
Cooking time: 12 minutes

Pumpernickel

2 cups rye flour

1 cup whole wheat flour

1 cup cracked rye

1 cup cracked wheat

½ cup unprocessed bran

1 tablespoon caraway seeds

1 teaspoon salt

2 tablespoons molasses

1 tablespoon oil

3 cups hot water

extra whole wheat flour

MAKES about 30 slices

1 Mix all ingredients except extra flour, cover and leave to stand overnight.

2 Next day, add extra flour to make dough dry enough to handle. Spoon dough into a well-greased, heavy-duty bread pan. Cover with foil and bake at 250°F for 3 hours. Remove foil and continue baking for a further 20–30 minutes or until dry and slightly shrunken from sides.

3 Cool thoroughly and keep for a day before serving in thin slices. Wrap unused pumpernickel in foil and store in refrigerator.

Nutritional information per slice: Protein 3 g; fat 1 g; carbohydrate 20 g; dietary fiber 3 g; 100 cals

Preparation time: 20 minutes + overnight standing time

Cooking time: 3½ hours

Corn Bread

1 cup self-rising flour

1 teaspoon baking powder

1 cup cornmeal

½ cup wheat germ

1 teaspoon dried thyme

1 egg

1¼ cups skim milk

2 tablespoons grated Parmesan cheese

2 teaspoons paprika

MAKES 16 slices

1 Sift flour and baking powder into a bowl. Tip bran remaining in sieve into bowl. Add cornmeal, wheat germ and thyme.

2 Add egg, milk, 1 tablespoon of Parmesan and 1 teaspoon of paprika. Mix well together and pour into a greased 7 inch-square cake pan.

3 Mix remaining Parmesan and paprika and sprinkle over top of corn bread. Bake at 400°F for 25 minutes. Serve with a crisp green salad or soup.

Nutritional information per slice: Protein 4 g; fat 2 g; carbohydrate 13 g; some dietary fiber 2 g; sodium 138 mg; 85 cals

Other features: Provides useful amounts of calcium

Preparation time: 15 minutes

Cooking time: 25 minutes

Cheese and Sage Damper.

Cheese and Sage Damper

3 oz low-fat Cheddar cheese

1 cup whole wheat flour

1 cup self-rising flour

½ teaspoon paprika

¼ teaspoon black pepper

1 teaspoon dried sage

1¼ oz low-fat/low-salt butter or margarine

1 cup evaporated skim milk

3 teaspoons milk

2 teaspoons grated Parmesan cheese

2 teaspoons poppy seeds

SERVES 8

1 Using food processor, grate cheese. Mix in flours, paprika, pepper and sage.

2 Add butter or margarine and process until crumbly. Add evaporated milk a little at a time and mix to a soft dough.

3 On a lightly floured surface, knead dough and shape into an 8 inch round. Using a sharp knife, cut almost through the dough into eight wedges. Brush top with milk and sprinkle with Parmesan and poppy seeds. Bake on a greased baking sheet at 350°F for 25–30 minutes. Cool slightly before serving.

Nutritional information per serving: Protein 11 g; fat 4 g; carbohydrate 22 g; good dietary fiber 3 g; sodium 395 mg; 175 cals

Other features: A good source of calcium, thiamin (B1) and riboflavin (B2) and provides some iron, zinc and niacin (B3)

Preparation time: 10 minutes

Cooking time: 30 minutes

Cracked Wheat Bread

½ cup bulgur
(cracked wheat)

½ cup cracked or whole
grain rye

¼ cup flaxseed (available
from health food stores)

1¼ cups hot water

2⅓ cups warm water

1½ lb whole wheat flour

½ teaspoon salt

3 packets dried yeast

1 Soak cracked wheat, rye and flaxseed in 1¼ cups hot water and leave overnight.
2 Next day, add remaining ingredients and mix well. Leave to stand for 3–4 hours. (In cold weather, cover bowl with plastic wrap.)
3 Pour into a heavy-duty well-greased bread pan and bake at 400°F for 1 hour. Tip out and leave to cool thoroughly before cutting in very thin slices to serve.

Nutritional information per slice: Protein 4 g; fat 1 g; carbohydrate 18 g; good dietary fiber 3 g; 100 cals
Other features: A good source of thiamin (B1) and provides some niacin (B3) and iron. Low sodium (33 mg)

Cracked Wheat Bread.

Preparation time: 10 minutes
+ soaking and standing time

MAKES about 30 slices

Cooking time: 1 hour

Cheesy Corn Bread

2 cups buttermilk

3 eggs

¼ cup oil

1 tablespoon lemon juice

1 teaspoon chopped chili

2 cups cornmeal

½ teaspoon baking soda

1 teaspoon baking powder

½ cup grated
Parmesan cheese

1 teaspoon paprika

2 teaspoons sesame seeds

1 Blend buttermilk, eggs, oil, lemon juice and chili.
2 Combine cornmeal, soda, baking powder and cheese. Add buttermilk mixture and mix well. Pour mixture into a well-greased non-stick 8 inch square pan.
3 Sprinkle top with paprika and sesame seeds and bake in a hot (425°F) oven for 25 minutes, or until a toothpick inserted into the center comes out clean. Leave to cool slightly and cut into squares to serve.

Nutritional information per serving: Protein 11 g; fat 15 g; carbohydrate 34 g; dietary fiber 2 g; 315 cals
Other features: Provides iron, calcium, niacin (B3) and vitamin A

Cheesy Corn Bread.

Preparation time: 20 minutes
Cooking time: 25 minutes

SERVES 8

Oat Cookies

1 cup quick-cooking oats

½ teaspoon baking soda

½ teaspoon cinnamon

¾ oz butter or margarine

1 tablespoon water

1 tablespoon honey

1 Combine dry ingredients.
2 Heat butter or margarine, water and honey until margarine melts. Pour into dry ingredients and mix well to make a dough.
3 Knead dough and pat to an 8 inch circle. Mark into eight wedges. Place dough on a non-stick baking sheet and bake at 350°F for 15 minutes or until lightly brown and crisp. Serve warm and with a low-fat spread, honey, jam or cheese.

Nutritional information per oat cookie: Protein 2 g; fat 3 g; carbohydrate 11 g; small amount of dietary fiber 1 g; 80 cals
Other features: Low sodium (26 mg)

MAKES 8 cookies

Preparation time: 10 minutes
Cooking time: 15 minutes

Raisin Oat Bread

1¼ cups whole wheat flour

1¼ cups self-rising flour

1 cup rolled oats

1 teaspoon baking soda

1 tablespoon brown sugar

¾ cup raisins

10 oz low-fat yogurt

½ cup orange juice

1 Combine all dry ingredients and raisins.
2 Add yogurt and juice and mix to a soft dough. Bake in a loaf pan or knead on a floured surface until smooth and place on a non-stick baking sheet. Bake at 350°F for 40–45 minutes or until the loaf has risen and sounds hollow when it is tapped underneath.

Nutritional information per slice: Protein 4 g; fat 1 g; carbohydrate 18 g; some dietary fiber 2 g; sodium 160 mg; 100 cals

MAKES 1 loaf
(about 18 slices)

Preparation time: 15 minutes
Cooking time: 45 minutes

Whole Wheat Lemon Griddle Cakes

2 cups whole wheat flour

1 tablespoon sugar

2 eggs, separated

1½ cups low-fat milk

1 tablespoon lemon juice

1 teaspoon finely grated lemon rind

1 Mix together flour, sugar, egg yolks, milk, juice and rind.
2 Beat egg whites until stiff. Fold in flour mixture.
3 Heat a non-stick pan until hot. Cook spoonfuls of the mixture until bubbles appear. Turn and cook other side until golden brown. Serve warm with whipped ricotta cheese or light cream cheese, or with a little lemon juice.

Nutritional information per griddle cake: Protein 2 g; fat 1 g; carbohydrate 6 g; small amounts of dietary fiber 1 g; 35 cals
Other features: Sodium negligible (11 mg)

Opposite, clockwise from left: Oat Cookies, Raisin Oat Bread and Whole Wheat Lemon Griddle Cakes.

MAKES about 30

Preparation time: 15 minutes
Cooking time: 10 minutes

Calcium has little effect on energy but greatly influences the density of bones. A lack of calcium – like a lack of iron – is mainly a problem for women. To keep bones strong, try to have some calcium-rich foods every day. Milk, yogurt and cheese are excellent sources and you can avoid their fat by using low-fat varieties. Other sources of calcium include fish with edible bones (such as canned sardines or salmon), almonds, fortified soy milk, tofu (soybean curd), tahini (the pale-colored kind made with hulled sesame seeds), oranges and green vegetables. Some of the low-fat fortified milks are concentrated sources of calcium – all excellent products for women's needs.

Opposite, clockwise from top: Apricot Almond Loaf, Banana and Carrot Muffins and Banana and Orange Scones.

Apricot Almond Loaf

6½ oz dried apricots

1 cup orange juice

1 egg

½ cup skim milk

2 teaspoons finely grated lemon rind

½ cup chopped almonds

½ cup wheat germ

½ cup whole wheat flour

½ cup self-rising flour

½ teaspoon baking powder

½ teaspoon cardamom

MAKES 16 slices

1 Place apricots and juice in a saucepan and bring to the boil. Cover and leave to stand until cooled slightly.
2 Combine egg, milk, rind, almonds and apricots and mix well.
3 Add wheat germ, sifted flours, baking powder and cardamom, tipping bran from sifter into mixture.
4 Pour into a greased loaf pan and bake at 350°F for 35 minutes. Turn out and cool before serving.

Nutritional information per slice: Protein 3 g; fat 3 g; carbohydrate 10 g; a very good source of dietary fiber 5 g; 80 cals
Other features: Useful amounts of potassium and some iron. Low sodium (64 mg)

Preparation time: 15 minutes
+ 30 minutes cooling time
Cooking time: 35 minutes

Banana and Carrot Muffins

1 large carrot

2 bananas, peeled

1 tablespoon dark brown sugar

2 eggs

¼ cup low-fat yogurt

1 teaspoon cinnamon

1⅓ cups whole wheat flour

2 teaspoons baking powder

½ cup unprocessed bran

MAKES 12

1 Using a food processor, shred carrot finely (there will be one cup of carrot, firmly packed).
2 Add bananas, sugar, eggs, yogurt and cinnamon to food processor and whiz until well blended.
3 Sift flour and baking powder into banana mixture, tipping husks into mixture. Add bran and mix quickly.
4 Place mixture into 12 greased muffin pans. Bake at 400°F for 20 minutes. Serve the muffins warm.

Nutritional information per muffin: Protein 4 g; fat 1 g; carbohydrate 15 g; good dietary fiber 4 g; 90 cals
Other features: Provides some calcium and potassium. Low sodium (95 mg)

Preparation time: 15 minutes
Cooking time: 20 minutes

Banana and Orange Scones

2 small bananas

1 teaspoon finely chopped orange rind

2 tablespoons non-fat dry milk

1 egg

1 tablespoon low-fat butter

2 tablespoons orange juice

¼ teaspoon cardamom

1 cup whole wheat flour

1 cup self-rising flour

½ teaspoon baking powder

MAKES 10–12 scones

1 In food processor, mix bananas, rind, dry milk, egg, butter, orange juice and cardamom. (Or mash bananas and mix well with other ingredients.)
2 Sift flours and baking powder into banana mixture, tipping bran into mixture from sifter. Mix lightly to a dough.
3 On a floured board, pat out to a circle and cut out 10–12 round scones. Place on a greased baking sheet and bake at 400°F for 12–15 minutes. Serve warm.

Nutritional information per scone: Protein 4 g; fat 2 g; carbohydrate 18 g; good dietary fiber 3 g; sodium 220 mg; 110 cals
Other features: Provides some calcium and potassium

Preparation time: 20 minutes
Cooking time: 15 minutes

Apricot and Almond Delight

5 or 6 fresh apricots
(or use canned apricots
without sugar)

1 cup orange juice

6½ oz low-fat yogurt

1 tablespoon sliced almonds

2 or 3 ice cubes

grated nutmeg

SERVES 2

Place all ingredients in blender and process until well mixed.
Sprinkle with nutmeg before serving.

Nutritional information per serving: Protein 8 g; fat 4 g;
carbohydrate 29 g; very good dietary fiber 5 g; 180 cals
Other features: An excellent source of vitamin C, a very good
source of vitamin A and potassium, a good source of calcium,
thiamin (B1) and riboflavin (B2). Provides some iron and niacin
(B3). Low sodium (85 mg)

Preparation time: 5 minutes
Cooking time: Nil

Peach Cooler

1 cup canned peach juice

1 cup buttermilk

2 tablespoons
non-fat dry milk

3 or 4 ice cubes

SERVES 2

Place all ingredients in blender and process until well mixed.

Nutritional information per serving: Protein 8 g; fat 2 g;
carbohydrate 24 g; no dietary fiber; sodium 125 mg; 145 cals
Other features: A very good source of riboflavin (B2) and
thiamin (B1), a good source of calcium and potassium

Preparation time: 5 minutes
Cooking time: Nil

Banana Smoothie

1 glass skim milk

½ cup low-fat yogurt

1 banana

1 teaspoon honey (optional)

1 tablespoon wheat germ

2 or 3 ice cubes

few drops vanilla

SERVES 2

Place all ingredients in blender and process until fluffy.

Nutritional information per serving: Protein 14 g; fat 2 g;
carbohydrate 41 g (or 36 g if honey omitted); good dietary fiber
4 g; sodium 175 mg; 235 cals or 215 cals without honey
Other features: An excellent source of riboflavin (B2), a very
good source of potassium and a good source of thiamin (B1) and
vitamin C. Also provides useful amounts of zinc. Rich in calcium

Preparation time: 5 minutes
Cooking time: Nil

Pink Drink

1 slice watermelon (about
8 oz) with seeds removed

2 bananas

4 oz strawberries

1 cup buttermilk

SERVES 2

Place all ingredients in blender and process until well mixed.

Nutritional information per serving: Protein 8 g; fat 3 g;
carbohydrate 33 g; very good dietary fiber 5 g; 185 cals
Other features: An excellent source of vitamin C, a very good
source of thiamin (B1), a good source of calcium, potassium and
riboflavin (B2) and provides some iron. Low sodium (72 mg)

Preparation time: 10 minutes
Cooking time: Nil

Opposite, clockwise from top:
Apricot Almond Delight,
Pink Drink, Peach Cooler
and Banana Smoothie.

Herb Sauce

This is an ideal sauce to serve with fish or chicken. For the most flavorful results, it really does need fresh herbs. However, you can vary the herbs used according to what is available – and to suit your taste.

1 cup chicken stock
1 piece lemon peel, about 2 inch
1 clove garlic, peeled
1 tablespoon chopped fresh parsley
1 tablespoon chopped fresh cilantro
1 tablespoon chopped fresh thyme
1 tablespoon cornstarch
¼ cup evaporated skim milk
freshly ground pepper

1 Heat chicken stock with lemon peel and garlic. Simmer, covered, for 2 minutes. Remove lemon peel and garlic. Add chopped herbs.
2 Mix cornstarch with evaporated milk. Add to hot stock, stirring constantly until sauce boils and thickens. Add pepper to taste.

Nutritional information per serving: Protein 2 g; no fat; carbohydrate 5 g; less than 1 g dietary fiber; 30 cals
Other features: Low sodium (45 mg)

SERVES 4

Preparation time: 5 minutes
Cooking time: 10 minutes

Spiced Raisin Sauce

This tangy sauce makes an excellent accompaniment to white meats like pork, veal and poultry, as it enhances their mild flavor.

1 cup apple juice
¼ cup red wine
4 cardamom pods
1 cinnamon stick, about 3 inch
6 cloves
1 piece orange peel, about 4 inch
1 cup raisins
2 teaspoons arrowroot or cornstarch
2 tablespoons water
1 tablespoon lemon juice

1 Heat apple juice, wine, spices and peel until boiling. Cover and leave for 30 minutes. Strain off liquid and reserve. Discard spices and peel.
2 Add raisins to liquid. Bring to the boil and simmer 10 minutes.
3 Blend arrowroot or cornstarch with water. Add to raisin mixture, stirring constantly until mixture boils and thickens. Add lemon juice.

Nutritional information per serving: No protein; no fat; carbohydrate 22 g; some dietary fiber 2 g; 85 cals
Other features: Some niacin (B3), potassium and vitamin C. Low sodium (20 mg)

Preparation time: 5 minutes
Cooking time: 25 minutes
+ 30 minutes standing time

SERVES 6

Tangy Lemon Sauce

A simple tangy sauce which is lovely served with fresh asparagus, broccoli or seafoods. It has all the flavor of a traditional Hollandaise sauce – and fewer calories!

2 teaspoons Dijon mustard

½ teaspoon dried
ground tarragon

¼ cup white wine vinegar

¼ cup lemon juice

1 egg, beaten

freshly ground black pepper

few drops of artificial
sweetener

1 In a small saucepan, mix mustard and tarragon. Add vinegar and lemon juice. Bring to the boil.
2 Stirring constantly, gradually add beaten egg to lemon mixture. Cook over a low heat until thickened. Add pepper and sweetener to taste.

Nutritional information per serving: Protein 1 g; fat 1 g; no carbohydrate; no dietary fiber; 20 cals
Other features: Low sodium (20 mg)

SERVES 4

Preparation time: 5 minutes
Cooking time: 15 minutes

Home-made Tomato Sauce

Home-made tomato sauce is the perfect accompaniment to burgers and barbecued foods and once you taste it, it is hard to go back to the store-bought varieties. It must be stored in the refrigerator in hot weather.

2 teaspoons olive oil,
preferably extra virgin

1 medium onion,
chopped roughly

1 clove garlic, crushed

½ teaspoon dry mustard

2 lb ripe tomatoes,
chopped roughly

¾ cup tomato purée

2 bay leaves

1 teaspoon dried oregano

freshly ground black pepper

1 Heat oil and add onion and garlic. Cover and cook over a gentle heat for 3–4 minutes. Add mustard and cook a further 1 minute.
2 Add remaining ingredients. Bring to the boil, cover and simmer for 10–15 minutes. Cool a little, purée until smooth. If you like, strain sauce through a sieve to remove tomato seeds. Bottle and store in the refrigerator.

Nutritional information per ¼ cup: No protein; no fat; carbohydrate 2 g; dietary fiber 1 g; 13 cals
Other features: Useful source of vitamin C. Low sodium (40 mg)

MAKES 4½ cups

Preparation time: 10 minutes
Cooking time: 20 minutes

EATING FOR VITALITY

THE RECIPES IN THIS BOOK DEMONSTRATE HOW varied and tasty a healthy diet can be. This section explains more about the roles of individual nutrients, how they work together and which foods provide them. And because dietary needs change according to a person's age, health and lifestyle, it includes diet advice for everyone from teenagers to athletes to older people – plus special guidance on effective weight loss and vegetarian diets. There is also a comprehensive guide to additives, with details of what they do and where they're used.

Carbohydrates and energy

Carbohydrates have had bad press over the last few years but their reputation as being fattening is quite unjustified. In fact, it is the complex carbohydrates in the diet that give the muscles the energy to work – and so to burn unwanted fat. Without carbohydrate we suffer fatigue and get flabby!

In Energy: what is it? (page 10) we saw that carbohydrates, proteins, fats and alcohol are all digested and metabolized to supply calories of energy which can be stored as body fat or as glycogen in the liver and muscles.

However, the energy from proteins is used by the body for different purposes than the energy obtained from fats or carbohydrates. The body prefers to use protein for growth and repair of body tissues. Any excess is stored as body fat. When we digest fats, their fatty acids can also be used for energy or stored as body fat for possible future energy needs.

Carbohydrates are broken down to sugars, and eventually to glucose. Some of this glucose replenishes the blood sugar level and provides energy for the brain and other organs. Some is converted into a storage form, known as glycogen, in the liver and larger quantities can be converted into glycogen in the muscles. Any leftovers are then converted to body fat.

The glycogen stores in muscles are expandable. If you lead a mostly sedentary lifestyle, every 100 grams of muscle can store up to one gram of glycogen. Athletes who train and eat plenty of carbohydrate can increase these glycogen stores fourfold to four grams of glycogen in every 100 grams of muscle. With such an increase in the use of glucose, athletes and other people who are physically active have little carbohydrate left for conversion to body fat. Not only that, once the muscles are well supplied with glycogen, exercise itself becomes easier. This means you can exercise more and the extra exercise will increase muscle. The extra muscle then uses more

glucose and so on. With plenty of carbohydrate in the diet and, therefore, plenty of glycogen in muscles, you can be more active without feeling tired.

Glycogen in muscles can be used only by the muscles. It cannot be sent to the blood to be turned into blood sugar.

If glycogen stores run out, you feel like crashing. Athletes call this feeling 'hitting the wall'. It occurs sometimes in marathon and long-distance events and the athlete is usually unable to go on. Without glycogen, you have no fuel to power your muscles.

Muscles can burn some fat for energy, but only when there is also some glycogen present. As an analogy, to produce power in the muscles you must burn fuel. Glycogen (or glucose from the blood) is like the kindling. Fat is like large logs. You cannot burn a log unless you first get the fire going with kindling. Without glycogen, you cannot burn fat.

On the other side of the coin, when glycogen stores are high, you can exercise longer without being fatigued. Even day-to-day activities suddenly seem easier with glycogen-filled muscles. Yet the typical Western diet lacks sufficient quantities of the raw materials so ideal for glycogen. We eat only about half the desirable amount of complex carbohydrate which would give us better glycogen stores. Slimming diets are often even more deficient in complex carbohydrate and are hopeless for anyone who wants to feel fired up and ready to go.

Most slimming diets 'work' by removing glycogen from muscles. If you don't eat carbohydrates, the body first uses up the stores of glycogen it already has. Liver glycogen lasts only a few hours

but muscle glycogen can last from a couple of hours in a person who is physically active to several days in someone who sits most of the time. Glycogen in muscles is heavy, mainly because every gram of glycogen is stored with almost 3 grams of water. So when you lose your glycogen stores (and the associated water), you think you are losing weight.

With most strict diets, you soon experience fatigue from a lack of energy. This is because the muscles have not been able to refill their glycogen so they have no fuel for activity.

Fast weight-loss diets are popular because you get a big initial drop in weight. They are foolish, as you can see, because the weight loss is not the fat you want to lose but is only glycogen and water from muscles.

Throughout the whole process, you lose any desire to be energetic and you still have your excess fat. Fast weight-loss diets have another, even worse, effect but to explain this we must first consider blood sugar.

Blood sugar

Blood sugar levels vary over any 24-hour period. After meals, they rise and then fall back to their previous level. The speed of the fall in blood sugar depends on the food eaten. Some foods, such as sugar, are quickly digested to give a sudden boost to blood sugar levels. This then causes the body to produce insulin, a hormone which takes sugar out of the blood and into other cells where it is used as an energy source. Sometimes, there is an overshoot of insulin and the blood sugar level does a temporary nosedive. Some people find this sudden drop makes them feel shaky, cranky, slightly nauseous or headachy and unable to make decisions. Fine coordination can also be affected during a temporary drop in blood sugar.

There are differences between foods, but, in general, whole grain products or foods with dietary fiber have a more gradual and gentle effect on blood sugar levels than more refined foods – and this effect is usually sustained for longer. Oats and beans (such as baked beans, kidney or other beans or dried peas) give the longest and most even stimulus to blood sugar levels.

There is no point in eating lots of carbohydrate to increase blood sugar levels beyond normal. Very high blood sugar is usually followed by plunging levels. These low levels are restored to normal even if you do not eat any carbohydrate because the body can convert liver glycogen and, once that runs out, protein (from food or from muscle) to glucose.

This leads to the other major problem with low carbohydrate, fast weight-loss diets. You need at least 100 grams (and usually much more) carbohydrate throughout the day to prevent muscle protein from being broken down to contribute some glucose to the blood. With these crazy diets, not only is muscle glycogen depleted but some of the muscle tissue itself is lost. Muscle is heavier than fat, so once again the scales may delight you but the truth is less pleasing. Muscle burns up lots of calories, even when you are sitting doing nothing. Less muscle means fewer calories are needed.

As an example, if a woman who normally needs around 1900 cals goes on a strict diet of only 800 cals a day, she inevitably loses some muscle tissue. This means that, after the diet, she will need fewer calories, perhaps only 1800 cals. If she goes back to eating a normal diet of 1900 cals she will gain weight. If she frequently tries the latest gimmick diet, she will eventually deplete her muscle to the extent that even 1200 cals a day may be too much for her. Dieting makes

her prone to fatness because it has led to a loss of her lean muscle tissue.

While we are talking about carbohydrates and glucose, let us consider in more detail the role of liver glycogen. This is a ready store of energy for the body. It can be mobilized fast to restore a flagging blood sugar level. When the blood sugar level is going through one of the normal wave-like motions, a drop stimulates you to feel a hunger pang. This is your body asking for something to eat. However, you may have noticed that after a few minutes a hunger pang disappears for a while. This is because the body

has used some of your liver glycogen for a quick 'fix'. After that is used, you get another hunger signal. If you ignore that too, some more glycogen is mobilized.

After a couple of hours, however, the liver glycogen is all gone. This is when the body turns to protein. Since you have been ignoring hunger pangs and have not eaten, there is no protein from food available. So the body converts some muscle protein to glucose in a process called gluconeogenesis.

If you want to keep all your muscle as muscle – a sensible idea if you want your body to remain

Potatoes certainly do not deserve their reputation of being 'fattening'. To gain two pounds from eating potatoes you would need to eat 86 large potatoes!

Breads, grains, legumes and pasta – the right kinds of carbohydrate foods.

firm – you should eat before you go through too many hunger signals. Apart from the discomfort, meal-skippers lose muscle. Sometimes we find athletes spending hours training to build up muscle but forgetting to eat for many hours at a time. Even though they may be training, they are losing muscle as fast as they are making it. It is always important to listen to the body's messages and eat something when you feel hungry. You do not need to overdo it – enough is as good as a feast – but neither should you ignore hunger pangs. Glycogen in muscles can be used only by the muscles themselves, so even if you do not want to exercise, the muscle glycogen cannot be changed to blood glucose.

Aerobic and anaerobic energy

The body gets energy from food by burning fats and glucose with oxygen. The products of these reactions are carbon dioxide (which we breathe out), water and energy stored in a molecule known as adenosine triphosphate (ATP) as well as energy that is given out as heat.

Normally combustion requires oxygen. Carbohydrates are special fuel for energy because they can provide short bursts of energy inside body cells when oxygen is unavailable. This is called anaerobic oxidation. It is important when a large amount of energy is needed fast, as in a sprint or during a sudden explosive movement such as serving in tennis or lifting a heavy weight. Anaerobic activities cannot last long as lactic acid accumulates in the muscle involved, causing quick fatigue. Anaerobic energy is only useful for physical activity lasting less than 60 seconds.

Most of the energy produced in the body is aerobic energy – that is, it uses oxygen. Aerobic oxidation is much more efficient and is able to capture much more of the energy in the glucose molecule. Aerobic energy can be used for any long or sustained physical activity.

Activity	% carbo-hydrate used	% fat used
walking	50	50
walking for long periods (more than 1–2 hours)	30	70
sprinting	80	20
running a marathon	15	85

Your ability to make the best possible use of anaerobic activity depends on the nature of your muscle fibers. Some people inherit muscle fibers which fire better without oxygen. To some extent, then, a good sprinter is born rather than made.

Your use of aerobic energy, however, can be increased by training. Fit people have more oxygen available for aerobic energy. Aerobic capacity is not something you inherit, but a feature you can develop.

Energy mix: fat or carbohydrate?

Under normal conditions, the body uses a mixture of fat and glucose as its fuel. Exercise can change the fuel mix and some types of exercise can increase the amount of fat used for energy. The duration of the exercise also alters the fuel mix (see the chart above). This is important for anyone who is overweight.

Intense activity cannot use fat as a fuel. Only carbohydrate (as glucose or from glycogen) can be used for any short, sharp burst of activity. On the other hand, exercise of low to moderate intensity, such as walking or long-distance swimming, uses fat as a prime source of energy. As soon as you start walking, specific hormones are released. These cause body fat to release fatty acids into the blood. The fatty acids and the carbohydrate then supply the energy for the muscles to keep walking.

Fats can be used as fuel unless there is a build-up of lactic acid (which occurs as the exercise becomes more intensive). Once lactic acid accumulates, glycogen becomes the favored fuel.

Moderate exercise is therefore more suitable for anyone who wants to burn fat as their major energy source.

The longer you exercise, the more fat is used as fuel. During a marathon, or any endurance activity, the percentage of fat burned increases.

Training increases the amount of fat used for energy. Untrained people accumulate lactic acid faster and therefore switch to using only carbohydrate for fuel. Trained marathon runners are able to make their precious carbohydrate stores last.

In all these activities, it is muscle glycogen which limits exercise. Even when using fat for fuel, some carbohydrate from muscle glycogen is also burned. Once the glycogen stores in the muscles are empty, you cannot exercise any more.

Sugar and exercise

Athletes are told not to eat sugar just before exercise. This is because eating sugar triggers the release of the hormone insulin. When insulin is present in the blood it stops fatty acids (from body fat) being mobilized. This means that little fat is used as fuel and glycogen stores must provide all the energy. Athletes need to preserve their glycogen stores – which is why it is unwise to eat sugar or glucose just before a sporting event.

Once exercise has been started, however, insulin does not flood into the blood so easily. Athletes competing in endurance events can therefore take sugar (usually as a weak glucose solution) during their event. This sugar can replenish the blood sugar and may even be helpful.

How protein fits into the picture

Proteins, present in every cell, are the 'building blocks' of the body

Proteins are made up of smaller units called amino acids. There are over 20 different types of amino acids which can be arranged in millions of ways to form different proteins. The average protein contains about 900 amino acids. Hormones, enzymes, skin, nails, hair, veins, arteries, bones, blood cells, tendons and muscles are all made of protein. Antibodies, which help fight infection (or cause allergic reactions), are also made of protein. Various proteins in the blood are also vital.

Every day, we damage body tissues. Amino acids from protein foods repair them. Growing children, teenagers and pregnant women build new tissue from protein. Each protein has a definite lifespan. Some enzymes may last only a few minutes, while red blood cells may last 120 days and some muscle proteins may last even longer.

Protein is rarely used as a source of energy, except during starvation or very strict diets. At such times, muscle is lost.

Many of the amino acids which make up proteins within the body can be made in the body. Some cannot. These 'essential amino acids' must be supplied by the foods we eat.

Animal vs vegetable proteins
Animal protein foods contain all the essential amino acids. Vegetable protein foods lack one or more of these amino acids. That does not necessarily make vegetable protein foods inferior because the amino acid missing from one vegetable food can be easily supplied by another.

Many of the traditional combinations of foods, such as rice and soy beans, corn and beans, rice and dhal, wheat and chickpeas, or nuts and grains (in a peanut butter sandwich) have a complete set of essential amino acids. An amino acid missing

from one food is supplied by the other. Any of these combinations is just as good as getting protein from animal foods.

Excess protein
Many people believe that extra protein will build big muscles. It won't. Muscles develop when they are used, and for that they need carbohydrates. Muscle fibers do contain protein and protein is needed for the repair of any damage to muscle fibers. But large quantities of protein are converted to fat, not muscle.

In children, too much protein can be dangerous. Proteins contain nitrogen and, when any excess is converted to fat, the kidneys must dispose of the resulting nitrogenous waste products. This can put a strain on an infant's kidneys.

High levels of protein can also interfere with the absorption of calcium. In Asian countries, where people eat less protein than in Western countries, more of the calcium in the diet can be absorbed. Some protein powder drinks and supplements are so

high in protein that they may stop some calcium absorption.

The worst feature of many foods with a high protein content is a high fat content and a relative lack of carbohydrate and dietary fiber. For maximum energy, then, the diet should have enough protein, but not at the expense of other foods which supply carbohydrate. It makes sense to get protein from foods like dried beans and peas which contain protein and carbohydrate. These products also have almost no fat.

Recommended protein	
infants: 0–5 months 5–12 months	2.2 g/kg body weight 1.6 g/kg body weight
1–6 years	1.2 g/kg body weight
7–14 years	1.0 g/kg body weight
15–18 years	0.9 g/kg body weight
19 +	0.8 g/kg body weight
pregnant women	an extra 10–16 g/day
lactating women	an extra 16 g/day

Above: Seafood Pizza (page 73) is a good source of protein.

Children and teenagers need much more protein in proportion to their size than adults.

Fat and cholesterol

Almost everyone thinks previous generations – with their daily breakfasts of sausages, bacon and fried eggs, and roast dinners followed by apple pie and ice-cream – ate much more fat. In fact, people in most Western countries today eat more fat than their predecessors, the major difference being that it is now concealed in fast foods, processed and take-out items.

Is fat essential?

Babies begin life drinking breast or formula milk in which 50 per cent of the calories come from fat. This is important for a baby's rapid growth and, for the first few years of life, dietary fat continues to be an important source of energy. Gradually, the need for fat decreases.

Everyone needs some essential fatty acids, such as linoleic acid and eicosapentaenoic acid (commonly called EPA). You won't find these in fatty meats, pastries, French fries or most fried foods. There are essential fatty acids in many foods without any obvious fat. Rabbit, turkey, chicken, fish, rolled oats, wheat germ, egg yolk, nuts, seeds and vegetables are all sources of the essential fatty acids needed by brain and nerve cells and to keep the membranes around all body cells healthy.

Most health authorities recommend that we eat no more than 20 to 30 per cent of our calories as fat. For an average man that translates to no more than 50 to 80 grams of fat a day and, for the average woman, a maximum of 40 to 60 grams a day. Children need smaller quantities but teenagers may be able to eat more during periods of rapid growth.

Why too much fat is harmful

A high fat diet is linked with excess weight, coronary heart disease, high blood pressure, diabetes, gallstones and some cancers. At 9 calories/gram, fats have more than twice as many calories as protein (4 cals/g) or carbohydrates (4 cals/g). Only alcohol, with 7 cals/g comes close to fat in calories.

To condemn fat still further, researchers have now shown that the body preferentially uses carbohydrates for energy and more easily converts fats in food into body fat. High levels of body fat then further increase the risks for all the conditions listed above.

Western diseases

In countries where the diet is low in fat, there is a very small incidence of 'Western diseases'. However, when people migrate, they pick up the host country's pattern of disease. Japanese people moving to the United States, for example, have an increased risk of developing problems associated with a high fat diet such as heart disease, diabetes, gallstones and cancers of the breast and bowel.

Eating saturated fat can cause the body to make too much cholesterol. This occurs more in some people than in others.

Excess dietary fat also increases the load on the heart so it must pump much harder. This can cause blood pressure to rise. Saturated fats create the greatest risk for high blood pressure. Saturated fats are also a risk factor in maturity-onset diabetes. For gallstones, all fats are a problem. In certain cancers, too much of any kind of fat – except for monounsaturated fat present in olive oil and fish fats – is also a potential problem.

Different kinds of fat – saturated or unsaturated?

'Saturated', 'monounsaturated' and 'polyunsaturated' refer to the chemical structure of fats. Foods always contain a mixture of many different fats but one type usually predominates. For example, a margarine which is labeled 'polyunsaturated' may have 35 per cent of its fat in the form of polyunsaturated fat, 45 per cent as monounsaturated fat and 20 per cent as saturated fat. Even polyunsaturated margarines thus contribute some saturated fat to the diet, a point often forgotten.

Some types of fat create more health problems than others. People living in Mediterranean countries eat a lot of olive oil but have long life expectancy with low levels of heart disease and cancer. Traditional Eskimos also had very low levels of heart disease, diabetes and many other

Major types of fat in different foods

Food	Sat fat (grams)	Mono fat (grams)	Poly fat (grams)
milk, 6½ fl oz	5	5	0
butter, 1 tablespoon	12	5	0
margarine, 1 tablespoon	2	5	4
polyunsaturated margarine, 1 tablespoon	2	5	4
olive oil, 1 tablespoon	3	14	2
sunflower oil, 1 tablespoon	3	6	10
palm kernel oil, 1 tablespoon	9	9	2
coconut oil, 1 tablespoon	18	1	0
pork fat, 1 tablespoon	5	6	1
beef, broiled, lean, 5 oz	6	6	up to 1
chicken breast, cooked, 5 oz	1	2	1
pork, steak, cooked, lean, 5 oz	3	3	1
lamb, trimmed, cooked, 5 oz	7	5	0
fish, broiled, 5 oz	1	1	1

health problems, even though their diet was high in fat. Their secret lay in fish fats. The high content of saturated fats in the typical Western diet seems to be responsible for many of our diet-related health problems.

Animal or vegetable fats?

Saturated fats are not synonymous with animal fats. Some animal fats, such as those in fish and game meats (like venison) are mainly unsaturated. On the other hand, many vegetable fats such as those found in chocolate, some margarines, coconut and palm kernel oils are highly saturated fats. When a food product lists 'vegetable oil' on its label, the ingredient is often palm kernel oil – a highly saturated fat.

Some saturated fats affect blood cholesterol more than others. Claims are sometimes made that chocolate contains stearic acid. This is a saturated fat which does not seem to raise cholesterol. However, chocolate is also one of the richest sources of palmitic acid, a saturated fat which does indeed raise blood cholesterol levels.

Which fat?

There is little doubt that saturated fats are undesirable while the monounsaturated ones are better, as shown by the long, healthy lifespan of those who eat a lot of olive oil. We know less about the polyunsaturated fats, as they have been consumed in large quantities only since the 1970s.

Cholesterol

Cholesterol is essential in small quantities for brain and nerve cells and for hormones. Some cholesterol comes ready-made in animal foods but most is made in the body. It is the body's excess synthesis of cholesterol which causes problems. When the diet is high in saturated fats, more cholesterol is made. Excess cholesterol in the blood leads to clogged arteries, especially the arteries to the heart and brain. Cholesterol can also block blood vessels to the penis and is the major physical cause of impotence in men.

Cholesterol is made up of both HDL cholesterol (high density lipoprotein) and LDL cholesterol (low density lipoprotein). HDL cholesterol is 'good' and represents cholesterol being taken back from the tissues to the liver. LDL cholesterol is 'bad' and correlates with fatty deposits in the arteries.

Ideally, blood cholesterol levels should be less than 200 mg/dL. The higher the percentage of HDL cholesterol the better. Endurance athletes, young women, and those from families who enjoy longevity tend to have high HDL cholesterol levels, generally ranging from 25 to 40 per cent of the total. Most men and most post-menopausal women have HDL levels less than 20 per cent of the total.

How to lower your cholesterol

Saturated fats lower protective HDL cholesterol and increase the nasty LDL type. Polyunsaturated fats reduce the LDL cholesterol. Monounsaturated fats can reduce the bad LDL cholesterol and may raise the good HDL cholesterol. These fats are therefore best. They are found in olive or canola oils, avocado and nuts like almonds.

In trying to reduce blood cholesterol, many people make the mistake of avoiding foods which contain cholesterol (such as eggs) while continuing to eat foods high in saturated fats. The best way to reduce your blood cholesterol is to avoid saturated fats and lose any excess weight. Stress can also be a factor in raising blood cholesterol levels.

Triglycerides

We convert excess fats, alcohol and sugar into triglycerides. After a meal, the level of triglycerides in the blood rises. Those not used for energy are stored as fat. If the blood level of triglycerides is still high after a 12-hour fast, it shows the body is not clearing fats properly. This may occur in those prone to diabetes. The high levels mean the blood is fatty and the heart must work harder.

This low-fat version of a Pasta Carbonara (page 85) is just as delicious as its traditional counterpart.

Fish fats

The small quantity of fat in most fish is rich in omega 3 fatty acids. These are chemically different from the omega 6 fatty acids in margarines and many varieties of vegetable oils.

The omega 3 fatty acids can prevent blood clots forming, make blood less 'sticky', lower blood pressure and triglyceride levels, and can play a role in reducing inflammation in some kinds of arthritis and eczema. They are also vitally important in the retina of the eye and in the development of the brain.

Omega 3 fatty acids are found in all seafoods. Some also occur in seeds and green vegetables, but the conversion of these to the same longer-chain omega 3 fats found in fish is not efficient if the diet is too high in omega 6 fats.

Currently we have about 50 times as much of the omega 6s as the omega 3s. The ideal ratio is thought to be closer to 6 parts of omega 6s to one of omega 3s. In practice, this means eating less margarine and polyunsaturated vegetable oil and more fish. One to three fish meals a week is ideal. Some of this should be fresh fish; some can be canned.

HEALTH TIP

Before having a blood test to determine your triglyceride level, make sure you have not eaten for 12 hours. Fasting is not necessary for cholesterol tests.

All about fiber

Dietary fiber was once called 'roughage' and was assumed to be indigestible fibrous material which went in one end of the body and eventually emerged from the other. Dietary fiber is much more complicated and undergoes important changes in the intestine. It has a part to play in many areas of health and longevity, including health of the intestine, diabetes or fluctuating blood-sugar levels, heart disease and cancer. However, not every kind of fiber has equal value in each of these areas.

Excellent sources of fiber include: black-eyed peas, this page; split peas, opposite at left; oats, center; and vegetables bottom right.

What is dietary fiber?
Just as there are many different vitamins, each with separate actions to perform in the body, so there are different types of dietary fiber with similarly varied roles. The old term 'roughage' was measured as 'crude fiber' and referred mainly to cellulose, one of the types of dietary fiber.

Roughage ignored the pectins, gums, hemi-celluloses and the saponins that all have a bearing on our health. These different types of fiber are found in different foods and you cannot assume your needs are being met just by eating, say, unprocessed bran or an apple a day.

Where is fiber found?
Dietary fiber occurs only in plant foods – grains, cereals (including breads and pasta), fruits, vegetables, legumes, seeds and nuts. Meat, fish and dairy products have other important nutrients, but they have no dietary fiber. To get the full range of the different types, you need to include a wide variety of plant foods in your meals and snacks each day.

What does fiber look like?
You can see strings of fiber in asparagus or spinach stalks, and the grainy fibers in some breads and cereal products. However, the gluey types present in oats and barley do not appear fibrous – and if you have ever added pectin to jam to help it set, you will know it is a fine white powder with no obvious fibers. Some foods which look fibrous, such as celery, have very little fiber, while others which have no obvious stringiness, such as bananas or potatoes, are good sources of fiber.

How much fiber?
The average daily Western diet has about 15 grams of dietary fiber. By contrast, people in some countries, and many who are vegetarians, have fiber intakes which may be three to four times

this level. In general a total of between 30 and 40 grams of fiber a day is recommended.

Soluble and insoluble
Dietary fibers which form a gel when mixed with water or with digestive juices in the intestine are classified as soluble fibers. This includes 'gummy' fibers and hemi-celluloses as well as pectins in fruits. Soluble fibers occur in barley, oats, apples, cabbage and some other vegetables, and in legumes. They can help lower cholesterol, regulate blood sugar levels and help in the prevention of colon cancer.

Insoluble fiber is found in whole wheat products such as whole wheat bread, whole grain cereals and wheat bran, as well as in vegetables. It is valuable in preventing constipation and may alter the bacteria in the bowel so that some substances implicated in causing breast cancer are removed from the body. For good health, try to have a mixture of soluble and insoluble fiber.

The digestion of dietary fiber
Dietary fiber is not broken down by the enzymes which digest proteins, fats and carbohydrates in the small intestine. Rather, most types of fiber are digested by bacteria in the large intestine. Soluble fibers are 100 per cent digested while insoluble ones are

How to change from a low-fiber to a high-fiber diet

Low-fiber choices	High-fiber choices
BREAKFAST	
corn flakes	rolled oats, whole grain wheat cereal or bran cereal
white toast with honey	whole wheat toast with marmalade
MORNING SNACK	
coffee and cookies	coffee and whole wheat fruit loaf
LUNCH	
chicken sandwich/white bread	chicken salad sandwich/whole wheat bread
apple, peeled	apple, unpeeled
AFTERNOON SNACK	
chocolate bar	banana
DINNER	
broiled steak	broiled steak
French fries	baked potato
green salad	2 or 3 vegetables
ice-cream	fruit salad
TOTAL	TOTAL
11 g fiber	**41 g fiber**

digested to varying degrees. Only one type of fiber, lignin, is not digested at all, although it may help remove some substances from the body.

While they are digesting dietary fiber, bacteria produce special acids, called short chain fatty acids. These provide a direct source of energy for the cells in the intestine. One acid causes an electrical stimulation in the bowel wall which helps the muscle wall propel food wastes along the intestine. Another has been shown to stop the action of the enzyme which colon-cancer cells need in order to multiply.

Constipation

Constipation is more common in women than in men, possibly because many women do not eat enough high-fiber foods. There may also be sex differences in the blood flow to the intestine and in the production of special gut hormones which help move foods along the intestine. In addition, a lack of water makes constipation worse.

Regular bowel movements are important but, in fact, it is the consistency of the stools which is more important than frequency. Small, hard stools constitute constipation.

Many people take laxatives. Those with anthroquinones (including some herbal laxatives) can damage the nerves in the bowel wall. The bowel is a muscular wall, so regular exercise in moving food along its length is important. Laxatives can destroy muscle tone and should not be used over long periods. A low fiber intake also tends to make the intestinal muscle walls become slack.

Increasing dietary fiber to 30 to 40 grams a day and drinking six to eight glasses of water will

prevent or cure constipation for most people. Those who have resorted to laxatives over long periods may find they also need the help of a mild faecal softener until their improved diet becomes effective.

Soluble and insoluble fibers work in different ways to increase stool bulk.

Insoluble fibers provide bulk and also absorb water to contribute to the stools. Soluble fibers cause useful bacteria to multiply by the million and their dead bodies are then excreted.

About 70 per cent of the weight of stools represents their water content; the other 30 per cent represents the dead bodies of bacteria which have digested soluble fiber, plus some undigested soluble fiber and insoluble fiber.

Flatulence

As bacteria digest fiber, they produce gases. This is normal and when you eat more fiber, you produce more gas. However, if you increase your fiber intake gradually, you will have fewer problems with excessive gas production.

Foods which produce the most gas include legumes, certain vegetables (cabbage, cauliflower, broccoli, Brussels sprouts) and apple juice. Soaking legumes and then discarding the soaking water helps. Eating the clear, outer husk on legumes also helps reduce gas because this coating contains substances which can bind the cause of some of the gas.

Gas and abdominal distension with pain may occur in people who cannot digest milk sugar, or lactose. The natural content of fructose and sorbitol in apple and pear juice also causes excessive 'gas' in some people.

Dietary fiber content of foods	
Food	Fiber (grams)
vegetables, average serving of any	3
beans, kidney or baked, 1 cup cooked	14
peas, average serving	4
sweet corn kernels, 1 cup	7
fruit, average piece	3
fruit, dried, 1¾ oz	9
nuts or seeds, 1 oz	3
coconut, fresh, 2½ oz	10
peanut butter, 1 oz	3
bread: white, 2 slices multigrain, 2 slices whole wheat, 2 slices rye, 2 slices	 2 3 5 3
cereals (average bowl): bran, 100%, ½ cup bran, processed wheat bran flakes corn flakes, rice krispies mixed cereals (flakes and fruit) muesli, natural oatmeal, instant cooked	 8.4 9 7 1 3 5 2
bran, unprocessed, 2 tablespoons	6
whole grain wheat cereal biscuit	2
wheat germ, 1 tablespoon	2
barley, cooked, 1 cup	4
pasta, cooked, 2 cups: white whole wheat	 4 9
rice, cooked, 1 cup: white brown	 2 3
wheat, cracked, cooked, 1 cup	5

*Right: Barbecued Vegetable
Kebabs (page 116) provide
vitamins C, A and the B group.*

Vitamins and minerals

They are needed only in tiny amounts, yet vitamins and minerals are vital to our well-being. Anyone eating a balanced and varied diet is unlikely to suffer from a lack of vitamins, but deficiencies or excesses of minerals can be a problem.

Vitamins

When some people feel worn out, they imagine they lack vitamins, so they buy vitamin supplements. Of course, if their diets really did lack vitamins, it would make more sense to improve their diets. In fact, vitamin deficiencies are rare in affluent Western societies and are seldom the cause of fatigue. Irregular meals and a diet with a poor balance of carbohydrate and fat are more common problems. And, in women especially, an iron deficiency may also be the cause of fatigue.

Vitamins are vital for good health but they are only needed in minute amounts. Once you have enough vitamins, there is no point in taking extra quantities. Some vitamins, in fact, are harmful in excess, while taking too much of others may mask the true problem. In addition, taking one vitamin or mineral means you may increase or decrease your body's needs for others. Vitamin supplementation, in other words, really is a minefield for amateurs.

Few people know how much of any vitamin they need. If the bottle says each pill contains 50 micrograms or 250 milligrams, they have no idea if these quantities are a lot or a little. Vitamin manufacturers do not always help, because sometimes they use 10 to 100 times as much of the vitamin as you need and other times they include only a fraction of the daily requirement.

The ideal way to get vitamins is from food. Contrary to the claims of some companies selling vitamin supplements, our food supply has plenty of vitamins. Our fruits, vegetables, grains, breads and cereal products are excellent sources, while protein foods such as meat, poultry, fish

and dairy products are also potent suppliers of essential vitamins and minerals. It is wrong to say that foods today do not contain vitamins. Analyses of foods show that even many fast foods are good sources of some vitamins and minerals. (This does not absolve fast foods of their excessive quantities of fat and salt and their lack of dietary fiber.)

If you decide to take vitamin supplements, they may do you some good, if:

❑ you are deficient in the vitamin in the first place (unlikely)
❑ you are taking some drug which destroys some vitamins
❑ you believe in them.

The attitude of vitamin-takers is important to their success. Those who think the vitamin will improve their health or sex life may find it does but so would a dummy pill. This is called the 'placebo response', which means that the belief in the product gives benefits rather than the specific substance consumed.

We have listed the major vitamins, why you need them,

their natural sources and how much would be unsafe if you feel you must take a supplement.

Vitamin A (also called retinol)
This vitamin exists only in animal foods. Carotenes, especially beta-carotene, in many fruits and vegetables can be converted to vitamin A in the body. Babies may not be able to convert carotene to vitamin A and may need some animal food (such as breast milk).

Why you need it For vision in dim light and to defend the body against infections. Vitamin A functions as an antioxidant to help the immune system. Carotenes may also give some protection against cancer.

Can it be harmful? Yes. Vitamin A is toxic in doses above 10,000 micrograms (or 10 milligrams) a day. Symptoms: dry red skin, eczema, fatigue, irritability, loss of appetite, joint pains, eventual liver damage.

Best sources For Vitamin A: liver, salmon and other seafoods, butter or margarine, cheese, milk. For beta-carotene: orange sweet potato, spinach, broccoli, pumpkin, red bell pepper, mango, apricots, pawpaw, peach and all green, red, orange or yellow fruits and vegetables.

Vitamin B

There are eight separate vitamins in this complex.

Thiamin (vitamin B1)

Why you need it Thiamin (B1) is needed by the enzymes which release energy from carbohydrates.

Can it be harmful? Unlikely to do any harm in excess.

Best sources All whole grain products (such as brown rice, whole wheat pasta, cracked wheat), bread (especially whole wheat), rolled oats, pork, Marmite or yeast extract, Brazil nuts, peanuts, breakfast cereals, dried yeast, ham, sweet potato, milk and fish.

Riboflavin (vitamin B2)

This is the vitamin responsible for the greeny-yellow color of urine after a multi-vitamin supplement has been taken.

Why you need it Riboflavin is essential in reactions involving proteins. It is also important for maintaining healthy skin and eyes.

Can it be harmful? Probably not. Any excess of this vitamin is quickly excreted in the urine.

Best sources Liver, kidney, dried yeast, Marmite or yeast extract, sardines, fish, milk, yogurt, almonds, pork, chicken, eggs, breakfast cereals, broccoli.

Niacin (vitamin B3)

Includes substances called nicotinic acid (no relationship to nicotine) and nicotinamide. Can also be made in the body from an amino acid called tryptophan.

Why you need it Niacin (B3) is essential in the release of energy from foods and needed to make some fatty acids and steroids in the body. Large doses will lower blood cholesterol. Important for healthy skin.

Can it be harmful? More than 1000 mg a day causes flushing and itchiness of the skin and may also cause gout or diabetes in some people. This vitamin also increases losses of glycogen from muscles so should not be used by endurance athletes.

Best sources Liver, tuna, chicken and all poultry, peanuts, sardines, fish and seafoods, beef, pork, lamb, Marmite or yeast extract, peanut butter, whole wheat pasta, brown rice, whole grain products and whole wheat bread, mushrooms, potatoes, peas, peaches and passion fruit.

Pantothenic acid (vitamin B5)

Why you need it Takes part in reactions involving fats and carbohydrates, helps produce hemoglobin in red blood cells and is involved in reactions in nerves and muscles. Contrary to popular belief, it will not stop hair going grey.

Can it be harmful? Very large doses (over 10,000 mg) may cause diarrhoea.

Best sources Liver, kidney, fava beans, mushrooms, salmon, watermelon, peanuts, chicken, pork, red meat, avocado, broccoli, oats, milk, bran cereals, and sweet potato. Royal jelly is a good source, too – but not good enough to justify its high price.

Pyridoxine (vitamin B6)

Like some other vitamins, this one comes in several forms: pyridoxine in vegetable foods and pyridoxal in animal foods.

Why you need it Pyridoxine takes part in reactions where amino acids are used for tissue repair. Also important in making red blood cells and in reactions in nerves and muscles. May be needed in higher quantities by some women taking the contraceptive pill.

Can it be harmful? Yes. Even though excess pyridoxine is excreted in urine, doses of more than 200 mg a day can cause damage to the nerve endings in hands and feet. This has occurred in women who have taken super-B capsules for premenstrual tension.

Best sources Fish, lentils and other legumes, bananas, pork, chicken, liver, red meats, avocado, walnuts, green vegetables, bran cereals and wheat germ.

Vitamin B12 (cyanocobalamin)

The most recently discovered vitamin. Also comes in several different forms and needs a substance secreted by the stomach for its absorption. After surgery to remove parts of the stomach, vitamin B12 must be given by injection.

Why you need it Needed for making the body's DNA and red blood cells. A deficiency leads to pernicious anaemia.

Can it be harmful? There are no reports of danger.

Liver and kidneys are both rich in iron. A 5 oz serving will supply almost a whole day's iron supply for a woman or two days' supply for a man.

Top left: Whole wheat breads are an excellent source of thiamin and niacin.
Left: Fish supplies thiamin, riboflavin and niacin.
Below: Eating plenty of fruit ensures adequate vitamin C.

Best sources Animal foods, such as liver, kidney, oysters, rabbit, cheese, red meat, chicken, milk, fish, yogurt and eggs. Mushrooms and fermented foods can provide some vitamin B12, but vegetarians may need a supplement.

Folate (folacin, folic acid)
Exists in several forms.

Why you need it Helps form new body cells. Involved in passing of information in genes and in making red blood cells. Action is intertwined with B12.

Can it be harmful? High doses may cause gastrointestinal problems and may mask a deficiency of B12.

Best sources Liver (especially chicken liver), dried yeast, green leafy vegetables, Marmite or yeast extract, peas, oats, avocado, oranges, peanuts and almonds.

Biotin (also known as vitamin H)
This vitamin is made by bacteria living in the intestine. Prolonged use of antibiotics may inadvertently wipe out these good bacteria. A substance called avidin in raw egg white also destroys biotin.

Why you need it Helps produce various fatty acids in the body and produces glucose in the blood when no carbohydrate is being eaten.

Can it be harmful? There are no toxic effects known.

Best sources Bacterial synthesis in intestine; found in chicken livers, liver, dried yeast, oysters, eggs, oats, artichokes and Marmite or yeast extract.

Vitamin C (ascorbic acid)
Captain James Cook was one of the first people to recognize the need for fresh foods on his ships so his sailors would not get scurvy. On his voyages he used limes and sprouted wheat grains to produce a fresh source of the vitamin at sea.

Why you need it Vitamin C is needed to make connective tissue which is important in bones, blood capillaries, cartilage, gums and teeth. It also helps iron to be absorbed from foods and functions as an antioxidant to help the body's immune system. It may also have an anti-cancer action. There is some evidence that it may reduce the severity of symptoms of the common cold – and about the same amount of evidence that it has no effect.

Can it be harmful? Taking more than 1000 mg a day may cause diarrhoea and may decrease the body's stores of copper and selenium.

Best sources Breast milk, liver and fruits and vegetables are the only sources. Highest levels in guava, red bell pepper, Brussels sprouts, broccoli, pawpaw, green bell peppers, oranges and other citrus fruits, cauliflower, kiwi fruit, rambutans, strawberries, mangoes, cherimoyas (custard apples) and cabbage. A serving of any one of these foods will provide more than you need for the entire day. Other fruits and vegetables also contain some. Some vitamin C is lost in cooking, so try to eat lightly cooked vegetables and include some raw products in your diet each day.

Vitamin D
Another vitamin which exists in several forms.

Why you need it Essential for the absorption of calcium and phosphorus into the bones.

Can it be harmful? This is the most toxic of all vitamins. Taking five times the normal daily requirement (see Table on page 163) can be dangerous, allowing calcium to be absorbed into soft tissues such as the kidneys and spleen.

Best sources Sunlight acts on a substance in the skin which forms vitamin D. (Tanning prevents any excess vitamin forming.) Also found in fish liver oils (such as cod liver oil), herrings, mackerel, salmon, sardines, tuna, eggs and dairy products and added to margarine.

Vitamin E
Occurs in several forms known collectively as tocopherols. The most potent form is d-alpha tocopherol.

Why you need it An important antioxidant which prevents the fatty acids in cell membranes being damaged by oxygen. Also important in red blood cells. There is no evidence that it will prevent ageing or encourage super sexual powers, as is sometimes claimed!

Can it be harmful? At very high doses of 300 mg, it may cause nausea. High doses in animals can stop the thyroid functioning normally but the effect in humans is not yet known.

Best sources Plant foods are the best sources, especially wheat germ oil and other vegetable oils (particularly cold-pressed oils), seeds (such as sunflower, sesame, poppy), avocado, wheat germ and nuts, plus seafoods.

Top: Avocado, nut butters and cold-pressed vegetable oils supply vitamin E.
Center: Most fruits contain vitamin C, but strawberries, mangoes and kiwi fruit are particularly rich sources.

Food and Nutrition Board—National Academy of Sciences
Recommended Dietary Allowances Dietary Reference Intakes

VITAMIN	INFANTS AND CHILDREN				BOYS			GIRLS			MEN		WOMEN	
	0–6 mths	7–12 mths	1–3 yrs	4–7 yrs	8–10 yrs	11–14 yrs	15–18 yrs	8–10 yrs	11–14 yrs	15–18 yrs	19–50 yrs	51+ yrs	19–50 yrs ● Pregnant ■ Lactating	51+ yrs
A (micrograms retinol equivalents)	375	375	400	500	700	1000	1000	700	800	800	1000	1000	800 ● + 0 ■ + 500	800
B1 (thiamin) (mg)	0.2	0.3	0.5	0.6	0.9	0.9	1.2	0.9	0.9	1.0	1.2	1.2	1.1 ● + 0.4 ■ + 0.4	1.1
B2 (riboflavin) (mg)	0.3	0.4	0.5	0.6	0.9	0.9	1.3	0.9	0.9	1.0	1.3	1.3	1.1 ● + 0.3 ■ + 0.5	1.1
B3 (niacin) (mg niacin equivalents)	2	4	6	8	12	12	16	12	12	14	16	16	14 ● + 4 ■ + 3	14
B6 (mg)	0.1	0.3	0.5	0.6	1.0	1.0	1.3	1.0	1.0	1.2	1.3	1.7	1.3 ● + 0.6 ■ + 0.7	1.5
Total folate (micrograms)	65	80	150	200	300	300	400	300	300	400	400	400	400 ● + 200 ■ + 100	400
B12 (mg)	0.4	0.5	0.9	1.2	1.8	1.8	2.4	1.8	1.8	2.4	2.4	2.4	2.4 ● + 0.2 ■ + 0.4	2.4
C (mg)	30	35	40	45	45	50	60	45	50	60	60	60	60 ● + 10 ■ + 30	60
D (mg)	5	5	5	5	5	5	5	5	5	5	5	10-15	5 ● + 0 ■ + 0	10-15
E (mg alpha tocopherol equivalents)	3	4	6	7	7	10	10	7	8	8	10	10	8 ● + 2 ■ + 4	8

Iron is best absorbed from animal products Consume vitamin C foods with iron to enhance absorption.

Vitamin K
Another vitamin which exists in several forms, some in plants, others made by bacteria and in some animal tissues.

Why you need it Essential for the normal clotting of blood.
Can it be harmful? Large doses of vitamin K may cause a type of anaemia.

Best sources Made by bacteria in the intestine. Also found in soy beans, spinach, cauliflower, cabbage, lettuce, broccoli and calve's liver.

Sources of iron	
HEME IRON	
Food	**Iron (mg)**
cooked clams, 3 oz	24
liver, 3½ oz	8.8
oysters, 1 dozen	7.2
beef, lean, cooked, 5 oz	4.7
lamb, chops, cooked, 2	4.0
veal steak, cooked, 5 oz	3.2
liverwurst, 2 oz	3.2
scallops, cooked, 3½ oz	3.0
sardines, 3½ oz	2.9
fish, cooked, 5 oz	2.1
salmon, canned, 5 oz	2.1
pork steak, cooked, 5 oz	1.8
chicken, cooked, 5 oz	1.8
NON-HEME IRON	
instant oatmeal, 1 packet (fortified)	6.0
lentils, dried beans or peas, 1 cup, cooked	3.6
breakfast cereal with added iron, average serve	1–16
cashews, 1¾ oz	3.0
peas, fresh or frozen, 1 cup	2.2
almonds, 1¾ oz	2.1
dried apricots, 1¾ oz	2.0
sunflower seeds, 1¾ oz	1.9
tahini, 1 tablespoon	1.8
peanuts, 1¾ oz	1.6
walnuts, 1¾ oz	1.2
whole wheat bread, 1 slice	1.0
broccoli, cooked, 3½ oz	1.0
vegetables, average serving	0.8
potato, 1 medium	0.8
wheat germ, 1 tablespoon	0.8

Minerals

Although vitamin deficiency is rare in affluent Western countries, there are people who lack minerals. Deficiencies of iron and calcium are the most common, although many people's diets also lack zinc. A lack of iron and calcium is common in women and teenage girls, mainly because they often shun the best food sources of these nutrients – meat (for iron) and milk (for calcium). You can make up enough of both these minerals without meat and milk but it takes some planning.

Iron

A lack of iron is a common cause of fatigue and lack of energy in women. Iron is needed for making hemoglobin, a pigment in red blood cells which carries oxygen to every cell in the body. If you do not have enough hemoglobin, less oxygen is delivered to each cell. The cells are then unable to produce their full potential energy level. The result, naturally, is a feeling of tiredness.

Iron deficiency occurs much more commonly in women because women need much more iron than men. This is because of blood loss each month with menstruation. During pregnancy and lactation, there are even greater losses of iron.

Traditionally, women have always eaten less meat than men so their diets have had less iron. Women also tend to eat less of other sources of iron such as whole wheat bread, cereals and grain foods.

If you feel constantly tired and irritable, you should ask your doctor to check your iron levels. This is done with a simple blood test to measure hemoglobin and ferritin (a storage form of iron). If these levels are low, it will explain any lack of energy you may feel.

It is easy to keep iron levels

Daily iron requirements	
men	10 mg
women:	
18–54 years	15 mg
54 and over	10 mg
pregnant	30 mg
lactating	15 mg
children:	
1–11 years	10 mg
12–18 years	12 mg

normal with a good diet but if they drop too low, it is best to take an iron supplement to get the blood levels back to normal as soon as possible. Iron needs vitamin C for its absorption, so choose a supplement which also contains vitamin C with the iron. Take it at mealtimes for best absorption.

Many people find that iron supplements make them constipated. You may be able to overcome this by increasing the fiber content of your diet and by drinking more water.

If that does not work, ask for a different iron supplement. The usual supplements contain ferrous sulphate but others available have ferrous fumarate which may be less constipating. The other alternative is to take half the recommended dose – some is better than none.

At the same time you should increase the iron content of your diet. Iron comes in two forms: heme iron in meat, fish and chicken and non-heme iron in vegetables, grains, legumes, nuts, seeds and eggs. You can absorb heme iron better than non-heme iron. Eating even a little bit of heme iron will increase the amount of non-heme iron you can absorb. So a small quantity of meat with your vegetables means you not only get iron from the meat but can absorb more of the iron from the vegetables.

The importance of calcium

The body needs a constant level of calcium in the blood for the normal action of nerves and muscles. A hormone released from the parathyroid gland controls this level by balancing calcium from the diet with stores in bones. If there is not enough in the diet, the parathyroid hormone stimulates the release of calcium from the bones. If there is more calcium than is needed to keep the blood level constant, the excess can be deposited in bones. Greater withdrawals than deposits mean that the bones gradually become less and less dense, until they are so chalky that they fracture from a slight fall, or just with the effort of standing. The loss of calcium happens so slowly that it is many years before weakness and chalkiness eventuate. There are no warning symptoms before a fracture occurs.

A number of factors govern calcium absorption into bones. The positive factors which are essential for its occurrence include:

❑ calcium in the daily diet
❑ normal levels of hormones (these are vital for calcium to be retained by bones)
❑ weight-bearing exercise (calcium goes into bones when muscles exert a pull on the bone during physical activity)
❑ vitamin D (usually from sunlight on skin).

Some factors also work against calcium retention. These include:
❑ too much salt (increases loss of calcium in urine)
❑ too much protein (reduces retention of calcium)
❑ nicotine from cigarette and cigar smoking
❑ very high levels of caffeine or

alcohol (small quantities are not a problem).

The chemical form of calcium may also be important. For example, we know that the type of calcium in milk and in dairy products is well absorbed. We do not yet know if the calcium in products such as soy milk is absorbed to the same extent.

Small, lightweight women have a lack of body weight and always have less pull of muscle on bone with weight-bearing exercise. They are more prone to weak, porous bones.

Blood tests are of little use in determining calcium levels in bone, because, as we have discussed, the body keeps its levels of blood calcium normal by withdrawing calcium from the bone. Blood tests will be normal, therefore, even when bones are dangerously thin. A special type of X-ray machine is needed to measure bone density. Such tests can be expensive but are recommended for women with a family history of fragile bones or spinal or hip problems.

General recommendations for calcium intake	
Age group	Calcium (mg)
infants:	
0–6 months	210
7–12 months	270
children:	
1–3 years	500
4–7 years	800
boys:	
8–10 years	1300
11–14 years	1300
15–18 years	1300
girls:	
8–10 years	1300
11–14 years	1300
15–18 years	1300
men:	
19–50 years	1000
51+ years	1200
women:	
up to menopause	1000
after menopause	1200
during pregnancy	1000
during lactation	1000

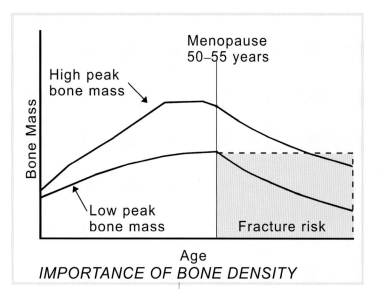

IMPORTANCE OF BONE DENSITY

Bone Mass / Age

High peak bone mass

Low peak bone mass

Menopause 50–55 years

Fracture risk

Osteoporosis

The condition of porous bones is called osteoporosis. It is very common in older women and is related to the fall in estrogen levels that accompanies menopause as well as a low-calcium diet, a lack of weight-bearing exercise and smoking. At the turn of this century, life expectancy for women was about 50 years, so few women lived long enough to develop osteoporosis. Over the past 20 or 30 years, many women have stopped working hard physically, no longer make a daily walk to the shops and carry home their food supplies, and have less calcium in their daily diet.

Among Western women, one in five can expect to be hospitalized for a severe fracture to the hip or spine between the ages of 50 and 70. This is a great expense for the community and an enormous burden for the many women who must endure the pain of such calamities. As many as 40 per cent of all women can also expect to fracture wrists, ankles and other bones as a result of a slight fall at some stage in their life. Osteoporosis is also the reason why many older people become stooped, have back problems and appear to 'shrink' with age. 'Dowager's hump' is often the first sign of osteoporosis.

How hormones control calcium in bones

In growing children, growth hormones ensure that calcium is deposited into bones. In adults, the sex hormones take over this role. At menopause, when the estrogen levels fall, calcium is no longer retained by the body. This may also occur in younger women and in female athletes if they lose so much body fat that their hormone levels change and their periods stop.

Osteoporosis also occurs in men, although the much slower loss of hormones and shorter life expectancy make it more rare.

Women at greatest risk of osteoporosis are those who:

❑ have had a low calcium intake throughout life;
❑ are small and/or light;
❑ have had little weight-bearing exercise.

To maintain bone density in women, most experts now recommend that those at risk of osteoporosis ask their doctor for hormone replacement therapy (HRT). This will cause their periods to continue past the usual menopause age but as they will be slight and regular, many women find it is worth the inconvenience to maintain their bone density.

Food	Calcium content (mg)
milk:	
regular or skim, 8 fl oz	300
low-fat (1 or 2 per cent fat), 8 fl oz	300
low-fat (1 or 2 per cent) fortified, 8 fl oz	350
buttermilk, 8 fl oz	300
cheese, 1 oz slice	230
cottage cheese, 1 cup	200
ricotta cheese, 1½ oz	215
yogurt:	
low-fat, 6½ oz	390
flavored, 6½ oz	310
salmon with bones, canned, 3½ oz	310
sardines with bones, canned, 3½ oz	380
crab, canned, drained, 3½ oz	155
fresh fish, 6½ oz serving	75
shrimp, 6 medium	120
oysters, 6	70
almonds, 1 oz	75
baked beans, 4½ oz	65
egg, 1	30
sesame seeds, 1 teaspoon	5
tahini, 1 tablespoon	35
soy milk:	
regular, 8 fl oz	35
fortified, 8 fl oz	290
broccoli, 3½ oz	30
cabbage, 2¾ oz	45
orange, 1 medium	30

Types of bone

There are two types of bone to consider in osteoporosis. Cortical bone in the long bones of the arms and legs is lost when there is insufficient calcium in the blood and the parathyroid hormone causes it to be withdrawn from bone. Cortical bone is also lost if we are lacking in vitamin D (from the sun). Trabecular bone is spongy bone which is found in areas such as the spine. It is lost when hormone levels change and when the diet contains too much salt. Over a lifetime, women lose half their trabecular bone and one third of their cortical bone.

Too thin? Too much exercise?

Dieting disturbs the hormone balance. Losing body fat often causes periods to stop. When this occurs, trabecular bone from the spine is lost. Strenuous exercise can have the same effect. This does not mean that women should stay fat and not exercise. Sensible, moderate dieting and increased exercise have a positive effect on health.

Girls and women with anorexia nervosa lose substantial amounts of bone and are at high risk of crushed vertebrae and other spinal problems and fractures. There is no evidence that a change to a better diet can undo the damage caused by periods of such intense dieting.

How much calcium?

The amount of calcium recommended for women varies. In the US, recommended dietary intake is 1000 mg per day. In some other countries, levels of between 800 and 1500 mg are recommended.

Many people think calcium is only important while children are growing. However, calcium continues to be absorbed into bones and peak bone density is not achieved until age 30 to 35 years. Women have so many bone problems after menopause that all young women and teenage girls should make sure they have plenty of calcium, some weight-bearing exercise and normal hormonal levels.

Women should not become so thin that their periods stop.

We are all genetically programmed so that different levels of body fat are appropriate for particular bodies. Any woman who is so thin that her periods stop has reduced her body fat to a level too low for her particular body. She may be fatter than someone else, but if her hormones are no longer functioning, she is too thin.

Sources of calcium

Dairy products contribute about 75 per cent of the calcium in most Western diets. In some Asian countries, calcium comes from small dried or fermented fish and from shrimp shells which are eaten with the shrimp or dried and powdered and used to give flavor to many other foods. Soy beans, nuts, green vegetables and oranges also contribute some calcium.

Some people do not digest dairy products well and, for them, milk, cheeses and the like are unsuitable food. Yogurt can be consumed without ill effect. Calcium is now added to orange juice and is another good source

Sesame seeds have been recommended as preferable to dairy products. However, they do not contain much calcium (see table) and it would be difficult to chew your way through the quantities needed to provide significant amounts of it. Some calcium values quoted for sesame seeds include the calcium present in the husks. Even if you could munch thoroughly enough for this calcium to be made available, the husks contain oxalic acid which forms a chemical complex with the calcium, tying it up so we cannot use it. Spinach also contains oxalic acid, so its calcium, too, is unavailable to the body. The only green leafy vegetable with bio-available calcium is kale. Making tahini is one way to grind enough sesame seeds to provide a richer source of calcium but as this paste is 50 per cent fat, it is not advisable to eat very much of it.

Raspberry Ice-cream (page 127) is a delicious source of calcium.

Understanding salt

Once considered a simple substance, salt is now confusing many people. Do we need it? How much do we need? Is it harmful? Should we choose sea salt, rock salt, vegetable salt, natural salt, sun-dried salt, iodized salt, cooking salt, salt substitute or just plain common salt? Or should we buy items that claim to be unsalted, have no added salt or are salt-free?

HEALTH TIP

Instead of using salt when cooking, add fresh or dried herbs, spices, a spoonful of lemon juice or lime. Use less water in casseroles and vegetables and you will lose less of the flavor of the ingredients and so need less salt.

Low-salt dishes can be full of flavor: try Chive and Pumpkin Soufflé (page 61).

Salt and sodium

Some people are confused by these terms. Salt is sodium chloride; the sodium makes up about 40 per cent of the salt molecule. Sodium occurs naturally in almost all foods, even in those to which no salt has been added. When salt is added to foods during processing, the total sodium content increases. Added salt contributes far more sodium than naturally occurring sodium.

If you are following a low-salt diet (for example, in order to reduce high blood pressure), do not add salt in cooking or at the table and avoid processed foods with added salt. Sodium which occurs naturally, however, is rarely a problem.

How much salt?

We all need the sodium and chloride found in salt. Along with potassium, sodium helps maintain the balance between water inside and around the cells, keeps blood volume normal and also controls the acidity balance in the body. Few people need to eat added salt since both sodium and chloride are found naturally in many foods. All seafoods, meats, eggs and milk are rich in these elements. Some vegetables are also adequate sources.

Most people eat too much salt and their kidneys must get rid of the excess sodium. This requires water and the thirst experienced after a particular salty meal is designed to make us provide the kidneys with the extra water they need to excrete excess sodium from the salt. The kidneys also look after the sodium balance at the other end of the scale. If we take in too little sodium in our diets, the kidneys will conserve it very efficiently.

Babies have great difficulty excreting salt and even a formula milk that is made up too strong will contain so much sodium that it puts an enormous strain on their immature kidneys. Babies do not inherently like salt and turn up their noses at their first salted foods. However, most adults keep giving salted foods to

children and their taste-buds become used to the flavor.

Eating heavily salted foods is also a cause of stomach cancer, which is the most common form of cancer in the world. Incidence of stomach cancer has decreased dramatically in Western countries since people began to preserve food with refrigeration and freezing instead of by salting.

Salt and blood pressure

The kidneys do a good job of getting rid of excess sodium but after years of effort they can fall down on the task and start to retain it. The extra water in the blood causes small blood vessels to become overly sensitive to signals which cause them to contract. The heart must then work harder to force blood through these narrow stiffened blood vessels and blood pressure rises. Not everyone is equally sensitive to the effects of excess sodium, but since we cannot yet predict who will become salt-sensitive, it makes sense for everyone to cut back on salt.

Daily needs for sodium

An estimated minimum requirement of 500 mg sodium a day is recommended for adults. Since about 40 per cent of salt is sodium, this equates to just 1.25 grams of salt a day.

Children under 10 years of age should eat a little less than this. One to five year-olds have a recommended daily minimum of 300 mg sodium, and six to nine year-olds 400 mg per day. Babies under 12 months should not have salt added to their meals; they will gain enough naturally occurring sodium from unprocessed foods. Salty breakfast cereals and other salted foods should not be a regular part of the diet. Prepared baby foods have no added salt.

It is best for everyone to avoid salt in cooking and at the table and to choose unsalted processed foods where possible. However, there is no need for most people to go to extremes of avoiding bread or even the occasional anchovy.

Taste

Once our taste buds become used to the flavor of salt, the liking for it tends to stay. If you decide to reduce the salt in your diet, you need to allow about three months for your taste buds to adjust and gradually learn to like the natural flavor of unsalted foods. Salt certainly adds flavor to foods – it adds the flavor of salt.

Try microwaving vegetables without water, steaming them or stir-frying them briefly either in concentrated chicken stock or in a little oil. You will find they retain so much of their original flavor that the need to add salt disappears altogether.

When making stews or casseroles, use less liquid. This leaves more flavor in the meat and vegetables so that little, if any, salt is needed. Herbs and spices, lemon juice and various vinegars can also give flavor without recourse to salt.

Where is the salt?

Almost everyone knows that anchovies or potato chips are salty. But few people realize how much salt comes in some breakfast cereals, savory crackers, certain breads or in foods such as cheese. There is nothing wrong with having a few of these foods and, if bread is the only salted food you eat, this will not cause any problems. But when every fast food and most prepared foods are laden with salt, the total intake can easily become excessive.

No add salt? Salt-reduced? Salt-free?

In response to changing palates, many food manufacturers are reducing the added salt in their products. Now for the confusion! 'No added salt' means just that. The only sodium present is that found naturally in the food. Bread with no added salt would have only the sodium from the flour, dry milk (if used) and any grains that have been included.

'Salt-reduced' means salt has been added but in smaller amounts than in the regular product. Salt-reduced breads have 30 to 60 per cent less salt than that in regular bread.

'Salt-free' is an old-fashioned term once used for foods without added salt. As almost all foods have some naturally occurring sodium; the term 'salt-free' is inaccurate and is no longer used.

Different types of salt

Many people pay more for 'sea salt' or 'vegetable salt', assuming they are somehow superior. All forms of salt are sodium chloride and should be used in moderation. Some vegetable salts have a strong flavor (usually from celery extract) so that you can use less of them than regular salt.

This may help reduce overall salt intake a little.

Salt substitutes

These products are mostly potassium chloride. Some have other additions to try to take away the bitter after-flavor which about 50 per cent of people experience from potassium chloride. No human population has ever eaten potassium chloride, so we have no long-term safety guidelines. For those who have certain kidney problems, potassium chloride may be harmful. It is probably better to make the effort to give up using salt altogether and let your taste buds enjoy the natural flavors of fresh foods.

Mineral water

A few years ago, many mineral waters had a high sodium content. Most have now changed. Look for those brands with less than 70 mg sodium/liter.

Rating the salt in foods (in terms of common servings)

High	Medium	Low
processed wheat bran	whole grain cereal	rolled oats
corn flakes	most mixed cereals	oat-bran cereals
processed rice cereal	milk	granola (home-made)
salted crackers	eggs	puffed wheat
prepared foods	bread, any type	salt-reduced bread
processed cheese	cottage cheese	quark
soy sauce	hard cheese	salt-reduced cottage cheese
processed meats	fresh meat	frozen or fresh vegetables
sausages	chicken	all fruits
salami, most deli meats	turkey	
most canned foods	canned vegetables	canned foods with no added salt
fast foods	home-made hamburger	
potato chips, snack foods	salted nuts	unsalted nuts
	butter	unsalted butter
	margarine	salt-reduced margarine
smoked fish	fresh fish	
fish canned in oil or brine	fish canned in water	

The facts about sugar

Breast milk is rich in the sugar lactose. Although lactose is not as sweet as regular sugar, it may well be the cause of many a lifetime love affair with sweetness. It is also likely that our early ancestors discovered that sweet-tasting foods were generally safe to eat, while bitter foods were often poisonous.

Natural?

Sugars occur in nature in many different forms. Milk has lactose, sugar cane has sucrose, fruits have fructose, sprouting grains and malt have maltose, honey has a mixture, predominantly of fructose, with some glucose and sucrose also present. In the context of their original food, any one of these forms of sugar could

Desserts don't have to be sinful: Winter Fruit Salad and Healthy Peach Crisp (page 133) will satisfy any sweet tooth.

be called 'natural'. However, the term 'natural' is not applicable when sugars are extracted from their natural source and concentrated to a level quite unlike their form in nature.

Other sugars

From time to time, some enterprising person tries to convince us that it is preferable to

use fructose or glucose or some other sugar in place of regular sugar. These sugars cost a lot more and, apart from a possibly more interesting taste, have no special value when they have been separated from their original food.

Fructose, when found in fruit, comes with many important vitamins, minerals and valuable dietary fiber. These other factors influence the way fructose is absorbed and used by the body. If we separate fructose from fruit, it loses its value just as sucrose loses any claim to nutritional worthiness once it is purified away from the valuable nutrients which accompanied it in the original sugar cane.

High-fructose corn syrup is a

popular substitute for sugar. It is simply another form of sugar. It is the major sweetener in soft drinks, but is also found in cake mixes and other desserts. Because fructose is a nutritive sweetener, recommendations for its use by the general public are the same as those for other sugars. It offers no caloric advantage.

Glucose is taken by some people for 'instant energy', especially before physical activity. The energy in muscles for physical activity depends on the carbohydrates eaten at least 12 hours beforehand. Glucose will raise blood sugar levels but may also stimulate an outpouring of insulin which will then cause blood sugar levels to fall again. Any excess glucose can also be converted to body fat. Glucose is useful for hospital patients after surgery. It is a waste of money for most other people and certainly for athletes.

Honey is a natural sugar, but nature intended it for bees, not humans. The quantities of vitamins and minerals in most honeys are ample for a small bee but insignificant in a human diet. Honey is very sweet so it can sometimes be used in smaller quantities than sugar to provide a sweet flavor.

Molasses is the least refined form of sugar from sugar cane. It has some iron and calcium but there is little data on how well these are absorbed.

Raw brown sugar in the US has been through a cleaning and purifying process, resulting in the loss of some nutrients and flavor. *Turbinado sugar* is a raw sugar with some molasses added to provide some color. Each of these sugars may give particular flavors but they have no special health benefits.

Problems with sugar

❑ Other carbohydrate foods also have vitamins, minerals, dietary fiber and, in many cases, protein along with their carbohydrate. Refined sugar is totally devoid of all of these important nutrients.

❑ Sugar, especially refined sugar, has the potential to damage teeth. Tooth decay is the most expensive diet-related health problem in western countries and many people regard it as almost inevitable. It is not. Tooth decay is entirely preventable.

❑ Sugar makes fats taste good. You would not eat chocolate, ice-cream, cakes, cookies or most pastries or desserts if the sugar did not sweeten and disguise the fattiness of the basic food.

❑ Sugary foods which do not contain fat, such as soda, many types of confectionery, popsicles and fruit drinks have no nutritional value. Most are loaded with artificial colorings and flavorings which may not be harmful for most people, but have no nutritional benefits.

❑ Sugary foods can easily displace other more nutritious foods in the diet. For example, many busy people will grab a candy bar at lunchtime rather than taking the time for a proper lunch of, say, healthy whole wheat sandwiches and fruit. Children will usually choose a sugary product – for example, if offered candy or apples, most children will choose candy. However, if there is no candy offered, they will happily eat apples.

❑ Because sugar is not filling, it is easy to consume large amounts inadvertently. For example, a glass of fruit drink is no more filling than a glass of water, even though it contains 18 grams of sugar.

Sugar and diet

For all these reasons, nutritionists recommend that sugar should have only a very minor role in the diet. In most Western societies, however, it plays a dominant role. This is often inadvertent. Most people are unaware of how much sugar is added to foods. Apart

from soda, fruit drinks, candy, cookies, cakes and some breakfast cereals, most individual foods are not high in sugar. But sugar is so ubiquitous that the total intake of sugar may average 240 teaspoons per person every week! More than 80 per cent of this sugar is in processed foods.

People with diabetes and those with raised levels of triglycerides must keep sugar consumption low and it makes sense for those who are overweight to cut back on sugar and take their calories from more nutritious foods.

Several committees have looked at the health effects of sugar and have come to the conclusion that, apart from its effects on dental decay, sugar is not solely responsible for any major health problems.

The major factor in eating sugar is moderation. Some recipes cannot be made without sugar but many dishes can be made with much less, especially if they have the natural sweetness and flavor of fresh fruits.

It is difficult to know how much sugar has been added to many foods as most food manufacturers are reluctant to tell you. They fear that the words, '55 per cent added sugar' on the breakfast cereal pack might turn consumers off the product!

You can get some idea of the amount of sugar added to a food from where sugar comes in the ingredient list. All food labels must list ingredients in descending order of magnitude. If sugar is one of the first few ingredients, it is present in large quantities. On the other hand, if it is listed below an ingredient such as salt or vanilla, it is unlikely that there is much present and you can ignore it.

Sugar and energy

Blood sugar, or blood glucose, is a major energy source for all body cells. We do not need to eat refined sugar as the body can easily convert all carbohydrates to glucose (see page 153). Proteins, either from food or from lean muscle tissue, can also be broken down to glucose. Fats cannot be

changed to glucose although excess sugar or glucose in the blood can easily be changed to fat.

The body strives to maintain blood glucose levels within normal limits because the brain needs glucose as fuel. Those with

Sugar content of foods

Food	Added Sugar (g)
cube sugar	4
granulated sugar, spoonful	8
jam, 1 tablespoon	17
fruit juice, sweetened, 8 fl oz	10
fruit drink, plus added water, 8 fl oz	18
flavored mineral water, 1 can	30
soft drink, 1 can	40
ice-cream, average serving	9
popsicle	16
gelatin dessert, ½ cup	20
chocolate topping, 2 tablespoons	25
cake, iced, average slice	30
apple pie, small	10
lemon meringue pie, 1 slice, 3½ oz	24
doughnut, iced, 2 oz	16
hard candy, 1¾ oz	43
licorice allsorts, 1¾ oz	34
cookies, plain sweet, 2	6
cookies, sandwich, 2	10
chocolate, 1¾ oz	26
corn flakes, 1 oz (small serve)	3
Coco-Puffs, 1 oz	12
granola, toasted, 2 oz	10
whole grain wheat biscuits, 2	1

fluctuating blood sugar levels or hypoglycemia may have a slight delay in restoring glucose levels to normal. In untreated diabetes, the level of blood glucose rises because glucose cannot move into the cells in the absence of insulin. If glucose 'spills over' into the urine, the blood glucose level may become dangerously low.

Losing weight

Weight reduction is sometimes said to be the most popular indoor sport for women. For many it is a semi-permanent game. They lose weight, put it back on, lose it again, and so on. With this pattern, there is a tendency for the final weight to creep upwards. Dieting actually makes them fatter. Some men also fall into this trap, although research shows that men make better dieters than women once they are persuaded they are too fat. This is not because men have stronger wills than women but is related to their reasons for losing weight. Most men who decide to lose weight usually do so for health reasons, at the instigation of their doctor. Most women want to lose weight for their appearance and make their own decision. A great many young women who make this decision are not even overweight to start with but, after years of strict dieting, they may well become so.

Weight or fat?

It is difficult to measure body fat under everyday circumstances. So we measure changes to body weight and hope they reflect decreasing or increasing levels of body fat. However, one problem with scales is that they do not distinguish between losses of fat and losses of water and muscle.

Overweight people do not have too much water or too much muscle. They have too much fat. Some women may accumulate extra fluid just before their period because of changes in hormones which affect sodium levels and water retention, but this is self-righting within a few days. Most people whose weight is above the healthy weight range (see page 14) have too much fat.

It is relatively easy to lose water from the body. For a start, up to two-thirds of the body's weight is water so there is plenty of it to allow fluctuations of a few pints (and a few pounds). Some water is also stored in muscles in association with a form of stored carbohydrate called glycogen. If you get rid of the glycogen, you lose a couple of pounds of water.

It is much harder to lose fat from the body. It won't melt and, contrary to the claims of some people, fat does not 'fall off'. Fat is only lost when it is burned for fuel. You can certainly help this process by getting a 'good fire' going but it is still relatively slow. Few people can burn off more than two pounds of fat a week,

and one pound is the maximum amount for many who are not very overweight or who are short. This is hardly what the diets promise with their claims that you can lose '10 pounds in 10 days' or that you can have 'thin thighs by Thursday'. These claims are false. You can lose weight fast but what you are losing is not fat but mainly water. Muscle is also much heavier than fat, so some muscle loss will also delude you into thinking you are doing well.

Before you dismiss the idea that half to one pound of fat is not much, imagine one or two large tubs of margarine. To lose that much fat from your body each week is quite a feat and not one to be dismissed lightly.

Why diets don't work

Most popular diets work on the principle of ridding you of water and muscle because the first results look impressive on the scales. If you want the scales to look good, you could cut of a leg! Absurd, yes, but so is the idea of trying to become slimmer by losing water. Fat people have a lower percentage of water than thin people. Excess water is not their problem.

It is these fast (water) weight-loss diets that have given carbohydrates such bad press. The diets 'work' by cutting carbohydrates to a minimum. This has several effects on the body. With less carbohydrate,

sodium balance changes and more water is excreted from the kidneys. Without carbohydrates in the day's meals, the body is also forced to use up its glycogen stores from muscles. As we have seen, glycogen not only has weight itself but every gram of glycogen has almost 3 grams of water stored with it. A low-carbohydrate diet forces the body to break down muscle tissue itself to replenish blood sugar levels and, since muscle is heavy, this looks good on the scales. These diets are useless for losing fat. Any weight lost is mostly from muscle and water, important components of the body you *don't* want to lose.

How to lose fat

The only way to lose fat is to eat fewer calories than your body burns for energy. There are a couple of conditions, however. Firstly, if you make the calorie deficit too large – in other words, if you cut back drastically on what you eat – the body will simply slow down the rate at which it burns energy. So it is important to cut back on the number of calories you eat only to extent that your body can still maintain its normal metabolic rate. Secondly, if your calories come from fat rather than carbohydrate, you will not burn up as much energy. The body finds it easiest to burn carbohydrates and hardest to burn fats. Any surplus fats are more likely to end up as body fat.

We mentioned earlier that the production of energy within the body is like a fire. Carbohydrates get the fire going. Without enough carbohydrate, fats are unlikely to be burned for energy.

Characteristics of a successful diet for fat loss:

❑ Relatively slow weight loss of one to two pounds a week.
❑ Has no gimmicks and promises no magic.
❑ Uses foods which are nutritious, readily available and can be incorporated into normal meals and snacks.
❑ Has a good balance of carbohydrate and protein with low levels of fat (about 60 per cent of calories from carbohydrate, 20 per cent from protein and 20 per cent from fat).
❑ Can be adopted (with slight changes) for life.

Counting calories

Many people pore over calories counters, totting up their daily total and making food choices accordingly. Calorie counters make interesting reading and can be useful in showing you how many calories there are in fast foods, pastries, fats and alcohol and how few are present in foods such as vegetables. However, counting calories ignores the source of the calories and takes no account of other important nutritional features such as dietary fiber, vitamins or minerals in particular foods.

Some people who count calories are also tempted to eat fewer and fewer calories. In practice, it is difficult to count calories without accurate data on weights of foods. The calorie book may tell you that a piece of steak has 200 cals and you may not realize the piece of steak they mean is not the same size as the one you're eating.

We cannot say that calories don't count. But it is probably fair to say that you should look beyond calories and take the kinds of food you are eating more into consideration.

Eating for fat loss

1. Look for high-fiber foods. Fiber is filling and one of the main reasons people eat fatty, sugary junk foods is because of an empty feeling. Dietary fiber is a natural obstacle to overeating.
2. Remember the Balanced Diet Pyramid. The principles are even more important.

❑ Eat most of breads, cereals (preferably whole grain), vegetables (including legumes), fruits, fish and seafoods.
❑ Eat moderately of high-protein foods such as lean meat, chicken, turkey, dairy products, eggs, nuts or seeds.
❑ Eat least of fat and sugar.

3. Within the categories of the Balanced Diet Pyramid, you can make choices. These are less important in the major category where all foods are desirable. In the middle category, choose the lower fat foods such as chicken or turkey without skin; low-fat meats such as veal, very lean cuts of beef, pork or game meats; and low-fat dairy products. In the 'eat least' category, be particularly strict.
4. Do not skip meals or fast. Without food, your metabolism will slow down and you will break down valuable muscle tissue to replenish your blood sugar level. This is undesirable, as muscle is active tissue that burns up calories.

Exercise

Exercise is almost as important as eating correctly when you are trying to lose weight. Exercise normalizes the appetite, increases metabolic rate, develops muscle tissue and burns up calories from body fat.

Over the years, people in affluent Western societies have not been eating much more than their forebears. Yet they have grown steadily fatter. The major reason has been the drop in physical activity and exercise. Our modern lifestyle is sedentary. We push buttons, drive cars, use labor-saving devices where our grandparents scrubbed, walked and worked physically hard every

day for most of their lives.

We have also decreased our intake of complex carbohydrate foods such as bread and potatoes and replaced them with fatty take-out foods. Many have shunned carbohydrates and then tried to exercise – but the exercise was unpleasant because energy stores in muscles were absent. As a result they believe exercise to be too tiring. Many women (both young and middle-aged) ask for any weight-loss program to

The principles of the Balanced Diet Pyramid are particularly important when you are trying to lose weight.

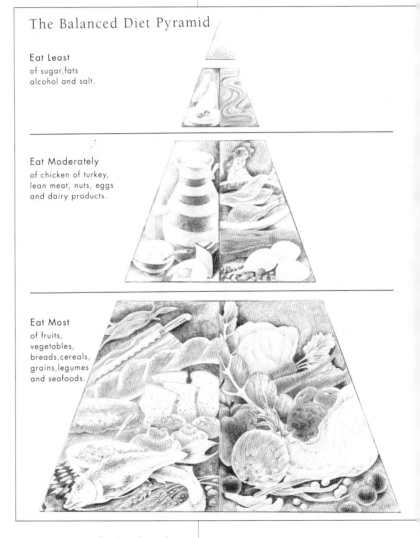

The Balanced Diet Pyramid

Eat Least
of sugar, fats alcohol and salt.

Eat Moderately
of chicken of turkey, lean meat, nuts, eggs and dairy products.

Eat Most
of fruits, vegetables, breads, cereals, grains, legumes and seafoods.

concentrate on food rather than exercise. Others have tried to lose weight sensibly by following a balanced diet which includes enough carbohydrate and have started exercising. They have found it to be an easy and enjoyable habit.

The ideal type of exercise for someone who wants to lose weight is of moderate intensity. Brisk walking, swimming, low-impact aerobics or water-aerobics are ideal.

Pregnancy and breast-feeding

There is an old saying that during pregnancy, you must 'eat for two'. It is true that a pregnant woman must eat the nutrients (such as protein, vitamins, essential fatty acids and minerals) for two but it does not mean she needs two adults' meals and snacks. The number of calories needed during pregnancy does not increase much. Pregnancy itself increases metabolic rate, which is why many pregnant women find they do not feel the cold as much as usual. However, most pregnant women reduce their physical activity as it is difficult to move as fast or as much as usual as they become bulkier. The drop in calories expended for activity balances the increased needs of the higher metabolic rate.

Because her nutrient needs are higher but her calorie requirements do not increase much, a pregnant women needs foods of high nutritional quality. Ideally, a woman who plans to become pregnant should have a top-quality diet for some months before pregnancy so she has good reserves of all nutrients before facing the nutritional stress of supplying the needs of a baby. If the diet is not adequate during pregnancy, the baby is at higher risk of low birth weight and possible abnormalities, while the mother may become deficient in iron or calcium.

Nutrients needed in extra quantities during pregnancy

Protein, B-complex vitamins (thiamin, riboflavin, niacin, B6, B12, folacin), vitamin C, vitamin D, vitamin E, iron, calcium, phosphorus, zinc, magnesium and iodine are all essential.

Shrimp and Citrus Fettuccine (page 88) makes a light nutritious meal.

Supplements or diets?

Theoretically, a good diet can meet the nutritional demands of pregnancy. In practice, however, few women can eat enough of iron-rich foods to supply the 15 mg of extra iron needed (normal requirement is 15 mg a day). Many women also fail to eat enough green leafy vegetables to supply their folacin needs. Stores

of this vitamin may be low in some women who have taken the contraceptive pill for some time before conception. Since a lack of folacin has been linked with abnormalities in the baby, many doctors routinely prescribe a supplement for iron.

Apart from iron and folacin, most women can get enough nutrients from a good diet and other supplements are rarely necessary. In any case, high-dose supplements should not be used in pregnancy. Their safety is not fully known and there have been instances of babies born with abnormally high vitamin requirements because their mothers took high-dose supplements during pregnancy.

Constipation

Many pregnant women become constipated. Extra fiber from plenty of vegetables, fruits and whole grain products should help. If the constipation is caused by taking iron tablets, a different variety of iron may help. (Try ferrous fumarate instead of the more common ferrous sulphate.) Drinking plenty of water and taking more exercise (such as walking or swimming) may also be of help.

Morning sickness

The nausea and vomiting which can occur in the first couple of months of pregnancy are caused by hormonal changes associated with the pregnancy. Some women never feel sick; others find the first three months consist of endless visits to the bathroom. Most 'morning sickness' (which can occur at any time of day) passes by three months.

Even when you feel nauseous, it is better to eat something. Dry foods are best – a piece of unbuttered toast, a couple of crackers, some boiled rice or a piece of fruit may help. Many women find it best if they eat one of these foods before they get up in the morning. It is best to eat small frequent snacks throughout the day rather than large meals.

Cravings

Some pregnant women crave particular foods during pregnancy. There is no evidence that these cravings represent any physiological inner wisdom. They are more likely to be psychological in origin. If you feel like strawberries at 3 am, or pickles with breakfast, go ahead and have them. If, however, you feel like eating whole boxes of chocolates or heaps of pastries, try to talk yourself out of the urge to indulge in large amounts of such fatty foods. If you want to eat dirt or chalk or some other non-food substance, resist the desire – it could be dangerous.

Drinks

Drinking plenty of water is just as important during pregnancy as at any other time.

There are doubts about the safety of large quantities of coffee during pregnancy and, until there is evidence that it is safe, it makes sense for pregnant women to keep levels of coffee low – say one or two cups a day. Weak tea seems to cause no problems.

Some herbal teas are not considered safe during pregnancy. Raspberry leaf tea is often recommended by some alternative health practitioners as being 'good for the uterus'. However, pharmacologists have warned that raspberry leaf tea causes the uterus to contract and this could, theoretically, cause a miscarriage. It is probably best avoided. Other herb teas which should not be used include comfrey tea, juniper, pennyroyal, sage, senna and yarrow. The safety of ginseng is also unknown, although most ginseng products contain so little of this oriental root that they are unlikely to do much harm.

Alcohol should also be avoided during pregnancy. Large amounts of alcohol can damage the baby but the safety of small doses is not fully understood. As a precaution, women who are pregnant or trying to become pregnant should avoid alcohol.

Weight gain

Too little weight gain in pregnancy may harm the baby: too much extra weight may be a problem for the mother after the baby is born. In general, women should aim for a weight gain of at least 25 to 35 pounds for the whole pregnancy. This may not be distributed evenly and many women find they do not gain much weight at all during the last month or so. As a general rule, weight gain of two or four pounds for the first three months and then two to four pounds a month is recommended. Some people tell pregnant women not to worry how much weight they gain but excessive weight gain will put greater strain on your back and can cause obstetric problems. It can also be a bit demoralizing to retain so much weight after the baby is born.

Breast-feeding

When feeding a baby, you need higher levels of nutrients and more calories. Over nine months or so of breast-feeding, an average of 1000 extra calories a day is needed for lactation. This is easier than the situation in pregnancy when large amounts of extra calories are not usually needed. During lactation, you simply eat more of the nutritious foods.

Most women find they are hungrier than usual once breast-feeding is established. This is normal and shows the body is asking for the extra calories needed to produce breast milk. Many women gradually lose any extra fat they accumulated during pregnancy. A few find their new, increased appetite overdoes things and they gain weight. The best idea is to eat more, but not so much that you gain weight.

Strict dieting is not appropriate when you are breast-feeding, as you risk losing your milk. However, if you need to lose weight, you can make sure you eat enough of the nutritious foods and avoid extra fat and sugar. This is usually enough for a slow, steady loss of body fat and need not affect milk supply.

If you are tired, you may find your breast milk supply is affected. Try to get enough rest, to include some exercise (take the baby for a walk) and eat only healthy foods. Relaxation techniques can also help fight fatigue, a common complaint at this time. If your milk supply does decrease, the best way to build it up again is to let the baby suck more frequently. Forget work for a while, or ask other family members or a friend, relative or neighbor for help so you can spend more time feeding the baby and relaxing for a few days. The milk supply will quickly re-establish itself.

Sample menu for a pregnant woman

Breakfast

Orange juice, ½ cup
Oatmeal, ½ cup
Whole grain cereal with fruit and low-fat milk
Whole wheat or enriched toast, 1 slice
An egg, if liked
Peanut butter, 2 tsp
Jam, honey or Marmite
Weak tea or low-fat milk
Decaffeinated coffee or tea

Morning Snack

Apple
High bran cereal, ¼ cup
Non-fat yogurt, ½ cup

Lunch

Turkey (2 oz) sandwich on rye or whole wheat bread with salad and 1 tsp mayonnaise or hot dish such as beans on toast or home-made soup
Green salad
Salad dressing, 2 tsp
Fresh peach
Non-fat or low-fat milk, 1 cup

Midafternoon

Non-fat or low-fat milk, or weak tea
Graham crackers, 4 squares

Dinner

Baked chicken breast, 3 oz
Baked potato with 2 T sour half-and-half
Peas and carrots, ½ cup
Green salad
Salad dressing, 2 tsp
Fresh pear

Evening

Non-fat frozen yogurt, 1 cup

Teenagers

At this stage, parents should stop taking responsibility for food choices and teenagers should learn to select their own food. Most will need some guidance and parents should still make sure healthy foods are available in the home. Teenage boys and girls often have different eating patterns, the boys being 'unfillable' and the girls eating little – and then, perhaps, bingeing on junk food. Surveys confirm that many teenage girls have poor diets, lacking enough complex carbohydrate, dietary fiber, iron and calcium. Because teenage boys eat so much more food, few lack any major nutrients. However, many teenage boys eat large quantities of fat and set themselves up for future problems with high blood fats, excess weight and high blood pressure. Half of the teenagers in the US already have high levels of blood cholesterol.

Fast foods are one of the major problem areas for teenagers. Eating fast foods occasionally does little harm, but a steady diet of such fatty foods is not good. Some fast food meals have enough fat to supply more than the maximum desirable level of fat for the whole day. Most will also supply about two days' desirable salt intake but lack dietary fiber and nutrients such as vitamins A and C and folic acid. This is because most fast food meals have little fruit or vegetables. If you have had a fatty fast food meal, it is important to include plenty of fruit and vegetables and very little fat or salt in the next few meals.

Teenagers also tend to eat erratically, mostly because their lives tend to be rather erratic. Friends become more important than family and what friends are eating becomes what they eat. Some stronger-willed teenagers, of course, maintain a healthy diet despite what everyone else is eating.

The most important feature of the teenage diet should be to follow the Balanced Diet Pyramid as much as possible. It does not matter if the foods are divided into three evenly sized meals or a series of snacks throughout the day and night. As long as the day's food keeps to the principles of eating most of fruits, vegetables, breads and grains and cereals, moderately of meat and dairy products (or alternatives),

and least of sugars and fats, there should be few problems.

Teenage boys

The growth spurt for teenage boys is usually spread over about four years, although there are peaks. It is not uncommon for boys to grow six or more inches in height in a year. This may occur at any time between 13 and 18 years of age. At such times, the well-known teenage appetite rears its head. Boys may eat breakfast cereal by the box, follow it with an entire loaf of bread and two hours later be back in the kitchen looking for more food! They devour any leftover food before it has had time to hit the refrigerator and watch with eagle eyes to see if anyone is going to leave anything edible on their plate. This is all normal, and necessary, behavior for a rapidly growing boy.

Most teenage boys need much more food than their fathers. Occasionally fathers resent this. Having been used to getting the biggest serving of food, they feel threatened by a youngster usurping their place and claiming the largest plate of food. An active teenage boy going through a growth spurt needs up to twice as much food as his father. Because they are growing so rapidly, teenage boys also have a high need for nutrients such as protein, iron, calcium and most other vitamins and minerals. To provide energy for sports

activities as well as growth, complex carbohydrate foods are important. Cereals, bread, muffins, rice, pasta and toast are important foods. So are fruits, lean meat and low-fat milk.

Some teenage boys do not need so much food, because they are not yet growing rapidly, or have stopped growing, are not destined to be tall or are not physically active. These boys still feel hungry and should eat according to their appetite. However, if they start to accumulate too much fat, they should limit foods such as all forms of fat, fried and fast foods, sugar, soft drink and juices, fatty snack foods, cakes, cookies and pastries, chocolate and candies. They should also make sure meats are lean and in moderate portions and that they do not consume too much cheese or milk. There is no need to limit foods such as bread (but skip the spread or use a low-fat variety), cereals (but use low-fat milk) or fruit (eating the whole fruit is preferable to drinking the juice).

Drinks are often responsible for excess weight in both boys and girls. It is difficult to eat 10 apples in an hour, but easy to take in all their calories by drinking apple juice. Once the fiber in fruits has been removed, it is easy to overconsume the product. Fruit juice is a healthy food, but in moderation only. Remember that two glasses of orange juice have the same number of calories as six slices of bread but it is much easier to drink the juice than to eat the bread. The calories from drinks add up very quickly. Soft drinks are also high in calories.

Some teenage boys also drink liters of milk. Milk is an excellent source of calcium, but one liter of low-fat milk a day is probably enough. Others take to coffee. A couple of cups of coffee a day does not do any harm, but too much coffee can give teenagers the jitters, interrupt sleep and eventually become a dependency. Weak tea or decaffeinated coffee are better choices.

Eating between meals is normal for teenagers. Toast, cereal, sandwiches, pretzels, muffins, low-fat milk smoothies or milk shakes (using fruit for flavoring), low-fat yogurt, pasta, hot unsweetened popcorn, rice or any kind of fruit all make ideal snacks.

For a break in study, a run around the block, a brisk walk or some other type of physical activity is a better energy booster than sweet foods or coffee.

Teenage girls

Some of the points mentioned for teenage boys also apply to girls. One of the major differences, however, is that girls' growth spurts tend to be over much more quickly than boys'. While they are growing rapidly, teenage girls are usually ravenous. Some maintain this appetite when their growth rate slows down and they no longer need so much food. If this happens, a girl is likely to start putting on weight unless she gets a lot of exercise.

Other teenage girls try to ignore their hunger and eat little in an attempt to get very thin. Most of these girls have poor diets and their lack of nutrients usually shows up in physical weakness and fatigue. The solution is to eat more. This is not as simple as it sounds because most teenage girls have a distorted body image and think they are much fatter than they really are. No cajoling or parental

pleading will make them eat more of the foods they think are fattening. Eating disorders can develop and can sometimes be serious.

Most girls with anorexia nervosa or bulimia nervosa are frightened of getting fat. Some have been plump in their pre-teenage years and want to remove any excess fat from their bodies. There is a continuum between a normal healthy desire to stay slim and an eating disorder. Just when the behavior changes from normal to abnormal can be difficult to diagnose. Some parents fear their daughters have anorexic tendencies when they are only behaving like most teenage girls. Others miss the clues to eating problems.

Many girls go on diets. Most have an occasional binge. Neither of these activities can therefore be classed as abnormal. However, when dieting or bingeing starts to dominate every waking moment for a teenage girl, the situation is out of control and you may need to seek professional help. Parents' nagging is unlikely to do any good. Many girls see their mothers as 'fat' and do not want to end up the same. This does not create a helpful environment for any useful dialogue between mother and daughter. If you suspect an eating disorder, try to see a dietitian who specializes in this area. A dietitian is usually able to iron out any dietary misconceptions and prevent a major eating problem from developing.

Part of the problem is the changing nature of the body. First a teenage girl develops breasts, a symbol of womanhood which our society applauds. Most girls do not mind these changes and those who are late developing are often the ones who have the greatest worries.

The same hormones which put fat on the breasts of teenage girls then put fat on the hips and tummy. About the same time, most teenage girls cut back on the amount of sport and physical activity they do. Suddenly they are conscious of their new body.

Our society has worshipped slimness. Models are often chosen when they are young so they will not have the normal fat deposits on hips and tummies. Other models half-starve themselves or exercise fanatically to prevent the slightest sign of a normal female bulge appearing.

Fruit Rounds and Apricot Squares (page 131) make better between-meal snacks than high-fat chocolates and cookies.

Girls of normal weight see these role models and feel they do not live up to the prescribed standard. The magazines they read tell them how to lose unwanted weight fast. Even those girls who have no excess weight begin to feel they must be the wrong shape or size.

Few people know much about nutrition and there are many misconceptions which have arisen from media hype and sensational stories about food. When teenage girls start to become conscious of their bodies and the effect food has on their weight, they may become victims of these wrong ideas. For example, most teenage girls think that bread and milk are fattening. They reject both but drink soft drinks and eat chips, chocolate and French fries, all of which are likely to contribute far more calories.

For teenage girls who are genuinely overweight, a sensible diet is important (see *Losing weight*, page 172).

Energy for older people

As people age, their need for nutrients does not decrease. If physical activity levels stay the same, the need for calories does not drop much, either. However, most people cut back on their physical activity as they grow older and this leads to a loss of muscle, lower metabolic rate and a reduced need for calories. The clue to keeping up energy levels is to maintain physical activity.

You may need to change the physical activity you do as you grow older. But there is no reason why walking, hiking, cycling, tennis, swimming, water aerobics, bowls or golf cannot become a part of your life. Many older people who are not overweight can also enjoy running, skiing or low-impact aerobics, with no ill effects on their health – and many benefits.

Unfortunately, our society values youth, and many older people feel they are not a welcome part of some sporting activities. It is time we changed such silly attitudes – but it is only by older people participating in various physical pursuits that society will change its expectations.

Those who work with older people are unanimous that the older people with the most energy are the ones who keep up physical activity, take care with their diet and don't smoke. Those who lack energy are the ones who do little, eat and drink too much and/or smoke. You can take your choice but the health and lifestyle of each group are vastly different.

Good nutrition and exercise can help defer the effects of ageing. This applies to the internal ageing of the body more than the external features. A healthy diet will not necessarily give you smoother skin or hair that doesn't turn grey. But a healthy diet can give you smooth clean arteries through which blood can flow freely to nourish all body cells and a body not overburdened with excess fat. You can also maintain normal blood pressure through diet and physical activity. These are more important signs of youthfulness than some of the unavoidable surface lines.

Many older people find they already have health problems such as high blood pressure, high levels of blood fats or diabetes. Each of these problems responds to a good diet and appropriate levels of exercise.

If you are overweight, follow a balanced diet (see page 172) and gradually lose your excess pounds. If you have any of the health problems mentioned above, you will need a drastic cutback in the amount of fat you eat. Make sure you use only low-fat products and eat plenty of healthy foods such as fruits and

vegetables, fish, whole grain products. With a better diet, you will also find that some walking or other exercise helps.

Those who have high blood pressure should also avoid added salt and choose low-salt products wherever possible. If your taste buds are already addicted to high salt levels, give yourself about two months to cut back on salted foods gradually. You will find your tastes change but it usually takes several months.

Constipation may also be a problem, especially in those who are not used to eating enough fiber. Adding fiber from fruits, vegetables, legumes, oats, cereals (including wheat or rice or oat bran cereals) and other grains such as barley, brown rice, corn or cracked wheat is preferable to taking laxatives.

Some older people ask if it is worth their while making dietary changes. That depends on how much you want to feel better and have more energy. If you are content to sit around for the rest of your life taking the appropriate medications, the answer is probably no. If, however, you want to enjoy life to the full and give your body the best fighting chance of making such enjoyment possible, then it is worth making the changes.

Healthy eating and exercise are not unpleasant – both become a joy once you get used to them. Most people who adopt a healthier lifestyle are glad they did. There are thousands of stories of those whose health was going downhill fast who have arrested the decline by taking responsibility for their own health. This does not mean taking 45 vitamin and mineral supplements a day. It simply means adopting a more prudent diet and exercise pattern.

Fish is an important ingredient of diet for everyone, especially for older people. A heart attack (still the most common cause of death in older people) occurs when a clot blocks an artery to the heart. This is more common in older people because their arteries are already partially blocked by fatty deposits and even a small clot will cause a blockage. Fish contains special fatty acids which help prevent blood clots forming. Studies have shown that even one to three fish meals a week can significantly reduce heart attacks in older people. As a bonus, fish fats may also give relief from inflammatory reactions in some forms of arthritis. You can eat fish fresh or canned, hot or cold (in sandwiches or salads) but do not cook it by frying in fat. Broiling, barbecuing, wrapping in foil and baking, cooking on a non-stick pan or microwaving are all fat-free methods of cooking fish.

Some older people spend a lot of money taking various supplements. At this stage, there is no good evidence that these reduce the effects of ageing. If you decide you want to take vitamins do not take more than the recommended daily intake (see page 163).

Frequently-asked questions
Question
Should older people take antioxidants to delay the effects of ageing?
Answer
Antioxidants are substances which prevent the harmful effects of 'free radicals'. These small, highly reactive particles try to stabilize themselves by attacking the membranes around cells.

Antioxidants such as vitamins A, C and E prevent the free radicals damaging the body. Many people take these vitamins to try to increase the life span of the cells in membranes. Research is continuing into the action of antioxidants but until we know these substances are safe in high doses, it is best to get natural antioxidants by eating plenty of fresh fruits and vegetables as well as foods like wheatgerm, seeds and nuts to supply vitamin E.
Question
If an older woman has not had sufficient calcium throughout life, will a supplement prevent osteoporosis?
Answer
Unfortunately, calcium is not well absorbed into bone after the menopause unless the hormone estrogen is also taken. Hormone replacement therapy plus calcium (preferably from low-fat dairy products) does preserve the strength of bones. However, calcium on its own is insufficient to replace calcium in bones in older people.
Question
How much should an older person eat?
Answer
It depends on size and physical activity. Those who exercise can eat more than those who do not.

Sample menu for older people

Breakfast

Oatmeal with wheat germ and low-fat milk
Whole wheat toast and low-fat spread with
sliced tomato or low-calorie jam, or Marmite
Tea

Lunch

Salad with plenty of fresh vegetables
Whole wheat bread
Fresh fruit
Glass of low-fat milk

Dinner

Fish or a small serving of lean meat or chicken (or use legumes)
Large serving of vegetables
Fruit, fresh, poached or canned without sugar
One glass of wine, if desired

Between meals

Water, some tea or coffee (not more than 4 cups a day), fruit

The older body still needs vital nutrients, so cut back on fats, sugar and alcohol rather than decreasing valuable foods such as breads, cereals, fruits, vegetables and low-fat dairy products. Older people need less meat than those who are younger.

Top: Fish and fresh vegetables are an important part of an older person's diet – along with the occasional glass of wine.

Vegetarian diets and other alternatives

Many people have adopted a vegetarian diet. Others follow a partial vegetarian diet, still eating fish and chicken but not red meat. Such diets usually have no nutritional problems. Other people simply omit meat and, although they may think they are eating more healthfully, their diets often lack nutrients. They do not eat meat but neither do they eat the legumes and the range of grains, seeds and nuts which are so important in a true vegetarian diet.

If a wide range of such foods is included, the vegetarian diet can be adequate – and may be healthier than that of meat-eaters. Nutritional risks can occur, however, with more extreme dieting strategies and these are outlined below.

Most of the world's population is vegetarian, either by choice or because of religious, economic, or practical considerations. In many places where there is no refrigeration, legumes, grains, nuts, seeds and fruits and vegetables keep well whereas flesh foods go bad.

Studies have shown that, compared to those on a typical affluent Western diet, vegetarians are less likely to suffer heart disease, stroke, diabetes and gall bladder disease and have a lower incidence of many types of cancer including breast and bowel cancer. This may be because

vegetarians are also less likely to smoke and indulge in other unhealthy behavior, but is probably because their diet has less fat and more dietary fiber.

There are two major types of vegetarian diet: (1) the lacto-ovo vegetarian diet, which includes milk, yogurt, cheese and eggs and (2) the vegan diet with no animal products. Nutritionally, either type of vegetarian diet can be adequate. In practice, it is much easier for a lacto-ovo vegetarian diet to supply enough nutrients because the dairy products and eggs have more concentrated nutrients. A vegan diet can also be adequate although some small children may have difficulty eating the quantities and varieties of foods needed for their requirements.

Lacto-ovo vegetarianism

A major advantage of any vegetarian diet is its high fiber content. But lacto-ovo vegetarian diets can still be high in fat, especially if considerable amounts of fried foods, chocolate, cheese and high-fat dairy products are used. Fiber will give protection against some of the harmful effects of too much fat, but cannot overcome them completely. It is also easy to kid yourself a meal is healthy just because it seems light and avoids meat – but, for example, a slice of spinach quiche and salad can have about six times as much fat and less dietary fiber than a piece of lean steak and some fresh steamed vegetables.

A lacto-ovo vegetarian diet can, in theory, provide all the necessary nutrients but there is some risk of deficiencies in iron, calcium, zinc and vitamin B12. The most common problem occurs with women, who are at risk of a lack of iron – a nutrient well supplied by meat. Legumes, nuts, fruits and vegetables, grains and green vegetables can supply iron to meet even the high requirements of women, but many women omit legumes and eat insufficient quantities of valuable foods such as whole wheat bread and vegetables, thus depriving themselves of iron. Iron supplements can help but some cause constipation.

Sources of iron are listed on page 164 and of calcium on page 166. From these tables, you can see that a vegetarian diet can supply adequate quantities of these nutrients.

Zinc is a mineral which takes part in many chemical reactions in the body. It is important for growth and sexual development and takes part in healing wounds and keeping cell membranes healthy. Zinc is not well absorbed from foods which have a high content of phytic acid – and these include many of the whole grain products. Zinc is also absorbed better from animal foods than from vegetable products.

Food sources of zinc for vegetarians include: eggs, cheese and milk (for lacto-ovo vegetarians) and lentils, Brazil nuts, peanuts, rolled oats (less phytic acid than whole wheat products), baked and other beans, whole wheat bread and breakfast cereals, walnuts and other nuts. Fruits and vegetables have little zinc.

It is unwise to take zinc supplements in large doses as excess zinc can interfere with the absorption of iron and copper.

Vitamin B12 is found mainly in animal products. Lacto-ovo vegetarians can get the vitamin from eggs, milk, yogurt and cheese. For young children who are no longer breast-fed, a vitamin B12 supplement may be advisable.

Children whose parents believe in a lacto-ovo vegetarian diet generally have few nutritional problems. However, it is important to allow them to have regular milk, yogurt, eggs and some cheese as well as a variety of grains, legumes, fruits, vegetables, seeds and ground nuts or nut butters such as peanut butter. For some children, a vegetarian diet may contain so much fiber that they develop loose stools. In such cases, use white rice, white bread and white pasta occasionally instead of whole wheat all the time.

Vegan diet

This is the true vegetarian diet and it omits all animal products. Legumes, grains, seeds, nuts, fruits and vegetables have to supply all nutrients. As long as enough is eaten and there is plenty of variety, a vegan diet can be quite adequate for an adult.

For children and those needing a high calorie intake (such as endurance sports people), a vegan diet can present difficulties. Small children may not be able to sit at a table long enough to eat sufficient food to meet their high growth needs and the high fiber content of the diet may be too much for their small intestinal tract. Athletes may be unable to devote the time and chewing effort necessary to eat the large bulk of food needed to fuel their very high calorie requirements. And, for those who do manage to eat enough, the high bulk and dietary fiber may be a problem.

In practice, vegans, often don't eat enough and are likely to be low in nutrients such as calcium, and iron. Foods such as almonds, soy products, soy yogurt and tahini can help increase calcium while legumes, grains and green vegetables will supply iron.

Vitamin B12 occurs mainly in animal products so can be in short supply in a vegan diet. Mushrooms and fermented soy products such as tempeh can provide some B12 and some medical researchers believe the vitamin may be made by bacteria within the intestine. Contrary to popular belief, comfrey does not contain an active form of vitamin B12. As it contains dangerous

---

Sample menus for vegetarians

LACTO-OVO VEGETARIAN

Breakfast

Fresh fruit
Oatmeal or whole wheat cereal with milk
Toast with peanut butter, jam, or Marmite
Egg or baked beans, if desired

Lunch

Whole wheat salad sandwiches with avocado spread and cottage cheese, cheese or egg or salad or vegetable dish with cheese and nuts or seeds
Fresh fruit

Dinner

Legume, rice, pasta or grain dish with seeds, nuts, cheese
Vegetables or salad
Whole wheat bread
Fruit and yogurt or custard

Snacks

Bread, fresh or dried fruit, nuts, seeds, milk, cheese or yogurt

Drinks

Water, milk, juices

VEGAN

Breakfast

Oatmeal or granola with soy milk or fruit juice
Fruit
Whole wheat toast with peanut butter
Baked beans or other legumes, or sweet corn if desired

Lunch

Whole wheat sandwiches with avocado, peanut or other nut butters, salad, or a legume, grain, pasta, rice or other grain or vegetable dish with seeds and/or nuts
Fruit

Dinner

Legume, tofu, grain, pasta or potato or other vegetable dish
Vegetables or salad
Whole wheat or rye bread with margarine or avocado spread
Whole wheat apple crisp or fruit with tofu ice-cream

Snacks

Breads, crisp breads, fresh or dried fruit, nuts, seeds, soy milk

alkaloids, it should be avoided.
Pregnant women on vegan diets
should take supplementary B12.

**Common questions
about a vegetarian diet**

Question

Is a vegetarian diet safe for
teenagers?

Answer

Yes, provided the growing
teenagers eat a variety of foods
including grains, seeds, nuts,
legumes and preferably some
dairy products. Many teenage
girls do not like eating meat but
also do not eat enough of the
foods listed above. As a result
they can become tired and cranky
(from a lack of iron) and fail to
deposit calcium in their bones.
Eventually they could develop
anemia and weak bones,
especially in the spine.

Question

Will a vegetarian diet help lower
high blood pressure?

Answer

Yes, studies have shown that
people with high blood pressure
can reduce it with a vegetarian
diet. The exact reason for this is
not yet known.

Question

Is a vegetarian diet safe for small
children?

Answer

Small children have very high
requirements for nutrients but
most do not have huge appetites.
This means that young children
need to eat foods which are fairly
concentrated sources of nutrients
without being too 'bulky'. A child
eating just fruits, vegetables and
bread would be unlikely to eat
enough of these foods to supply
sufficient nutrients. If a
vegetarian diet includes milk,
yogurt, cheese or eggs as well as
legumes (or legume products
such as fortified soy milk and
tofu), it can be adequate and safe
for children.

Question

Can canned beans be used in
place of dried beans?

Answer

Yes, canned beans are nutritious
products. Their only drawback is
their salt content. You can now
buy reduced salt beans and

| Food combinations to supply complete protein—the following vegetable foods go well together to give a complete mix of amino acids ||
Combination	Example
legumes + grain (wheat)	baked beans on toast
grain + leafy vegetables	tabbouleh
legumes + corn	tortilla with beans
peanuts + grain (wheat)	peanut butter sandwich
tofu + seeds	tofu with sesame seeds
legume + grain (wheat)	couscous (chickpeas and cracked wheat)
legume + grain (rice)	soy beans and rice
legume + grain (wheat)	falafel in pita bread
legume + grain (wheat)	dhal with chapatis
legume + seeds	chickpea dip blended with tahini
legumes + seeds	peanuts and sunflower seeds
legumes + grains (rice)	lentil curry and rice
legumes + grains (wheat)	lentil burger
grains + seeds	bread with added sesame seeds
nuts + tofu	tofu with stir-fried cashews
nuts + seeds + grain	granola
dairy products + grains	pasta and cheese or granola and milk or rice pudding cooked with milk

the salty liquid from other beans
can be drained and discarded.

**No fat, no cholesterol, no salt,
no sugar, no alcohol diet**

Many people have adopted a
spartan approach to diet and
religiously avoid fat, cholesterol,
sugar, salt and alcohol. As well as
following this strict dietary
approach, some people also
increase their amount of exercise
in order to achieve reduced
blood-cholesterol levels, weight
loss, falls in high blood pressure
and blood-triglyceride levels.

Such extreme approaches
certainly work but a modified
approach is likely to produce
equally good results.

Diets such as the Pritikin
program are not suitable for

infants and young children.
Breast milk derives 50 per cent of
its calories from fat; it also
contains cholesterol. These are
important to the rapidly growing
infant and a sudden change to a
diet with only 10 to 15 per cent
of its calories coming from fat is
too drastic for one so young.
During periods of rapid growth
and relatively small capacity for
food, fat is an important
concentrated source of
calories.

Eating is also an important
social aspect of life. While there
are many delicious recipes which
fit the very strict criteria of the
Pritikin life-style – some are
included in this book – such a
diet can make eating out in
restaurants and with friends very

difficult. The task of finding the right foods can dominate life.

While there are no nutritional hazards in striving for minimum levels of sugar, salt and alcohol, the effort to reduce fat to minimal levels can lead to a lack of minerals such as iron, calcium and zinc. Some essential fatty acids may also be low in diets which restrict the consumption of all foods containing fat.

There is no doubt that fatty diets are unhealthy. The balanced solution may be to have very little fat and to make sure that it is of high value. Foods such as fish, very lean meat or poultry and a little olive oil can supply essential fats without making the level of fat in the diet too high.

Macrobiotic diets

Like vegetarian diets, a macrobiotic diet can be a healthy choice or it may lack certain nutrients. This depends on the type and quantity of foods chosen.

A macrobiotic diet aims to create a balance between 'yin' and 'yang'. Yin represents the negative, passive and, some claim, feminine, side of life whereas yang is positive, strong and masculine. Foods are classified as either yin or yang and a desirable balance of five parts yin to one part yang is said to promote health and balance of mind and body. Climate, exercise, stress and state of health are all taken into account in deciding the ideal balance for each individual.

At the center of yin and yang are vegetables and cereals. These foods form the bulk of the macrobiotic diet. The foods which are highly yin include sugar, liquids of all kind, alcohol, fruit and dairy products. Chemicals and drugs are also regarded as yin. Yang foods are meat, fish, poultry, eggs and salt. Very few raw fruits, raw vegetables or liquids are suggested. Miso soup, made from fermented soy beans, salt and brown rice plays a prominent role in the macrobiotic diet and is believed to contain enzymes which assist the digestion.

The macrobiotic diet is actually a series of diets ranked according to various levels. The initial levels consist of a fairly wide selection of foods with the greatest emphasis being placed on vegetables and whole grains with some fish, meat or poultry. The ultimate level (usually the seventh or 10th level) is brown rice only and a 10-day diet of brown rice is recommended at frequent intervals to 'cleanse' the body. Brown rice is supposed to have the ideal balance of yin and yang. Liquids are strictly limited.

Nutritionally, the early levels of macrobiotic diets can be quite well-balanced. However, this diet may easily be inadequate for children and the high salt content of miso is unwise for those with, or at risk of, high blood pressure.

The brown rice level is nutritionally unbalanced and would lead to severe nutritional consequences over time.

Food combining

Back in the 1920s, it became popular for people to eat certain types of foods separately – protein at one meal, carbohydrate at another. Much of this theory originally stemmed from a misunderstanding of digestion. In the 1980s, the theory of food combining again rose to prominence. Again you were not supposed to mix proteins and carbohydrates. Proponents claimed that the body could not digest both types of nutrient at once. Some went even further and claimed that fruit could not be digested if any other food was present in the digestive system.

The mistake made by the supporters of this theory (who are not qualified in nutrition) is to assume that digestion occurred in the stomach. They ignored the small intestine where almost all digestion occurs.

The body is perfectly capable of digesting carbohydrates and proteins at the same time. Every day, we produce some eight quarts of digestive juices containing enzymes to break down proteins, fats and carbohydrates – and all can be present at the same time. If this were not so, we would not be able to digest foods such as bread, cereals, legumes, seeds, nuts or milk, which all contain both proteins and carbohydrates. As most of the world's population lives on such foods, the idea that we cannot digest proteins and carbohydrates together is obviously absurd.

HEALTH TIP

One tablespoon of peanut butter will supply one-third of an eight-year-old's daily intake of vitamin B2.

Stuffed Tomatoes, (page 106) and Chickpea and Avocado Salad (page 110) are both excellent sources of protein for vegetarians.

The sporting life

Athletes need lots of energy to perform at their peak. Endurance athletes have the highest needs of all. The realization that nutrition can affect performance just as much as regular training has given many athletes an opportunity for greater physical achievement. Both the type and quantity of foods eaten must be taken into account.

As we discussed earlier (see page 154), physical activity is either anaerobic (without oxygen) or aerobic (using oxygen). Anaerobic activity is intensive and only glucose or glycogen are suitable fuels. Anaerobic energy can only be used for short periods because glucose is not used efficiently and a waste product called lactic acid builds up. This stops the muscle fibers from contracting and you can feel fatigue in the muscles concerned. Most anaerobic reactions are short – less than 60 seconds.

For all longer-lasting physical activity, oxygen is used and the glucose molecules can be burnt much more efficiently. The muscles can keep contracting much longer. This is the kind of energy used for most sports and physical activity, although some kinds of activity combine the two. Playing football, for example, you would use aerobic activity most of the time but for a short, sharp burst of intensive effort, anaerobic energy would also be used. Aerobic activity can use either glycogen or free fatty acids for fuel.

Glucose is available from blood sugar which, in turn, comes mainly from the carbohydrates in the diet. During times of fasting or starvation, or if you have skipped a meal, the body can turn some muscle protein into blood sugar.

Glycogen is stored in muscles and the liver and is made when the diet contains enough carbohydrates. Liver glycogen is not used directly for energy but is converted to blood sugar if necessary. If you increase the carbohydrate content of the diet, glycogen stores in muscles can be increased fourfold. Once glycogen stores in muscles run out, you can no longer keep going. Intense fatigue sets in at once, a condition which runners call 'hitting the wall'.

Free fatty acids come from fats eaten in foods or from body fat stores. Even lean people have enough fatty acids stored in body fat to run 620 miles (though this would turn out to be impossible because glycogen stores would run out and fats are not burnt efficiently when there is no glycogen or other carbohydrate available). Still, you do not need to eat fats to supply energy from fatty acids. The body makes its own each day from the foods we eat.

The fuel mix used for any activity depends on the intensity of the exercise. Moderate exercise burns a higher proportion of fat. Short, sharp bursts of activity burn only glycogen.

Training also changes the fuel mix. As you train, muscles develop the ability to store more carbohydrate, if the diet has enough carbohydrate. In addition, as you become fitter, you can perform aerobically at higher intensities. This means you can use more fat for energy and glycogen will last longer.

Diet also influences the fuel mix. Eating more carbohydrates, most especially complex carbohydrates, increases glycogen stores. Eating more sugar is less advisable as it lacks other valuable nutrients. It is also easy to eat so much sugar at once that the blood sugar level can rise sharply. This may overstimulate the production of insulin, which in turn will remove too much sugar from the blood and leave the blood sugar level too low. Some sugar can be used, with other foods, as a source of carbohydrate. For example, whole wheat bread with honey or jam would be suitable as the bread supplies the nutrients which are not present in the sweet spread.

Caffeine

Caffeine is a drug found in coffee, tea and cola drinks. It stimulates the central nervous system and has been shown to stimulate fat cells to release free fatty acids into the blood. These can be used for energy, allowing glycogen supplies to last longer. The stimulus to the central nervous system can also increase alertness, at least temporarily. (Caffeine cannot, however, undo

---

2050 cals diet
Suitable for a female athlete, for example a ballet dancer, gymnast or swimmer with a small frame.

Breakfast

Whole grain wheat cereal, a banana and 10 fl oz low-fat milk

Lunch

2 tuna fish salad sandwiches (4 slices whole wheat bread, no butter or margarine)
2 pieces of fruit
Juice

Dinner

Medium serving lean red meat or fish or chicken
1 cup cooked rice or pasta or 1 large potato
At least 2 other vegetables or salad
1½ cups fresh fruit salad

Between meals

1 glass of skim milk
1 piece fruit

2900 cals diet
Suitable for a male athlete, for example a tennis player, ballet dancer, gymnast or football player, or a female endurance athlete

Breakfast

Whole grain wheat cereal, banana and 10 fl oz low-fat milk
3 slices toast with low-fat spread (honey or jam on two,
Marmite or yeast extract on one)

Lunch

1 tuna fish sandwich (2 slices multigrain bread)
1 baked potato
2 pieces of fruit
Juice

Dinner

Medium serving lean red meat or fish or chicken
1½ cups cooked rice or pasta or 2 medium potatoes
At least 2 other vegetables or salad
1 slice bread
2 cups fresh fruit salad

Between meals

1 glass of skim milk
1 piece fruit
2 slices bread with peanut butter and raisins
1 oz dried apricots
1 glass fruit juice

the effects of alcohol – it merely makes you a wide-awake drunk.)

Many athletes use caffeine as a stimulant (in events such as pistol shooting) or to preserve glycogen (in endurance events). Because it is a drug, only certain levels of caffeine are allowed in competitive sports and urine tests are performed to check how much caffeine has been consumed by the competitor.

A major concern for endurance athletes is to preserve glycogen as long as possible. Some use caffeine for this purpose. The downside, however, is that endurance athletes also tend to run out of water and dehydration of body cells is a fast route to failure. Caffeine is a diuretic and stimulates the kidneys to secrete water into the bladder. This is obviously undesirable for endurance athletes. Weighing up the pros and cons of using caffeine, most endurance athletes decide not to use it.

The athlete's ideal diet
At least 60 per cent of an athlete's calories should come from carbohydrates, with fats and protein making up the rest. To achieve this balance, athletes need to choose low-fat foods and have a predominance of breads, cereals, pasta, rice and other grains, potatoes and fruits in their diet. Low-fat milk will also contribute some carbohydrate without providing a lot of fat.

The diets on these pages show how the balance can be achieved for athletes requiring different levels of calories.

The 2050 cals diet provides 19 per cent of its energy from protein, 13 per cent from fat and 68 per cent from carbohydrate. It meets the recommended daily intake for all essential nutrients.

The 2900 cals diet provides 18 per cent of its energy from protein, 15 per cent from fat and 67 per cent from carbohydrate. It meets the recommended daily intake for all essential nutrients.

Pre-event meal
Most of the glycogen in muscles comes from the carbohydrates eaten the day before an event. The food you eat on the day of the event will not influence these stores much. However, the food you eat before an event will influence blood sugar and liver glycogen levels. It is important to keep these levels normal, as blood sugar controls the brain and nervous system and has an effect on fine coordination and reaction times.

Features of the pre-event meal should include the following:
❑ Eat two or three hours before an event so that you can digest the food and avoid a full stomach. (Note: rapidly growing children need to eat a little closer to an event than this or they feel hungry when the event begins.)
❑ Drink plenty of water. Diluted fruit juice is also suitable but avoid anything but water in the hour before an event begins.
❑ Eat carbohydrate foods but avoid fat. Suitable foods include cereals with low-fat milk, pasta (without a creamy rich sauce), rice, potatoes (not French fries), bread, muffins with jam or honey (avoid margarine or butter) or fruit (especially bananas).
❑ Avoid high-protein foods as most also contain fat. Protein also takes longer to leave the stomach than carbohydrate.
❑ Eat foods which you like. Avoid any which give you gas.
❑ Avoid eating sugar or glucose in the hour before an event as sugars can increase the blood sugar level, stimulate insulin and cause a more rapid loss of glycogen from muscles.

Sample pre-event meal

Glass of water
Breakfast cereal
with sliced banana
and golden raisins.
Low-fat milk
Toast, muffins, pancakes
(made without fat)
or rice with honey
Fruit juice

Advantages of exercise include better muscular strength, less body fat, more flexible joints, better lung and nerve function, less risk of heart disease and greater resistance to depression.

What is in foods

When cooking at home it is easy to keep track of what you're putting in your food. However, when using processed or canned foods, or eating out, it is not so simple. Although all processed foods must list their ingredients on the label—the major ingredient is listed first, followed by the next prominent, and so on—the exact percentage of most ingredients is not given. You can read the labels and avoid buying foods containing ingredients you are allergic to, but take-out foods and restaurant menus do not have to list their ingredients. Take-out Chinese food may be loaded with MSG and you wouldn't know unless you asked and the chef was honest. These pages explain what additives are used for.

In some countries, such as Australia, foods may contain specific additives only if they are permitted for that particular type of food. A food coloring, for example, may be allowed in candy, soft drinks and popsicles but not in bread. This provides a small amount of control over the food additives in the diet. Other countries, including the United States, have removed such controls and allow an approved additive to be added to any food the manufacturers desire.

Types of food additive

Anti-caking agents help stop powdered products such as salt, coffee whitener or confectioners' sugar sticking together in lumps. They are convenient but not strictly necessary.

Anti-oxidants preserve foods such as margarines or oils so that oxygen from the air does not turn them rancid. They are also used in some fruit products and in mashed potato flakes. Anti-oxidants are useful because they stop harmful compounds forming in foods.

Artificial sweeteners are a permitted, calorie-free alternative to sugar. They are useful for those who want or need to avoid sugar, but still want some sweetened foods or drinks. The full name of the sweetener used is listed on food labels.

Bleaches are used to whiten products such as flour. They are not permitted in some products and it is hard to justify their use, except on the dubious grounds of consumers wanting white products. However, if bleached flour is used in bread, the flour is listed but the bleaching agent is not.

Colorings are used only for visual appeal. They have no essential role and many artificially colored foods have little nutritional value and it is difficult to justify their use. The permitted list of colorings has been steadily reduced in most countries as various ones are suspected of being undesirable.

Emulsifiers are used to keep fats evenly distributed through foods. They may be added to foods such as margarines, salad dressings, peanut butter, sauces, breads, processed cheese and frozen desserts. In some cases, emulsifiers may be essential to the nature of the product. Other foods, such as peanut butter, do not really need emulsifiers as we could easily mix in the oil which settles out if no emulsifier is used.

Enzymes are sometimes added to breads and to tenderize meats. All living organisms contain enzymes, so they are not 'unnatural' in any way. Enzymes used in foods include papain (derived from papaya), ficin and bromelain. They are listed in ingredients by name or as 'enzyme'.

Flavorings are used to mimic the taste of a real ingredient. They are not a problem themselves but they are usually added to products which have little or no nutritional value. There is no permitted list of approved flavorings, since most natural and artificial flavorings are made up of a complex mixture of chemical compounds. Look for the words 'artificial flavor' on the label.

Flavor enhancers are used to bring out the flavor in foods. Since many people are sensitive to flavor enhancers such as MSG, there is little justification for the continued use of it and similar substances.

Food acids are used to provide a 'tang' (for example, to counteract the large quantity of sugar in soft drinks). They also stop browning in fruits and vegetables and may be used in products such as jams. They are quite safe, but if omitted from soft drinks the large quantity of sugar could be reduced since the drinks would be too sweet without the food acids.

Gums extracted from plants are used to give texture to desserts, confectionery and milk products. They are a valuable type of dietary fiber although the quantity present may be too small to be significant.

Humectants prevent dryness in foods such as fruit cakes and confectionery.

Minerals are added to increase the nutritional value of products like breakfast cereals, soy bean milk and iodized salt. Some may be in a form not easily absorbed into the body. For example, the iron added to breakfast cereals is not as well absorbed as that in lean meat.

Mineral salts are added to hold water or air in products like cakes or processed meats.

Preservatives help to control molds, bacteria and other micro-organisms in foods. In most cases, preservatives are a much better alternative than micro-organisms. Using modern preservatives may also allow greater retention of nutrients than traditional methods of salting and drying foods. No preservatives are needed in canned foods, as the exclusion of oxygen and heat treatment kill micro-organisms. Preservatives are used in a wide range of foods and drinks. In some cases, they make valuable foods safer to eat.

Propellants are used in foods in aerosol containers. We do not need such packaging for foods and there is no justification for the use of these additives. They are listed as 'propellant' with their name.

Thickeners are made from starch or gelatin and are used to give texture to sauces, baby foods and various meals and desserts. Most are probably harmless. They are not given names but are described on the food label as 'thickeners'.

Vitamins are usually added to replace losses from processing (in breakfast cereals, bread or fruit juices), or to add value to a product (margarine). They can be useful, although not all vitamins lost during processing are added back to a food. The heating, puffing and popping of breakfast cereals, for example, causes a loss of many vitamins; only four are added back. Vitamins are listed by name on food labels.

Caffeine

Caffeine is the most widely used drug in the world. It is addictive and some are more sensitive to it than others. Those who consume a lot develop a tolerance, while those who rarely use the drug find that a single cup of coffee may keep them awake at night. Giving up caffeine can produce withdrawal symptoms ranging from headache to nervousness.

Caffeine stimulates the central nervous system, affecting the brain, heart, muscles and respiratory system. About 15 to 30 minutes after drinking coffee, most people report they can think more clearly. Levels of caffeine in the system peak about an hour after drinking it and it is excreted 12 to 16 hours later.

Caffeine can be of benefit to asthmatics as it may relax smooth muscle and dilate the breathing passages. It also increases the production of stomach acid, a potential problem for those with gastric problems such as ulcers.

For most adults, three or four cups of average strength coffee (or tea) a day seems to do little damage. Those who have difficulty sleeping should avoid caffeine in the late afternoon and evening. Children should have little or no caffeine.

Many people think coffee gives them energy, but it only increases wakefulness. Using caffeine as a stimulant instead of eating is unwise. Coffee or tea is no substitute for a balanced meal.

Pesticides

Pesticides are chemical substances which present great hazards, especially to pests. Because they are 'chemicals' over which the ordinary consumer has little control, many people fear pesticides. Yet we dig our graves sinking our teeth into piles of fatty, sugary and salty foods without a second thought. This may be because we can blame someone else for pesticides whereas we have only ourselves to blame for our overindulgence in food and drink.

Pesticides are used to prevent fruit flies infesting fruits, vegetables and grains. It is difficult to feed an urban population cheaply without using some form of pest control. Pesticides are potentially a problem if they are misused.

There are no safe substances, only safe quantities. Tests in countries like the US show very low levels of pesticide residues in human foods – lower than in the past. They do not currently present a problem for humans. If the pesticide residue from eating two million apples would be harmful, it does not follow that eating one apple is risky.

The real menace of pesticides in use today may be to other species of animals for whom a much smaller dose presents a danger. We may be unaffected by the pesticide remaining on, say, an apple, whereas birds or animals eating the remains of the apple may be harmed. We need to press for the use of smaller quantities and safer pesticides for the sake of the environment. For ourselves, we should direct our attention to the very real hazards of a poor choice of foods, rather than being sidetracked by fears or fueled by ignorance.

Check the caffeine content of your beverage.	
Beverage	**Caffeine content (mg)**
brewed coffee, 1 cup	85–120
instant coffee, 1 cup	60
strong tea, 1 cup	80
weak tea, 1 cup	20–30
cola drink, 1 can	35–55
cocoa powder, 2 teaspoons	20

HEALTH TIP

Different forms of fat in foods may appear on the label as, beef and/or vegetable fat; vegetable oil; shortening; coconut oil; butter fat; monoglycerides; diglycerides; cream.

HEALTH TIP

A cup of strong tea has as much caffeine as a cup of instant coffee. Weak tea may have less than half as much caffeine as instant coffee, while brewed coffee usually tops the bill.

USEFUL INFORMATION

All our recipes are tested in an approved Australian test kitchen. Standard metric measuring cups and spoons approved by Standards Australia are used in the development of our recipes. All cup and spoon measurements are level. We have used large 2 oz eggs in all recipes. Sizes of cans vary from manufacturer to manufacturer and between countries – use the can size closest to the one suggested in the recipe.

Measures

Dry Measures

1 oz	=	30 g
8 oz	=	250 g
1 lb	=	500 g

Liquid Measures

1 fl oz	=	30 mL
4 fl oz	=	125 mL
8 fl oz	=	250 mL

Linear Measures

¼ inch	=	6 mm
½ inch	=	1 cm
1 inch	=	2.5 cm

International Glossary

bell pepper	capsicum
aubergine	eggplant
raw shrimp	green prawns
all-purpose flour	plain flour
mange tout	snow peas
whole wheat	wholemeal
courgette	zucchini

Conversion Guide

1 cup = 8 fl oz (250 ml)

1 US tablespoon = 15 ml (3 teaspoons)

1 Australian tablespoon = 20 ml (4 teaspoons)

Note: We have used 20 ml tablespoon measures. If you are using a 15 ml tablespoon, for most recipes the difference will not be noticeable. However, for recipes using baking powder, gelatin, baking soda, small amounts of flour and cornstarch, add an extra teaspoon for each tablespoon specified.

Cup Conversions

1 cup sugar	= 8 oz (250 g)
1 cup shredded coconut	= 3 oz (90 g)
1 cup low-fat yogurt	= 8 oz (250 g)
1 cup pearl barley	= 7 oz (220 g)
1 cup all-purpose flour	= 4 oz (125 g)
1 cup prunes	= 7 oz (220 g)
1 cup raisins	= 4 oz (125 g)
1 cup self-rising flour	= 4 oz (125 g)
1 cup whole wheat flour	= 5 oz (150 g)

Oven Temperatures

Cooking times may vary slightly depending on the type of oven you are using. Before you preheat the oven, we suggest that you refer to the manufacturer's instructions to ensure proper temperature control.

	°F	°C	Gas Mark
Very slow	250	120	½
Slow	300	150	2
Warm	325	170	3
Moderate	350	180	4
Mod. hot	375	190	5
Mod. hot	400	200	6
Hot	425	220	7
Very hot	450	230	8

NOTE: For fan-forced ovens check your appliance manual, but as a general rule, set oven temperature a little lower than the temperature indicated in the recipe.

RECIPE RATING

Easy

A little care needed

More care needed

This edition published in the United States and Canada by Whitecap Books.
Published by Murdoch Books®, a division of Murdoch Magazines Pty Ltd, 45 Jones Street, Ultimo NSW 2007.

Recipe Origination and Text: Rosemary Stanton. Editors: Lynn Humphries, Juliet Richters, Jane Sheard, Stephanie Kistner. Design and layout: Annette Fitzgerald. Photography: Ray Joyce, Andrew Furlong. Step-by-step Photography: Ray Joyce. Food Stylists: Jo Anne Calabria, Silvia Sieff. Food Stylists' Assistants: Kerrie Carr, Melanie McDermott, Kerrie Ray. Home Economists: Voula Mantzouridis, Kerrie Ray. US Editor: Kerry MacKenzie. US Nutritional Adviser: Marjorie Freedman.

CEO & Publisher: Anne Wilson. Associate Publisher: Catie Ziller. International Sales Director: Mark Newman.

A catalogue record for this book is available from the National Library of Australia.
ISBN 1-55110-847-X.

Printed by Toppan Printing Pte. Ltd. This edition first printed 1998.
PRINTED IN SINGAPORE.

Distributed in Canada by Whitecap Books (Vancouver) Ltd, 351 Lynn Avenue, North Vancouver, BC V7J 2C4, Telephone (604) 980 9852, Facsimile (604) 980 8197 or Whitecap Books (Ontario) Ltd, 47 Coldwater Road, North York, ON, M3B 1Y8, Telephone (416) 444 3442, Facsimile (416) 444 6630
Distributed in the USA by Graphic Arts Centre Publishing, PO Box 10306, Portland, OR 97296-0306, USA Telephone (503) 226 2402, Facsimile 1 503 294 9900

The Publisher wishes to thank the following companies for their generous assistance in the photography of this book: Accoutrement, Art & Frame, Avalon Interiors, Avalon Sports Store, Bloomin' Newport Florists, Casa De' Fiori, Country Floors, Country Trader, Crafts Council, Essentials, Fragrant Garden, Hampshire and Lowndes, Home Sweet Home, Immaterial Fabrics, Les Olivades, St James Furnishing, Season's Gallery, The Bay Tree, The Little Company Guest House, The Reject Shop, Village Living, Villeroy and Boch, Waterford Wedgwood, Whitehall Silver & Plate Company, Wilson's Fabrics. All New South Wales.